# Business Groups in Punjab

All organisations go through two types of changes: continuous and discontinuous. Continuous changes are incremental and evolutionary, and the process is slow. They are the first order changes where the new state of things have the same nature but with different features. Continuous changes may include better services, innovative products, new markets and locations, and improvement in quality whereas discontinuous changes are radical and abrupt with a new state of things having a substantially different nature from the old pattern. Discontinuous changes usually involve redefining and reconstructing corporate business, organisational structure, mission, and objectives. This book is an effort to compile both kinds of changes in the context of Punjab's economy.

Punjab stands out as a symbol of hard work and entrepreneurial skills of its citizens. The phenomenal growth of agriculture, business and industry in Punjab is emulated as a role model across India.

The present book places on record the achievements of Punjab's entrepreneurs in the industrialisation of India in general and that of Punjab in particular. It documents and consolidates the contribution of enterprising business groups of Punjab in placing this State on the industrial map of India. The book would prove useful for students of management and commerce, business executives and market analysts. It will also serve as a catalyst for present and prospective entrepreneurs who will get an insight into the rough and tough world of business and industry.

# Business Groups in Punjab

*Chief Editor*
Dr. K.N.S. Kang

PCTE

Punjab College of Technical Education
Ludhiana

New Century Publications
New Delhi, India

NEW CENTURY PUBLICATIONS
4800/24, Bharat Ram Road,
Ansari Road, Daryaganj,
New Delhi-110 002
Tel.: 23247798, 55396605
E-mail: indiatax@del2.vsnl.net.in

Editorial office:
34, Gujranwala Town, Part-2,
Delhi - 110 009
Tel.: 27247805, 27138192
Fax: +91-11-27464774



---

**First Published 2004**

ISBN: 81-7708-070-9

Published by New Century Publications and printed at
Singhal Print Media, Delhi -110 007

PRINTED IN INDIA

## Punjab College of Technical Education (PCTE)

Punjab College of Technical Education, Ludhiana, started functioning in August 1999. Affiliated to Punjab Technical University, Jalandhar, it is approved by AICTE, New Delhi. PCTE conducts the following courses: Master of Business Administration (MBA), Master of Computer Applications (MCA), Bachelor of Business Administration (BBA), Bachelor of Computer Applications (BCA), and Ph.D. programmes. PCTE has a student base of over 700. Being situated in Ludhiana, the industrial hub of Punjab, the College has a proven advantage of being at arm's length from the industry. It has a strong interaction with the industry for research and consultancy projects.

PCTE is the first B-school of India to get entry into Limca Book of Records for its unique mutual fund exercise being managed by SWAP (Students Welfare Association of PCTE). Similarly, PCTE is the first ISO 9001:2000 certified institute, rated best B-School in Punjab by AIMA survey in association with Business Standard.

The foreign presence of PCTE is established by the visits of students and delegations from other countries. Of late, these visits have included six students from South Africa, Pakistan delegation from National College of Business Administration and Economics, Lahore, participation of Pakistan delegation in Ehsaas-2004 (the fifth inter-college literary-cum-cultural festival of PCTE), and delegation from Shahid Zulfikar Ali Bhutto Institute of Engineering and Technology, Islamabad

In a short span of time, PCTE has achieved various distinctions in the field of academics and cultural activities. Since its inception in 1999, the College has won 6 Gold Medals out of 7 awarded by the University so far. PCTE is also proud of 100 per cent placements for all its successful MBA students. No exaggeration, the College can be ranked as one of the best B-School of Northern India.

## About the Editor-in-chief

Dr. K.N.S. Kang, an academician, an entrepreneur and an achiever is basically an electrical engineer, with Post-graduation in business management and doctorate in marketing management. A unique mix of an intellectual, a sportsman and artist, Dr. Kang has always achieved merit and distinction in education, sports and cultural activities throughout his student life. Fourth position holder in state higher secondary examination, national level athlete and a winner in inter-university level cultural events, Dr. Kang was conferred with the prestigious Shaheed Bhagat Singh State Youth Award for overall excellence by the then Governor of Punjab, honourable Mr. S.S. Ray. Dr. Kang worked as an Assistant Professor in the Department of Business Management, PAU, Ludhiana and has fourteen years of professional experience to his credit. He had been the advisor to All Indian Management Association Nodal Centre for imparting post-graduate level management education in Ludhiana for four years. His fields of expertise include marketing management, international business and advertisement management. He has been guiding various research projects on different management problems and current business environment. He is a consultant to various industrial houses in the city and is a member of several committees and associations working in the field of education and business. Dr. Kang has some other important portfolios such as: Chairman (Board of Studies), Computer applications for BCA and MCA; Member, Interim Council, Distance Education Programmes of PTU and Executive Member, Ludhiana Management Association.

## Acknowledgements

We wish to place on record our gratitude to all the executives of various industries who readily extended their support by way of providing material for this book. Thanks are also due to the key personnel of the companies covered in this volume who spared valuable time to attend to the PCTE team that visited them for collecting material and supporting information about their respective organisations. Without their co-operation this compilation would not have been possible.

**PCTE Team**
**Ludhiana**

## PCTE Team

| | |
|---|---|
| **Editor-in-chief** | Dr. K.N.S. Kang |
| **Editors** | Sandhir Sharma |
| | Pavitar Parkash Singh |
| | Samarjeet Kaur |
| | Pawan Taneja |

**Contributors**

| | |
|---|---|
| **Auto Parts** | |
| GNA | Sukhjinder Bath |
| GS Auto | Cheenu Garg and Anshu Dhansoia |
| **Cycle and Cycle Parts** | |
| AVON Cycles | Arunesh Garg and Gautam Bansal |
| Bhogal Group | Sandeep Bazaz and Irenpreet Singh |
| Eastman | Pallavi Dawra and Shweta Kapoor |
| Hero Cycles | Sandeep Bazaz and Irenpreet Singh |
| **Steel Industry** | |
| Aarti Steels | Anshu Dhansoia and Cheenu Garg |
| Upper India Steels | Sandeep Bazaz and Irenpreet Singh |
| **Textile, Yarn and Hosiery** | |
| Duke | Samarjeet Kaur and Sandhir Sharma |
| JCT | Sukhjinder Bath |
| Malwa | Arunesh Garg and Gautam Bansal |
| Nahar | Pallavi Dawra and Shweta Kapoor |
| OCM | Sukhjinder Bath |
| Vardhman | P P Singh and Sandhir Sharma |
| **Tyre and Tube Industry** | |
| Hindustan Cycles and Tubes | Pallavi Dawra and Shweta Kapoor |
| Metro | P P Singh and Sandhir Sharma |
| Ralson | P P Singh and Sandhir Sharma |
| **Others Industries** | |
| Amrit Vanaspati (Food) | Sukhjinder Bath |
| Bharti (Telecommunications) | Pallavi Dawra and Tanisha Jolly |
| F C Sondhi (Sports Goods) | Pavitar Parkash Singh |
| FMI (Measurement Tapes) | Cheenu Garg and Anshu Dhansoia |
| International Tractors | Sukhjinder Bath |
| Leader Valves (Machinery Parts) | Pavitar Parkash Singh |
| Ranbaxy (Pharmaceuticals) | P P Singh and Arunesh Garg |
| Shreyans (Paper and Textiles) | Arunesh Garg and Gautam Bansal |

# Preface

Enterprise and endeavour are the two words which symbolize the essential spirit of the people of Punjab. Since Independence in 1947, the State of Punjab has earned its epithet of *India's Granary* through the enterprising spirit, and untiring toil of its people. Its average growth rate of 10% is amongst the highest in the country, clearly reflecting the progressive economy of the State. Punjab also boasts of a 58% literacy rate and the highest per capita income in India. Since the recent liberalization of India's economy, Punjab has started making its mark on the global business mainstream, with major players from around the world forming joint ventures in the field of agri-business.

Privileged by nature and the dynamism of its people, Punjab is a land of rivers, fertile soils and steady achievement. With its inimitable style of transforming every potential opportunity into a success story, the State was the first to translate agricultural technology into the *green revolution*, recording highest growth rate in food production. From a minor producer, it emerged a major rice surplus State. Providing the impetus for the *White revolution*, during Operation Flood, it was Punjab that recorded the highest per capita availability of milk.

Presently, Punjab has over 1.97 lakh of small and medium industries with an investment of Rs. 4,509 crore, employing 9 lakh persons, and about 653 large-scale industries involve fixed capital investment of Rs. 17,594 crore. It leads in the manufacture of machine and hand tools, printing and paper cutting machinery; auto parts and electrical switchgear. The State also meets more than 75% of the country's requirement for bicycles, sewing machines, hosiery and sports goods, pipes, footwear, medical instruments, and tractors. Punjab is rapidly moving up in the production of engineering goods, pharmaceuticals, leather goods, food products, textiles, electronic goods, sugar, machine tools, hand tools, agricultural implements, paper and paper packaging. At par with the highest quality standards in the world, these products have carved a niche for themselves in markets across the globe. Exports from Punjab are estimated to be more than Rs. 4,800 crore per annum.

The present book places on record the achievements of business groups located in Punjab. What these business houses are? Where are they now? What are their future plans? These and other questions are answered in this book.

For the purpose of this book, members of PCTE team contacted more than 50 business houses of Punjab to collect information. These business houses were selected and approached according to their brand image and popularity in the market. However, in spite of best efforts, necessary information could be collected from 25 business groups only. The information was collected through primary and secondary sources. The present exercise is merely a compilation work and does not include any comments on or analysis of any organisation.

We believe that this compilation will serve multiple purposes. Firstly, it will provide the prospective entrepreneurs the necessary inspiration to venture into the rapid changing business environment. Secondly, it places on record the contribution of enterprising groups to the development of not only Punjab but also of India. Thirdly, it provides us at PCTE with a feedback to extend the coverage of the business/industrial groups to make it more comprehensive Fourthly, the book will prove immensely helpful for the students, research scholars and academicians for their references in academic pursuits. Lastly, it will spread awareness beyond the northern region of India as to how Punjab achieved its prime glory as the nucleus of business and industrial activities in India.

We wish to place on record our gratitude to the members of the business groups in Punjab who readily extended their support by way of providing material for this book. Thanks are due to the key personnel of the companies covered in this volume who spared valuable time to attend to the PCTE team that visited them for collecting material and supporting information about their respective organisations. Without their co-operation this compilation would not have seen the light of the day. Thanks are also due to those companies which refused to provide us the necessary information but still exist in our list of endeavours. They will continue tc inspire us to come up with another volume of the work.

K.N.S. Kang
Director
Punjab College of Technical Education
Ludhiana
June 2004

# Contents

**Preface** **ix**

## Section 1: Introduction

- Macro Economic Overview of Indian Economy **3**
- Industries in Punjab **9**

## Section 2: Auto Parts Industry

- Indian Auto Parts Industry **17**
- Guru Nanak Auto (GNA) Enterprises **20**
- GS Auto International **32**

## Section 3: Cycle and Cycle Parts

- Indian Cycle and Cycle Parts Industry **41**
- AVON Cycles **44**
- Bhogal Group **52**
- Eastman Industries **58**
- Hero Cycles **65**

## Section 4: Steel Industry

- Indian Iron and Steel Industry **85**
- Aarti Steels **87**
- Upper India Steels **92**

## Section 5: Textile, Yarn and Hosiery

- Indian Textile, Yarn and Hosiery Industry **99**
- Duke India **102**
- JCT **108**
- Malwa Industries **116**
- Nahar Industries **127**

- OCM 136
- Vardhman Spinnings and General Mills 142


## Section 6: Tyre and Tube Industry


- Indian Tyre and Tube Industry 163
- Hindustan Cycles and Tubes 166
- Metro Tyres 173
- Ralson India 178


## Section 7: Others Industries


- Indian Edible Oil Industry 187
- Indian Telecommunication Industry 189
- Indian Sports Industry 192
- Indian Pharmaceutical Industry 194
- Indian Paper Industry 197
- Amrit Vanaspati (Food) 200
- Bharti (Telecommunications) 208
- F C Sondhi and Company (Sports Goods) 225
- FMI (Measurement Tapes) 244
- International Tractors 250
- Leader Valves (Machinery Parts) 259
- Ranbaxy Laboratories (Pharmaceuticals) 268
- Shreyans (Paper and Textiles) 299

# Section 1: Introduction

- Macro Economic Overview of India
- Industries in Punjab

# Macro Economic Overview of India

According to data for 2001-02, released by the Central Statistical Organisation (CSO) on January 31, 2003, Gross Domestic Product (GDP) at factor cost at constant 1993-94 prices grew at 5.6 percent in 2001-02, as against 5.4 percent projected in February 2002. The higher growth estimate for 2001-02 is particularly significant as it comes against the backdrop of a revised estimate of a more moderate growth deceleration for 2000-01 than originally apprehended. In 2000-01, GDP at factor cost at constant 1993-94 prices grew at 4.4 percent, as against the previous estimate of 4.0 percent.

The pick-up in growth of the Indian economy observed in 2001-02 was stronger than what had been initially anticipated. Data on quarterly GDP at factor cost at constant 1993-94 prices, available only for the first half of 2002-03, indicated that in the first and second quarters of the current year, year on year, GDP grew by 6 percent and 5.8 percent - rates that are markedly higher than 3.5 percent and 5.3 percent respectively, registered in the corresponding periods of the previous year. The monsoon failure, however, affected agriculture severely, with agriculture and allied GDP declining by 3.1 percent, as per the advance estimates released by the CSO on February 7, 2003. Overall GDP growth in the current year is likely to be only 4.4 percent. This agriculture-pulled deceleration in growth, in 2002-03, clouds an across-the-board improvement in the growth performance of industry and services from 3.3 percent to 6.1 percent, and from 6.8 percent to 7.1 percent, respectively, between 2001-02 and 2002-03. Indications are that, in spite of a severe monsoon deficiency, the rebound in growth observed since 2001-02 gained momentum in industry and services sectors in the current year.

The growth recovery was accompanied by continued macroeconomic stability in terms of low inflation, orderly currency market conditions and comfortable reserves. In the past, droughts, with their impact on price and availability of foodgrains, have been particularly harsh on the poor. In the current year, notwithstanding the deficient monsoon, there were no shortages in availability of essential commodities, or flare-ups in their prices. The 52-week average inflation rate based on the Wholesale Price Index (WPI) was only 2.6 percent in mid January 2003.

While merchandise exports have grown well in 2002-03, services exports have also been an important area of success reflected in net invisible inflows of US $14 billion in 2001-02. India's share in world commercial services trade is larger than India's share in world merchandise trade. While software exports is a well-known success story, India is now an important venue for many tasks in services such as financial accounting, call centres, processing insurance claims, and medical transcription. The future potential for growth in these areas appears to be considerable.

The strengthening of the balance of payments has impacted on the monetary sector, with net foreign exchange assets (NFA) of RBI emerging as an important source of reserve money. From 9.1 percent as at end-March 1991, the share of net foreign exchange assets in reserve money, which had reached 78.1 percent by the end of 2001-02, became 100.7 percent on January 24, 2003, which is close to a currency board situation.

Capital markets continued to be subdued. The NSE-50 index, which was at 1,087 in January 2002, was at 1,073 in January 2003, showing no significant change. This weakness in the secondary market led to a small volume of issuance on the primary market. However, the drop in the Indian equity market in the period after December 2001 is smaller than that in many other countries. Unlike the heavy inflows in the preceding years, there was a small outflow of foreign portfolio investment from India between April to November 2002.

**Production**

The share of services in GDP has gone up by 12.8 percentage points from 36 percent in 1980 to 48.8 percent in 2001. This increase in the share of services is strikingly similar to the corresponding rise in services' share in GDP in many other Asian countries between 1980 and 2001.

The relative performance of agriculture and industry and their contributions to growth are likely to be quite different in 2001-02 and the current year. A robust performance by agriculture (5.7 percent) was instrumental in the acceleration of GDP growth by more than one percentage point in 2001-02. Industry, by contrast, had a relatively disappointing record in 2001-02, with lower growth being registered by all industry groups compared with the preceding year.

Industry has experienced a significant revival, with IIP growth of 5.3 percent in April-November 2002-03. This has been a broad-based recovery, comprising of 5.7 percent in mining and quarrying, 5.4 percent in manufacturing and 4 percent in electricity. The two key elements which led this growth were capital goods, which grew by 9.9 percent, and consumer non-durables, which had growth of 12.7 percent.

Two industries, which have experienced striking revivals in the current year, are steel and cement. World steel prices rose from December 2001 onwards. Domestic demand for steel and cement was supported by the highway construction taking place under the aegis of NHAI, and housing sector growth spurred by easy access to housing finance and a favourable tax regime. Improvements in technology and cost reductions have made India more competitive in exporting steel and cement. For these reasons, steel output grew by 19.8 percent in 2001-02, and a further 24.5 percent in April-November 2002. In the first half of 2002-03, cement production grew strongly by 9.5 percent.

The textile industry is a key area where India has an opportunity for labour-intensive exports. Textile products showed a strong growth of 14.8 percent in April-November 2002. A key element of this growth was an increase of 11.6 percent in exports of readymade garments in dollar terms. The powerloom segment accounted for most of the growth in fabrics.

Assisted by low interest rates, growth in consumer finance, and strong export demand, the automobile industry is experiencing sound growth. The number of vehicles exported during April-December, 2002, was 2,15,318, compared with 1,28,119 in the corresponding previous period, thereby registering a buoyant growth of 68 percent. Most major international companies in this industry now have operations in India, and are increasingly using India as a platform for export-oriented production. All elements of the automobile industry are functioning soundly in India, ranging from components to various kinds of vehicles, sophisticated inputs of design, research and consulting.

In the oil and gas industry, a significant development is gas discovery in new blocks. Preliminary estimates of the in-place reserves from the recent discoveries in the Krishna-Godavari offshore, and in the Rajasthan block, are about 220 million metric tonne (MMT) of oil and oil equivalent gas. In late 2000-01, there was enough refining capacity in India relative to domestic demand, to result in India exporting petroleum products in net terms of 3.08 million tonnes in 2001-02, and 2.08 million tonnes in April-October 2002.

India continues to make progress on export-oriented production in electronics and computer technology. Software exports have grown at a compound growth rate of over 50 percent per year for the last five years. There are now signs of headway being made in the field of hardware exports as well. Hardware exports grew sharply in 2000-01 and 2001-02, reaching a level of Rs.5,871 crore in 2001-02, with growth of 22.6 percent over the previous year.

**Issues and Priorities**

The current year is the first year of the Tenth Five Year Plan (2002-07), which envisages an average annual growth rate of 8 percent. While the growth performance in recent years has been lower than this target, international evidence, as well as India's own experience, demonstrate that the target is indeed feasible. Malaysia, Republic of Korea, and Thailand, among other East Asian countries, sustained annual growth rates at levels equal to, or higher than what India is seeking to achieve in the Tenth Plan, for several years, before the outbreak of the East Asian crisis. The People's Republic of China, a large country like India in terms of both area and population, has been one of the best performers among the major economies of the world during the 1980s and 1990s, and has been maintaining high growth (7 percent plus) despite the recent slowdown in global economic activity.

The drivers of change and rapid growth acceleration have to be technology and competition, together with benchmarking to the best international practices. India is now taking advantage of all three factors. Technology is getting upgraded rapidly and competition in the market place has become fierce. The IT revolution, and the vibrant

IT industry in the country, have been critical factors in making information available about state of the art technology and in bridging the technological divide in some sectors. With quantitative restrictions on imports a thing of the past, customs duties progressively coming down, and foreign investment - both direct and portfolio - liberalized, integration of India into the global economy is also progressing.

The automobile sector, previously under a strict licensing regime, has been a direct beneficiary of competition and technology in the new liberal regime. Not only has automobile output grown at double digit compound rates, but the sector has become a sizeable exporter. Major international auto-companies now have operations in India, and are increasingly using the country as a platform for export-oriented production. There is also a strong set of upstream firms, producing ancillaries for, and providing design consultancy to the automobile industry. The telecommunications sector provides another illustration of a virtuous interaction between technology and competition. While mobile telephony is rapidly raising teledensity, price competition between two technologies, namely Global System for Mobile (GSM) and Code Division Multiple Access (CDMA), has yielded price benefits to the consumer.

# Industries in Punjab

The level of industrial development generally determines the economic development of a nation or a region. Punjab, which has done remarkably well in the field of agriculture, is now well on its way to rapid industrialization through coordinated development of Small, Medium and Large scale industries. It leads in the manufacture of machine and hand tools; printing and paper cutting machinery; auto parts and electrical switchgear. The state also provides more than 75% of the country's requirement for bicycles, sewing machines, hosiery and sports goods, pipes, footwear, medical instruments, and tractors. Punjab is rapidly moving up in production of engineering goods, pharmaceuticals, leather goods, food products, textiles, electronic goods, sugar, machine tools, hand tools, agricultural implements, paper and paper packaging.

Punjab has essentially an agrarian economy with a low industrial output. The absence of basic minerals is the main reason for low level of industrial progress. A notable feature of the industrial scenario of the Punjab is its small-sized industrial units. There are 194,000 small scale industrial units in the state in addition to 586 large and medium units.

**Important Industries in Punjab**

Industrial units in the state are namely divided into three:

- Agro-based industrial units: These may be classified as food products, beverages, cotton, wood and paper industries.
- Machinery units
- Chemical units

Some notable industries are:

### Cotton Textiles

Punjab produces about 70 percent of the best quality cotton in India. The easy availability of the raw material facilitates the localisation of this industry in Punjab. In spite of several advantages, there is one main disadvantage that the total spindlage capacity of the state is only 1.5 percent of the country.

The cotton mills are located at Abohar, Malout, Phagwara, Amristar, Kharar and Ludhiana. Malerkotla, Abohar, Malout and Bhatinda are important for cotton ginning and pressing and about 25.3 lakh bales of cotton are pressed annually over here. About 97 million kgs of yarn and 36.5 million metres of cloth were produced in the cotton textile mills of Punjab.

### Sugar

Sugar mills in Punjab are located at Batala, Gurdaspur, Bhogpur, Phagwara, Nawanshahar, Zira, Morinda, Rakhra, Dhuri, Fazilka, Nakodar, Budhewal, Bhatinda and Jagraon.

A salient feature of the Sugar industry is that out of the 14 mills, 12 are in the Co-operative sector and only two are privately owned. Compared to Uttar Pradesh and some other states, the size of the sugar mills in Punjab is small. The Co-operative sugar mill at Morinda is the biggest in the state with a daily crushing capacity of 4,000 tonnes of sugarcane.

### Dairy

The primary source of milk and other dairy products in the state is the buffalo. Punjab ranks at the top in the country in the availability of milk. A major part of the milk produced in the state is consumed at the individual household level, only a limited quantity of milk is produced and processed in the milk plant.

In Punjab there are milk plants in the Public Sector, Private sector and Co-operative sector. The plants are mainly located at Verka (Amristar district), Ludhiana, Mohali, Jalandhar, Patiala, Hoshiarpur, Gurdaspur, Ferozepur, Sangrur, Bhatinda, Faridkot, Nabha, Moga, Kot Kapura and Hamira. The plant at Moga, known as Food Specialities, is the biggest plant in the state with a processing capacity of 435 thousand litres of milk. This plant produces a variety of milk products like ghee, sweets, lassi etc.

**Vanaspati Ghee**

The Vanaspati ghee industry is based mainly on the production of groundnut. This industry is not very big, as the oilseeds for the country are brought from other states. The Vanaspati ghee units are situated at Amritsar, Ludhiana, Khanna, Doraha and Rajpura.

**Woollen Textiles**

Woollen textile industries are situated at Amritsar, Ludhiana and Dhariwal.

**Hosiery**

Punjab leads the whole of the country in the manufacture of hosiery products. Most of these units are located in Ludhiana. This industry is a major foreign exchange earner.

**Sports Goods**

The sports goods industry of Punjab became well known only after 1947. Jalandhar is the main centre for the production of sports goods. This industry plays a major part in earning foreign exchange.

**Engineering Industries**

In the absence of basic minerals, the heavy engineering industry is almost absent in the state.

- **Bicycles:** Punjab now ranks at the top of the bicycle industry. Main centres are Ludhiana and Rajpura.
- **Sewing Machines:** Punjab not only fulfils the home requirements for sewing machines but also exports the same. Ludhiana and Bassi Pathana are important centres for the production of sewing machines and machine parts.
- **Agricultural Implements And Machine Tool:** The important centres for manufacture of agricultural implements are Batala, Ludhiana, Phillaur, Jalandhar, Phagwara, Goraya and Amristar.
- **Tractors And Combines:** The state has a tractor plant at Mohali and a combine harvester plant at Bhadson.

**Feed and Concentrates**

To develop livestock and poultry industries, it is of utmost importance to develop the feed industry on a priority basis. The possible sources of feed and concentrates are oilseed cakes and the by-products of milling and the cereals.

**Wheat Bran:** This is a by-product of the roller flour mills and there are about 11 such mills in the state.

**Oilseed Cakes:** The cotton seed is preferred as such by the farmers for feeding the milk animals. Cotton seed is utilised for oil production which is a costly product and is in great demand.

**Rice Milling:** About 80 percent of the paddy produced in Punjab is marketed and processed in different types of rice mills. There are about 2,200 hullers mostly in rural area,148 shellers and 43 hullers-cum-shellers. The major by-products of rice milling are two percent germ, five percent bran and 23 percent husk

**Wheat Milling:** There are about 15 roller flour mills in the Punjab with a capacity of flour lakh tonnes. Local consumption of wheat is to the tune of 20 lakh tonnes, mostly as atta.

**Bakery:** The bakery industry is in its infant stage. There are mechanised bakery units in the Punjab which produce biscuits and bread.

**Barley Processing and Malting:** Barley is the chief cereal which is prepared for malting. There are two malt factories in Punjab. Considerable export of malt extract is now contracted by a Punjab malt factory.

**Maize Processing:** Two private factories in Punjab manufacture starch and starch products from maize. One modern maize processing plant has been set up at Sangrur. Cornflakes are a popular breakfast food which can be manufactured as part of the maize processing mills in the malt factories. It is also possible to utilize maize for malting purposes.

**Cereal Based Nutritive Foods:** Manufacture of nutritive food is important to counter the widely prevalent malnutrition. Several high protein rich foods such as Bal-Ahar, Multi-purpose food, Nutro Biscuits, Bulgar wheat, Vegetable Milk and Fortified Bread can be produced.

**Cotton Seed Crushing:** Cotton seed is highly valued for its protein and oil contents. It is high in protein and its oil content varies from 12 to 18 percent. Besides extracting oil, protein-rich flour can also be produced.

**Meat and Poultry Processing:** One modern chicken dressing plant was installed at Chandigarh. Other such plants are in Ludhiana, Jalandhar and Amristar.

**Fruit and Vegetable Processing:** Punjab has a good market for pickles and preservers. It has wide scope for processing units for the production of juice concentrates and dehydration factories for vegetables.

# Section 2: Auto Parts Industry

- Indian Auto Parts Industry
- Guru Nanak Auto (GNA) Enterprises
- GS International Limited

# Indian Auto Parts Industry

The auto component industry is today one of the jewels in crown of Indian Industry. The auto component industry consists of over 400 key players, besides a number of very small and tiny manufacturers participating either directly or indirectly in its activities. With an investment of Rs. 13,500 crore and annual sales of Rs. 34,500 crore, this sector provides direct employment to over 2.50 lakh persons.

In the last five years, this sector has made significant strides in quality improvement. The number of companies with quality certification ranging from ISO 9000 to TS 16949 is about 350, which represents 83 per cent of the membership of the Automotive Component Manufacturers Association of India (ACMA). The export performance of this sector has been growing at a rate of over 25 per cent in the last few years. Last year, the export figure was $800 million.

## Challenges and Opportunities

In the first few years since 1991, like many other sectors, the auto components industry did not fully comprehend the impact of the World Trade Organization regime. However, the following events slowly but surely changed the strategic direction of the industry.

**Arrival of Auto Giants:** The arrival of players like Ford, Hyundai and Toyota changed the performance parameters in the component industry. The expectation that these organizations brought to India, based on their experience elsewhere was of a much higher order, as is borne out by the measurement of quality in PPM (parts per million) rather than in percentage, as was the practice in the industry earlier on. The importance of Just In Time (JIT) delivery made the component industry review the entire manufacturing system. Every aspect including packaging methods and modes of delivery had to be reviewed and often improved upon.

**Overcapacity:** In the mid-1990's there was a short period of euphoria created by a sudden spike in the growth rates of the auto industry and fuelled by two factors. The first was an overly optimistic forecast by a leading international management consultant. The second was what can be called the bandwagon effect of global auto majors coming to India without a proper market survey. The resultant overcapacity coupled with the enormous clout of the original equipment customers started exerting severe cost and margin pressures on the component industry.

**Cost Advantage:** The component industry in the European Union and North America has reached a point where the rate of increase of employee cost is sharper than the rate of increase in productivity. The industry in these regions had invested heavily in automation during the 1980s and 1990s. But the increasing range of products that the market demands today is not amenable to extremely rigid automated manufacturing. This being the scenario, these organizations have started looking at India as potential outsourcing destinations.

**Huge Export Potential:** The global trade in auto components is estimated at $1 trillion. The Indian export of *$800* million is less than one per cent of this potential. More auto component manufacturers are now joining the export club. However, there are issues and developments in the global world trade that India needs to address. There are still many impediments to rapid progress in the Indian system.

**Technology and Tariffs:** The policy makers must appreciate that there is a direct linkage between the level of technology flow and tariff levels in the country. India will still need at least a decade to catch up with the latest technology in the auto industry before it can risk the stoppage of technology flow due to very low import tariffs. A profile study of Indian exports would indicate that they score higher on products where there is labour intensity and products that involve environmentally hazardous processes (castings and forgings). Incidentally many of these Industries are also power intensive. However the reforms in the area of power in India have not taken off. The reasons are obvious. Unless this sector is made competitive, the cost of power would continue to be a major eroder of competitiveness.

**Threats from WTO:** As the developed countries had a major say in the formation of the WTO, there is an inherent bias in their favour in the whole scheme of things. If one were to look at the recent proposal under NGMA (Negotiating Group on Market Access) guideline, auto components were supposed to be one of the selected items on which WTO members would have to lower tariffs to zero over a period Indian industry and the Indian government this time have resisted the same at Cancun. The stated objective of this proposal was to help developing countries increase their exports. One is unable to understand how this can happen. India must guard against any further rapid reduction of import tariff for manufactured items below 20-25%.

**Incorporation and Integration**

Efforts combined with knowledge and tenacity is the springboard of accomplishment. In today's marketplace, the key to success is quality; we need to show that our products and services meet our customers' requirement and expectations. Operating in a competitive environment, GNA Enterprises is an auto component manufacturing plant, founded in 1946 by legendary Late Sardar Amar Singh spread on an area of 60,000 square meters with 15,000 square meters of covered space in hamlet - Bundala, Jalandhar. At the hub of its high quality of finished products through computer aided designs coupled with advanced Statistical Techniques strengthens company's ability to deliver defect free product at no extra cost to the global automobile industry.

**A Tribute to Late Sardar Amar Singh (1908-1996)**

The great values shown by him still guide the Group on the paths where the company have not treaded before. Business ethics, which he wrote and cherished for, still bolster stumbling steps. It was his great dream to establish a workplace amidst the people and the land to which they belong with a single-minded aim that people don't have to exodus from the place of their birth. It was he who brought workplace close to the people rather than people leaving their families in the villages and migrate towards cities. In the process he led the great revolution of industrialization of Indian villages and thus saving many lives from inhumane conditions of cities.

In a diverse society as ours it became almost imperative to run an organization on the egalitarian platform. As a true statesman he understood this fragile societal fabric well and welded an organization with dedication, skill and dexterity.

Scientific temper with saint at heart, rare combination, he set the new dimension for the generations to follow and emulate. A true leader is the one who strives towards achieving super-ordinate goals rather than ordinary goal. His legitimacy to the leadership was borne out of business ethics and values he stood for.

His company today is dedicated to the pursuit of excellence. It places high emphasis on continuously improving its systems, processes, product as well as environment. It's obtaining the prestigious QS 9000 and ISO 9002 certification reflects its ability to take the challenges from the front.

His company is today the largest integrated auto component manufacturing company in the Indian sub-continent with its product seeing more and more Pacific and Atlantic rim countries.

The journey started by him is still continuing and fathomed many miles since he left us in 1996 without any sign of effeteness. The company today as group salute him for all he has done to alter destinies.

**Company Profile**

Operating in a competitive environment, **Guru Nanak Auto Enterprises Ltd.** is an auto component manufacturing plant, founded in 1946 by legendary Late Sardar Amar Singh. It is spread over an area of 60,000 square metres with 15,000 square metres of covered space in Bundala, Jalandhar. Expanding continuously ever since under the stewardship of Mr. Jagdish Singh, Managing Director, the Company, today, has become the largest integrated plant of its kind in the Indian sub-continent with committed employment strength of 600.

To keep pace with modern times, the Company expertly applies breakthrough technology snapshots by providing innovative art-to-part engineering, state-of-the-art lean, flexible manufacturing with world-class infrastructure and on-time delivery of components like Rear Axle Shafts, Brake S'Cam Shafts, Torsion Bars, Steel Forgings, Wheel Spindles & Clutch Shafts from passenger cars and light trucks to heavy commercial vehicles.

Still further, the company provides in-depth support that can cut development time, improve process efficiency and help rewrite product quality and performance standards.

At the hub of its high quality finished products through computer aided design via I-DEAS and Computer Aided Manufacturing coupled with advanced Statistical Techniques like SPC, PMEA, PPAP, APQP and MSA empowers company's ability to deliver defect free product at no extra cost to the global automobile industry.

**Mission**

At Guru Nanak Auto Enterprises Ltd., the company is dedicated to enhance productivity and technology to stay on top of the quality ladder on every step of the way with an aim to be a true Global Operating Company.

The company measures growth by how well the company aligns itself to the needs of customers to achieve the highest level of customer satisfaction.

**Certifications**

The global quality standards of the company are attested by Underwriters Laboratories Inc. (UL), Melville, NY,

USA, which has certified the company's facility for QS 9000 & ISO 9002 in 1998.

**Performance and Product Profile**

From the modern facilities in Bundala, the company as a totally integrated facility produces in excess of one million auto parts in a year engineered to the demanding specs of its customers. The components include Rear Axle Shafts, Torsion Bars, Brake S Cam Shafts, CV Shafts, Pivot Pin, Output Shafts, Clutch Shafts, Wheel Bearing Spindles, Steel Forgings etc for LCV/MCV/HCV/SUV/Passenger Cars and Jeeps. Its unshackling commitment to the excellence in every aspect of their manufacturing has won the confidence of the leading automobile manufacturers across the globe. The company presently is OEM supplier to TELCO, Toyota-Kirloskar, Spicer India Ltd., Automotive Axles Ltd. (Meritor), Mahindra & Mahindra, Maruti, Eicher, Kirloskar, Swaraj Mazda, Dana Corporation – USA, Chrysler, Ford and Iveco of Turkey to name few.

**Conglomeration**

Today GNA as a group is a **conglomeration** of four companies namely **GNA Enterprises, GNA Udyog, GNA Duraparts and GNA Axles.** Expanding continuously ever since under the stewardship of dexterous sons of Late Sardar Amar Singh, GNA has reached to the level of terming itself a truly global class manufacture that has exhibited before the world what determination and perspiration can achieve.

**Journey**

The story of GNA can be easily compared to that of India. Both took birth almost simultaneously, former in 1946 and latter in 1947. Both at the outset were devoid of infrastructure and technology to present them before the world. However both had in their kitty the hard work and the perspiration which they were ready to put in to set an example of shining glory before the world. If Pandit Nehru gave the mantra of self realisation to built the foundation of the country, it was Sardar Amar Singh who with little infrastructure and skill he inherited from his father and grandfather laid the sapling of great Banyan tree which today is known in the industrial world as GNA. The two again in 1990s gave new direction to their sailing boat when India embarked on the path of globalisation and GNA simultaneously gave new impetus to the exports when they touched giants in the automobile industry like MMC-Japan, Dana Corporation-USA, Ford, Iveco and Chrysler of Turkey.

**Values**

One of the things noticed in the company through talks with Jagdish Singh is the respect and care his management shows toward its employees whom they term as team members. The Managing Director admitted, "It is the commitment, dedication and hard work of employees that are the basis of company's success in the highly competitive automobile industry. The company continually strive to develop a work culture that encourages continuous improvement in teamwork, safety, high quality and enhanced productivity by using the knowledge and skills of all employees."

**Operations and Strategies**

Manufacturing management dealing with the planning and control of manufacturing systems activities usually focuses on the operation activities in an industry. However the strategic aspect of manufacturing systems assumes a more important role in the dynamically changing, globally competitive circumstances. In this age of "market-in" rather than "product-out," it is essential to grasp the exact market needs and reflect them on the production processes.

To become or to remain the best manufacturer in the world is not the responsibility of the manufacturing management alone. Every level in each branch of an organization must aggressively pursue the common goals of increasing the productivity and return on investment at the same time reducing the operating costs.

To stay or to become the world's best and biggest, every manufacturer working on the product and process development must strive to upgrade existing facilities to the level or even beyond current world class manufacturing performance. Since the achievement of the world-class status is not enough, the new hallmark of excellence must be the continuous improvement to maintain the superior position

**Reliability and Customer Satisfaction**

GNA manufacturing facility employs the latest Statistical Process Control (SPC) techniques. The company have also established Statistical Quality Standard Measurement at every key stage in the manufacturing process

GNA products have longer life, greater strength, better resistance to heat and detonation, greater embedability and conformability.

The Company insists on compliance with international quality standards. However GNA can develop and supply customer specific requirement.

To satisfy the demand of after market, GNA has sales force that covers completely the whole of India. It has direct support from plant and an experienced team that provides technical assistance. The company offer a wide variety of products to service after market on time and with excellent quality.

**Product Range**

- **Rear Axle Shafts**
- **Brake S'Cam Shafts**
- **Torsion Bars**
- **Steel Forgings**
- **Wheel Spindles**
- **Clutch Shafts**

**Customers and Market**

The company serves both Indian and overseas markets for its various products.

**(In India)**
**For Light Commercial Vehicles**

| CUSTOMER | KNOW HOW |
|---|---|
| Tata Engg & Locomotive Co. Ltd. | Mercedes Benz, Germany |
| Swaraj Mazda Ltd. | Mazda, Japan |
| Eicher Motors Ltd. | Mitsubishi ,Japan |
| Mahindra and Mahindra | Nissan, Japan |

**For Medium, Heavy Commercial Vehicles**

| | |
|---|---|
| Tata Engg & Locomotive Co. Ltd. | Mercedes Benz |
| Automotive Axles Ltd. | Meritor |
| Dana Spicer Ltd. | Data Corporation Ltd. (USA) |

**For Cars & Jeeps, Pickup & Utility Vehicles**

| | |
|---|---|
| Maruti Udyog Ltd. | Suzuki Corp Ltd Japan |
| Premier Auto Ltd. | Peugeot France |
| Tata | |
| Mahindra & Mahindra | Willys |
| Toyota Kirloskar Motors | Toyota Motors, Japan |

**(In Overseas)**

| OEM | | |
|---|---|---|
| Ford, Turkey | | USA |
| IVECO, Turkey | | Italy |

| After Market | | | |
|---|---|---|---|
| Mercedes Benz | Land Rover | Willy's Jeep | Chevrolet GM |
| Chrysler Dodge | Bedford Vauxhall | Ford | British Leyland |
| Toyota | Nissan | Mazda | Suzuki |

**Testing Facilities**

- Metallurgical Microscope with image analyzer
- Metascope
- Ultrasonic Flaw Detectors
- Micro Hardness Tester
- Profile Projector
- Surface Roughness Testers
- Magnaflux Testing
- Torque Testing Machine
- BHN, HRC & Vicker Hardness Testers
- Co-promoter of Institute of Auto parts Centre, a joint venture of UNDP/UNIDO & Punjab State Government, having testing facilities-
- Fatigue Testing (MTI make)
- Universal Testing
- Spectrometer
- X-Ray Fluorescence spectrometer.
- 3D- CMM

**Management's Perspective**

Gurinder Singh, promising son of illustrious father very clearly forecasted the future strategy with which every Indian company has to gear up with if the same wants to stay in the business. He stated "The survival strategy for the coming industrial scenario includes reducing cost of manufacturing, stable manufacturing process that is devoid of both internal and external quality failures, reducing significantly the new product development time and capability of doing right first time. There is stronger need to automate the process, mechanisms and systems in order to achieve repeated quality standards at all levels of the industry. One area the company is overlooking but must not is area of research & development. More effort and bigger investment in this sector is certainly going to pay us the rich dividends. The need of today is to strive hard to widen ones marketing horizons and make forays into untapped and potential export markets. The company require motivated people to work with hand, brain and heart to get better results. The manager of the industry has to foresee the future in advance."

Gurinder Singh further narrated his strategy in the forthcoming years clearly stressing focus on diversification, exports & more outlay for the research and development activities. His self confessed aim is to become important and strongest link to the overall supply chain management in the years to come.

Jagdish Singh admits that slowly the government of India has realized the potential Indian auto components makers in the field of exports. Welcoming the new medium-term export strategy of GOI, he confessed that if implemented effectively, has the potential to take exports of auto components to one billion dollar from the current level of 600 million dollars in the next four years. This three pronged strategy will focus on to boost auto component export through leading overseas vehicle manufacturers in the in the country, buyback arrangements with global tier-1 manufacturers in India and direct exports to overseas after markets. He however very categorically reminded that the auto component sector is worried over the World Trade Organization regulations being put into effect, as it would result in flood of imports of components, thereby affecting the indigenous industry. He wanted to convey through this medium to finance ministry to maintain the customs duty levels on imported components at the current level of 30% for at least another three years, so that the domestic industry gets sufficient time.

True are the concerns shown by the man whose company has seen many ups and down in the last 55 years. It deserves an attention all the more when the company realize that Indian automobile industry has become Rs 50,000 crore investment industry, an industry which employ 4.5 lakh people directly and more than 1 crore people indirectly and also contributes nearly 5 percent of the industrial output in the country.

It is really heartening to know that company is all prepared to go for EMS-Environment Management System and NABL accreditation of its inspection and testing facilities in line with overall dream of becoming truly global competitive company.

GNA is a pride of India and India is proud of its shining star. It was perhaps because of these greats the statesman like Arnold Toynbee once said :It is already becoming clear that a chapter, which had a western beginning, will have to have an Indian ending if it is not to end in the self-destruction of human race. The 19$^{th}$ & 20$^{th}$ century was the period of European and American expansionism and dominance. The nationhood, which India acquired in the 20$^{th}$ century, fulfilling the dreams of Ashoka and Akbar, has now brought it to the threshold of great power status at the beginning of the 21$^{st}$ century. It is widely accepted that the new century will be Asian one in which India will play dominant role."

**Diversification**

GNA Engine Component Division is a division of Guru Nanak Auto Enterprises Limited, a company established over 50 years ago, engaged in manufacturing of various types of automobile components such as Rear Axle Shafts, Brake S' Cam Shafts, Torsion Bars, CV Shafts and steel forgings, having strong presence for OEMs, Government Institutions & Export applications.

GNA has now diversified into manufacturing of Bimetal Bushes and Thrust Washers, Piston Pins, Rocker Shafts for all automobile applications including Trucks (both LCVs & HCVs ), Tractors, Cars, Air Compressors, Diesel Engines, Locomotives, Marine Engines & Pumps etc. Also introducing Main & CR Bearings for all types of vehicles very soon.

The company has latest technology incorporated in the production of modern Engine Bearings in very close tolerances & is committed to the implementation and achievement of ISO 9000 & QS 9000 norms and the standards of excellence.

| **Snapshots** |
|---|
| **Name of the Company**<br>Guru Nanak Auto Enterprises Ltd.<br>**Year of Establishment**<br>1946<br>**Located at**<br>Bondala, Goraya, Distt. Jalandhar, Punjab.<br>**Main Products**<br>Rear Axle Shafts, Brake S'Cam Shafts, Torsion Bars, Steel Forgings, Wheel Spindles & Clutch Shafts<br>**Total Turnover**<br>Rs. 270 crore: Domestic 55%, Foreign 45%<br>**Quality Certification**<br>The global quality standards of the company are attested by Underwriters Laboratories Inc. (UL), Melville, NY, USA<br>**Flagship Company**<br>Guru Nanak Auto Enterprises Ltd.<br>**Main domestic market**<br>Through out India<br>**Foreign market:** Germany, Japan, USA, France, Italy |

**Incorporation and Integration**

The origin of the present GS Group dates back to1948 when late Baba Gurmukh Singh Ji started manufacturing bicycle components. Baba Gurmukh Singh Ji was a self-motivated person, devoid of parental love & education. He started working as an apprentice in a smithy shop in his native village near Machiwara just at the age of 12 years. Later on he started a venture of his own and soon started making automotive components of the improved vehicles. Flagship Company of the group GS Auto International was private Ltd. Firms till 1985 and was known as GS and Sons (P) Ltd. However, it was converted to public Ltd. Company afterwards.

The GS group has constituent companies namely GS Auto International Ltd., GS Radiators, GS Sales Corporation, Ryait Exports, GS Foods Ltd. and Music Division.

**About the Group Companies**

GS Auto International Ltd. is the flagship company of the group started in1948 today GS Auto International Ltd. has got a team of 1000 young dedicated technicians, which are looking for excellence in quality and workmanship. Sound engineering skills honed over a period of 50 years in the armoury of its people is the best weapon in the GS armoury. Cost effectiveness and customer service is at its best when coupled with latest state of art equipment supported by Computer Aided Design (CAD), Computer Aided Manufacturing (CAM) and Computer Aided Engineering (CAE). Centre bolts, U-bolts, Hub bolt King Pins, Computer Aided are passed through numerous steps at stages of design, raw material procurement process.

All the guidelines from quality manual are followed and GS Auto International is having quality certifications both in forms of ISO 9002 and QS 9000.ISO 9002 was obtained by the firm in 1997 –1998 and QS 9002 in 2000. QS-9000 is a Quality certification on the theme of ISO 9000 but with a difference.

GS Auto has joined a cluster of fourteen Indian companies in January 2001 under the program initiated jointly by ACT, CACMA Centre of Technology and CII (Confederation of Indian Industry). The mission of this program is to bring about improvement in the production processes by way of concept propagated and practiced by major automotive companies the world over. Under the joint program the cluster member companies are required to carry out self-audition and improvements in house based.

**GS Radiators Limited**

Started in 1992 GS Radiators is carrying out manufacturing operations by adopting the latest technology from Calsonic Llanellc Radiators Ltd, UK .It has developed a wide range of radiators for almost all vehicle manufacturers in India like: -Telco, Ashok Leyland, Swaraj, Mazda, Swaraj Tractors, Mahindra & Mahindra and Hindutan Motors.

The plant is equipped with full fledged design facilities with expert design skills, calibration facilities with expert design skills, calibration facilities as well as tool room having latest machines with high level precision. Facilities are also available for prototype development and testing. Due to these R&D efforts GSR has developed and supplied Radiators for latest generation vehicles like VOLVO, Saab and Mazda 626.The total investment in GS radiator stands at

Rs.358 lakh and total turnover of the firm is over Rs.1608 lakh.

**GS Sales Corporation**

The firm was started in 1994 to provide a platform to the local units by exploring synergies .The products under exploring synergies. The products under "GSC" (GS Sales Corporation) include a range of truck & tractor parts. The components are being marketed throughout India.

**Ryait Exports**

Year 1990 saw the start of Ryait exports. Presently the company is engaged in Export of handtools, automotive components, machine tools and steels, handicrafts and agricultural implements are also being exported by Ryait Exports.

**Product Profile**

**Automotive Components**

**Cast:** Shakle, Brackets, Plates, Clamps (2 Kg-12 Kg)

**Forged:** Wheel/Hub bolts, Washers, High and Castle nuts (hot as well as cold)

**Machined:** King pin kits, Spring Pins, Axle Studs, Check Nuts, Bushes, U-bolts, Centre bolts

**G.S. Radiators Ltd.**

Radiators for all Automobiles mainly Telco. Ashok Leyland, Swaraj, Hindustan Motors, M&M

**G.S. Sales Corporation**

Marketing of Truck 7 Tractors parts under brand name GSC throughout India outsourcing from domestic manufacturers

**Ryait Exports:** Exports of Hand Tools, Automotive components, Machine Tools & Steels, Handicraft & Agricultural implements.

**Certifications**

G S Autos is accredited with QS 9000 and ISO 9002 certifications by BVQI, U.K. Each component passes through numerous tests at the stages of design, raw material inspection and of course throughout the manufacturing process. Conformance to the quality begins at the shop floor, with each worker following the quality guidelines as laid down in the quality manual. The following quality requirements are taken care of at GS Autos for conformance to quality standards, on time delivery, maintaining product quality and handling customer's complaints.

- APQP (Advanced product quality planning)
- PPAP (production part approval process)
- FMEA (Failure mode effect analysis)
- SPC (Statistical process control)
- MSA (Measurement system analysis

**Distribution Network**

Presently group is endorsing its presence through a vast dealer network with more than 500 dealers mapping the whole nation as well as making marks abroad via sales officers. Group is presently operating in OEM and replacement markets and is also growing overseas .The clients of the group who have shown faith in competitiveness of GS include Ashoka Leyland, Hindustan Motors, Delphi Automotive Systems and Daewoo Motor. GS Group has made its presence felt in countries like Holland, Malaysia, Egypt, Kenya, Germany, Iraq, Kuwait, U.A.E., Morocco, and United Kingdom etc.

**Management's Perspective**

The management views that in order to succeed in life one must be enthusiastic and dynamic to deal the various facets of life. One of the important function of management i.e. motivation, also plays an important role to reach the heights. At the same time quality consciousness also holds true because quality is the important criteria considered for evaluation in this competitive era. GS is in lead as compared to its competitor by reducing manufacturing cost, material handling etc. and maintaining a competitive pricing edge. GS Group has also adopted new advancement in the arena of computers and thus strengthened the information flow.

GS group has distinction of adopting various statistical techniques like PPC, Inventory Control to bring co-ordination at various stages of manufacturing and thus reducing the processing time. GS Group quickly adopt the latest changes, which is clearly implicit in the decision to impart in house training to the employees for nine months by IBM. Although conditions have improved a lot since beginning of reforms in 1991 but till date we must admit a lot of red tapism is still hindering the entrepreneurs in different ventures.

Globalization is considered as an opportunity by GS Group. Modern techniques can always help and real issue is getting different techniques and concepts into act .GS group always responded to global challenges and presently we are having both ISO 9001 and QS 9001 certifications to our credit. Recently 5s is being implemented in the group factories and implementation phase is almost over and the results are just wonderful and improvements have to level of 100% in each section on various counts. Mushrooming of technical education is quite seen but hampering the growth of engineers because of lack of practical exposure. If one is not through with working and maintenance of the machine one cannot be a good technicians. During their professional courses, students from various engineering and management institutes have to undergo internship but the question arises, how many actually benefited from it. The need of the hour is to bring some prescribed standards and then only training completion certificates should be issued to the trainees.

GS foods limited, is another feather in the cap of GS Autos, which deals in the trading activities In a span of coming 10 years GS Group would like to be leader in auto component manufacturing so we are looking up to some expansion in our capacity and we hope GS Auto will conform to 'Factory of Future" concept by adding latest technology like Computer Integrated Mfg. (CIM), Robotics and Flexible manufacturing system with adding of latest facilities and equipment's. Social responsibility is given due importance by GS Group by its involvement in education and social concern. Guru Nanak Public School, Ramgarhia Girl's College, Ramgarhia Middle School and Ramgarhia Senior Secondary School are prominent educational institutions being run under the patronage of the group in Ludhiana.

| **Snapshots** |
|---|
| **Year of Start**<br>1938<br>**Located at:**<br>G.T. Road, Ludhiana.<br>**Automobile Components**<br>(Cast, Forged, Manufactured): Radiators, Tea, Hand Tools,<br>**Total Turnover**<br>Rs.60 crore, Domestic Turnover: 55%, Foreign Turnover: 45%<br>**Certifications:** ISO 9002&9000<br>**Major Collaborations:** Calsonic Zlanelli Radiators (UK) for Radiators<br>**Flagship Company:** G.S. Auto International Ltd.<br>**Main Markets being served Domestic**<br>All over India, main markets are Maharashtra, MP & UP<br>**Foreign Market:** UK, Germany, Holland, Africa |

# Section 3: Cycle and Cycle Parts

- Indian Cycle and Cycle Parts Industry
- AVON Cycles Limited
- Bhogal Group
- Eastman Industries Limited
- Hero Cycles Limited

# Indian Cycle and Cycle Parts Industry

With an annual turnover of more than 14 million bicycles, the bicycle industry in India is one of the most established the country has today. It has raised the country's position to that of the second largest bicycle manufacturer in the world, next only to China. Today not only is the Indian bicycle industry well accepted but is also widely recognized for its quality standards in international markets.

The Indian bicycle industry came into existence when East India Company came to Calcutta in the year. It was at that time that the English people brought bicycle technology to' India. At that time, the parts were imported, assembled and then marketed in India. In 1953, the scenario changed entirely, when some of the noted companies like Hero and Avon were given the license to manufacture bicycles.

After almost four decades, in the post 1991 scenario Indian industries are free to breath in the global environment. But at the same time this change has thrown up a number of challenges before the local industrial houses. In the presence of high tax rates, bureaucratic control and poor infrastructure the home industry finds it tough to stand upto global competition. Despite all these adversities, the cycle industry has grown to 10 million cycles a year and is growing at the rate of 11 percent per annum.

The bicycle industry is currently in the midst of making endeavors for enhanced and increased bicycle exports since the scope for export of Indian manufactured bicycles in the international market is significant. As per public reports the present level of exports fall within the range of Rs. 150 crores.

Some facts about the Bicycle Industry

- Between January and April 2000: 270000 bicycles were produced in India and only 10,000 were imported.
- During 1998-99 the export bicycle and parts was worth Rs. 60 million.
- During 1999-2000 the export of bicycle and parts increased to Rs. 70 Million.
- Out of total production of bicycles in India about 60% of the bicycles are produced in Ludhiana only.
- More than 80% of total Bicycle parts production is also produced in Ludhiana district.
- Hero Cycle Limited is the world record holder in bicycle production in 1987 registered in Guiness Book of World Records by producing 2,494,649 units in a year.

**Challenges before the Industry**

- Rising Price of Steal
- Heavy Taxation By Government
- Work Force Strikes
- Competition from China
- Competition from other Motor Bikes industry.

**Future of the Industry**

The bicycle industry in India is registering a continuous growth year after year. Aspirations and expectations of consumers have witnessed a lot of change thereby the overall scenario in this industry has undergone a visible change. The bicycle industry has also taken necessary steps and has prepared itself fully to adapt this change. The future of Indian bicycle industry seems to be quite bright. The socio-economic scenario appears to be favorable for the country to improve its performance making its impact visible in the industry as well. There will be a change in the demand pattern linked with consumer's changing aspirations and choices. This industry is already witnessing this to some extent. The newer segments of the market, like fancy bicycles, will grow far more rapidly. It would not at all be surprising if by 2010 the fancy bicycles and roadster bicycles have almost equal market share against existing 20% market share of fancy bicycles.

# AVON Cycles Limited

**Incorporation and Integration**

The group was incorporated in 1952 with an initial investment of Rs.50000/- and started manufacturing bicycle forks. The turnover today has reached a staggering Rs. 600 crore. AVON Cycles Limited has four divisions:

| Division | Location | Product |
|---|---|---|
| Unit – 1 | Ludhiana | Cycle Parts - Handle, Chain, Pedal Hub etc. |
| Unit – II (Head Office) | Ludhiana | Bicycles & Cycle parts - Fork, Frame, Chain cover |
| Unit – III | Ludhiana | Steel pipes |
| Unit – IV | Ludhiana | Rim |

**Background and Historical Perspective**

One among pioneers in Bicycle Industry in India with a strong presence in the world market, AVON Cycles Limited is based at Ludhiana. Three Pahwa brothers founded the group: Mr Hans Raj Pahwa, Mr. Jagat Singh Pahwa and Mr. Sohan Lal Pahwa. The unit started manufacturing forks as a small-scale industry in 1952. Today the company is a major player in bicycle and bicycle parts in the large-scale sector

The company's head office and manufacturing units are located in Ludhiana, a bustling industrial city located in the state of Punjab, the Bicycle capital of the world. AVON Cycles comprises of four units. Established half a century ago, AVON today is a household name. Consistently providing the common man with his means of transport at affordable prices, the house of AVON has contributed significantly in satisfying his need for mobility in a pollution-free and user-friendly manner

Each bicycle made by the company is a testimony to top quality craftsmanship bicycle parts products by AVON are certified by ISI. Also, AVON is the only manufacturer of bicycles in India certified by ISI. AVON celebrated its 50 years of existence in 2002.

**Avon group comprises of the following five companies:**

1. Avery Cycle Industries Ltd. Ludhiana
2. Avon Cycle Ltd. Ludhiana
3. Pahwa Cycles Private Ltd. Ludhiana
4. Pahwa Chains Private Ltd. Chandigarh
5. Avery Free Wheels Pvt. Ltd. Chandigarh

The company's Head office and manufacturing units are conveniently located on the G.T. Road at Ludhiana, a buzzing industrial city in the northern state of Punjab. The city is well connected with other major cities and ports by Rail, Road and Air. The national capital Delhi is 300 kms. away.

Beyond the Indian shores, AVON goes to more than 80 countries worldwide. In Bicycles and Bicycle parts, the company distinguishes itself as the Largest Exports from India. That the company has enjoyed this status now for five years running speaks of the brand's ever growing popularity overseas. Avon is recognised by the Government of India as a 'Golden Trading House'.

## Profile of the Company

### Product Profile

| | |
|---|---|
| **Range:** | 1. Bicycle of 50+ description and even greater number of combinations;<br>2. Exerciser, junior and senior;<br>3. Bicycle parts, wide range. |
| **Bicycle Models:** | To satisfy all Age Groups: from the starry-eyed urge of a toddler reaching for his first pedals, all the way up to the excitement and thrill as a 21-speed sturdy MTB_Avon has one, made just right for you! |
| **Application:** | Wide spectrum: commuting, touring, transport, adventure, fun & sport, vending/delivery operations, physical fitness, group pursuits etc. The machine`s capability to perform anywhere out of nowhere, allows it an unimaginable number of applications. |
| **Customer Focus:** | In addition to the customer specified requirements, We ensure those not specified but considered necessary with reference to the intended use and any regulatory and legal requirements. |
| **Quality Management System:** | ISO 9001:2000(E) |

**Marketing Profile**

**Philosophy:** For every AVON product to be an excellent value For Money (VFM) proposition the company adopts a proactive role to determine level of satisfaction and understand the changing consumer aspirations. `Aap ne sujhayi, hum ne banayi` meaning `We made it exactly as you wanted us to` has been the company's regular advertising refrain.

**Distribution:** Inland, through a well-established network of about 1,500 AVON authorised dealers in cities and towns of India. A dedicated force of more than 12,000 sub dealers supports the dealership`s operations.

Overseas operations are conducted through Representatives in respective countries / regions. The company`s executives are regularly visiting overseas markets, Trade fairs and Exhibitions.

**Logistics:** For safe and speedy delivery to the dealership points spread across the length and breadth of the country the company employs a number of reputed transporters and hauliers on a sub-contracting basis. For multiple delivery point trips thc company`s accompanying attendant ensures correct and proper delivery.

**Production**

| | |
|---|---|
| **Technology:** | Regularly updated responsible and sustainable cleaner production technologies are employed. |
| **Planning:** | PPC department co-ordinates with the Inland and Overseas wings of the Marketing department to ensure correct and timely shipments. |
| **Work environment:** | Clean, congenial and commensurate environment keeps the work force motivated. Workers Participation in goal setting makes them exceptionally self-driven. |
| **Human resource:** | Recruitment and training hings on the principle of right man for the right job on agreeable terms. On-job training, orientation training and HRD training is a continuing process. |
| **Product Realisation:** | The process and machinery employed are consistent with the Quality Management System in place. Periodical customer feedback on quality, level of satisfaction and servicing of complaints is relied upon as a regular input for improvement. |

**Certifications**

Avon has obtained the coveted ISO 9001certifications from TUV –Germany and Golden Trading House certificate from Ministry of Commerce, Govt. of India.

**Foreign Presence**

AVON Cycles Limited is the largest manufacturer exporter of bicycles and bicycle parts from India. AVON goes to more than 80 countries worldwide. AVON Cycles Limited bagged the Top Exporter Award for fifth year running. To the overseas buyer, the company offers a choice of 50 plus models of bicycles and spares to suit a wide variety of market specifications. Quality at affordable price is made possible by a state-of-the-art manufacturing plant supported by most modern techniques and superior logistics.

AVON is recognized by the Govt. of India as a 'Star Golden Trading House'.

Major export destinations include: UK.Africa, Germany, Switzerland, UAE, Egypt, Bangladesh and Nepal.

**Competitors**

The competitors of AVON cycles limited are:

1. Hero Cycles Limited
2. Atlas Cycles
3. TI Cycles

**Management's Perspective**

Management is highly indebted to its laborious and sincere employees who have strived hard and put in their best efforts to make Avon earn a name in the Cycle Industry. Avon Cycle put in a lot of emphasis on the development of its human resource. Workshops, Conferences, Executive and Workers development programmes are regular features in the organization. management of Avon Cycles consider their employees as part of their family and HR policies of the organization give due concern to employees' welfare.

Management admits whole heartedly that Information Technology has contributed substantially to the changed face of the organization. Computers are being used in every department of the organization. Company has hired computer professionals and employees of the organization are also being trained to equip themselves with expertise in this field. Due to high competition and market saturation, the company is focusing on cost reduction measures to reduce the cost of production. Avon Cycles has also kept its profit margin quite low to have an edge over its competitors in the market. The same has resulted in products at cheaper rates leading to the increase in market share of the company.

However, the company gives equal importance and preference to in-house R&D facilities so that it can improve upon its products and incorporate new features.

Management is of the opinion that Indian cycle industry in the light of low cost competition from China has enough capabilities to combat any threat from anywhere in the world. Industrialists of India are very enterprising and innovative and have the potential to excel in any kind of situation. Avon. Cycles is proceeding with the immediate expansion and up gradation of the existing facilities. Indians are capable enough to face challenges of globalization. Government should contribute by more positive and long-range policies.

Keeping in view the changes in the present business environment and emerging challenges before the corporate, management of AVON cycle believes that role of professional education in present times is highly crucial and important. It becomes the foremost responsibility of the professional institutes to deliver best of the input to the industry in the present competitive environment. Along with industry should also encourage the participation and seek support of academicians to solve their day-to-day problems. Industry and academia if joins hand together, there is no doubt that India will be a super power in 2020 as envisioned by Hon'ble President of India.

| **Snapshots** |
|---|
| **Year of Start**<br>1952<br>**Located at:**<br>G.T. Road, Ludhiana<br>**Main Products/Operations**<br>Bicycle & Bicycle Parts<br>**Total Turnover**<br>Rs. 600 crores<br>**Domestic Turnover**<br>60%<br>**Foreign Turnover**<br>40%<br>**Certifications**<br>ISO 9001 from TUV-Germany<br>**New Ventures**<br>Upgradation and expansion of existing manufacturing facilities<br>**Flagship Company**<br>Avon Cycles Limited<br>**Domestic Market**<br>All over India<br>**Foreign Markets**<br>U.K., Africa, Germany, Switzerland, UAE, Egypt, Bangladesh, Nepal |

# BHOGAL Group

## Incorporation and Integration

The Bhogal group was started by Sardar Karam Singh Bhogal -1938 as a small manufacturing company dealing in bicycle components. It is counted among the first Indian companies who ventured into manufacture of bicycle components. This is one of those conglomerates, which can boast of being totally Indianised or indigenised company and has survived very well in the face of stiff competition.

This has been possible through maintaining strict Quality standards, cutting edge technology and cutting cost efficiently. But as said "Rome was not built in a day", this formidable giant started off as Chakkar & Company by two partners namely Sardar Karam Singh and Sardar Channan Singh. The company initially produced cycle parts like Hubcone, BBAxle and auto parts. This company started off with 6-10 employees. The initial employees were none other than youth who were formally thinking of entering military as soldiers. Thus the company was also one of the companies who gave the right direction to jobless yet efficient youth.

S. Mohinder Singh Bhogal s/o S. Karam Singh Bhogal separated from the parent company and launched a new company - Bhogals Sons - in April, 1948. Bhogal Sons, and Bhogal Exports, the exporting arm of the group, together consist of 5 companies spread over 25,000 Sq. Mtr. of area and employ more than 600 people.

## About the Company

Bhogal Group is a group of companies engaged in the manufacture of engineering goods. Established in 1938, Bhogal Sons (Regd.) was amongst the pioneers in India to manufacture Bicycle components. Today BHOGAL is a known brand in National as well as International markets. Bhogal is exporting to Europe, USA and other countries since 1960.

Today, Bhogal is spread over 25,000 sq. meters of area and employs more than 600 people, with its turnover touching 460 Million Rupees. Bhogal Exports, which is an Exports House recognized by the Govt. of India, is accredited with ISO 9002 by the prestigious DNV of Holland.

**Mission of Bhogal Group**

Bhogals will continue to evolve its resources, both intellectual as well as infrastructural, to cater to the requirements of customers. It will also strive to provide solutions, which are simple, usable, and functionally superior.

To evolve our resources, both intellectual as well as infrastructural, to cater to the requirements of our customers by providing them high quality products and prompt services.

**Product Profile**

**Complete Range of Bicycle Parts**

Cotterless Bottom Bracket Axle ■ Bottom Bracket Axle ■ Bottom Bracket Bearing Cups ■ Bottom Bracket Bearing Cups with Ball Retainer Front ■ Rear Hubs with Quick Release ■ Hub Axles with Quick Release ■ Chains ■ Chain Tensioners ■ Chain Wheels (Single and Multiple Speed) ■ Free Wheels (Single and Multiple Speed) ■ Hub Cones ■ Auto Parts ■ Wheel Pulley Mbk ■ Wheel Pulley Pgt ■ Vehicle Lowering and Lifting kits (2 wheel drive and 4 wheel drive) ■ Engine Mounts ■ Aluminium components for automotive shock absorbers.

## Bhogals' Family Chart

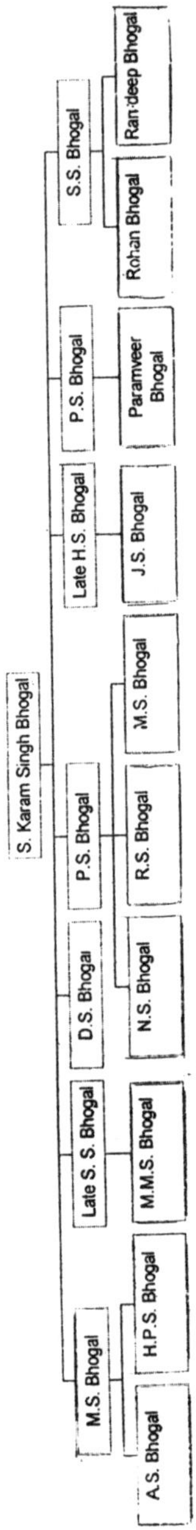

**Awards/Certifications**

Best Industrial Unit in the State (1965-66) (Before the Division of Punjab) ■ Shield by Director of Industries, Punjab (1966) This award was given for manufacturing Bicycles, Sewing machines and Quality components. They had 100% indigenous self designed machines ■ Export Special Award (1980-81) (For Producing New Product BB Axle) ■ A.R. Bhatt Entrepreneurship Award (1984) ■ District Level Productivity Award (1985) ■ National Award for "Best Lab for Quality Product"(1995) ■ ISO-9002 Accreditation by DNV for Bhogal Exports.

**Management's Perspective**

Bhogals started off under the flagship of Sardar Karam Singh Bhogal. The main aim of the organization was to stop foreign goods from taking the marketshare. Charan Singh was the partner in the partnership firm named Chakkar and Company. The initial product mix launched in the market was BBAxle, Hubcone , Paddle Axle. Hub Cub was started in 1948.The partnership firm Chakkar and Company was located near Rekhi Cinema. The employees were the ones who were initially going to be recruited in army. Sardar karam Singh imparted free service and free know how to them so that they could work in the firm.

Their main strategy was to get local workers at less wages. This seemingly small firm grew to become a conglomerate. Currently they have 4 factories and one Exporting unit. Bhogal Exports, their exporting branch exports to U.K., Germany, Holland, France, Belgium, Italy, Switzerland, Spain, Portugal, Mexico, Uruguay, New Zealand, Australia, Japan, USA, Canada, etc..

The group is focused to improve the quality of goods and earn a good name for the country. Their total turnover from domestic and foreign sales at present is Rs. 460 Million. Their Product Portfolio has increased considerably .At present their Product-Mix comprises of BBAxle, BB cup, Hub parts, Hub, Paddle, Free Wheel (on contract), Steel Bar (Product quantity of o/s not more than 100 P.C packet sealed). All products are carefully sealed, thus the chances of product getting lost by theft are nil. The_Bhogals have recently launched a range of cycle and kickcyles for teenagers.

Bhogals have diversified into manufacture and Export of Automotive Lowering and Lifting Kits meant for offroad vehicles and SUV's & MUV's. Currently these are exported 100% to the U.S. after-market.

Regarding the competitors, they believe that there is no direct competition so long as their products are of high quality. This they ensure by Stringent Quality tests in Lab and high Pricing by having uniform pricing policy. They ensure that the prices of their product remain the same through out the country by way of their chain of stockists.

The company believes in Quality. Bhogals have been awarded IS09002 certification by the International Standards Organisation. Thus the Quality Policy has been implemented throughout the organisation. The company believes in Customer care. If any Product is defective, it is immediately sent back to the company. This speaks a lot about their company which values Customer & its relationship with the company. Their products are used throughout India. But in terms of Quantity their main market is Uttar Pradesh.

In terms of the foreign market, they conform to the European market requirements. Bhogals attribute the success of their business to Quality and regular hard work. Mohinder Singh has a firm belief in the maintenance of quality of his goods He often says "Do not let the quality of goods to deteriorate, otherwise you would not survive." This adage has led to the development of 3 more sister concerns such as Bhogal Sales corporation, Bhogals Exports and Bhogals Private limited.

In the light of liberal imports from China, Bhogals are of view that there is absolutely no problem from China. It is felt because of the not-so-good quality of the Chinese products. A possible loophole that is working in favour of China is that Chinese Labour laws are not stringent. Their labour law consists of just 9 pages. Labour has to work in 2 shifts of 10 hours each. Working hours are flexible in terms that working time can be increased from 10 to12 hours No extra payment is made for extra hours put in. There is no holiday or Sunday in China.. In India the labour scenario is not very bright since here labour work for 8 hours in 3 shifts.

| Snapshots |
|---|
| **Year of Start**<br>1938<br>**Located at:**<br>G.T. Road, Ludhiana<br>**Main Products/Operations**<br>Axels, Hubs,_BBAxle, BB cup, Hub parts, Hub, Paddle, Free Wheel, Steel Bar<br>**Total Turnover:** 460 Million Rs.<br>**Certificates:** ISO 9001( Bhogal Exports)<br>**New Ventures**<br>Ice Cream carts / Kids Cycles / Automotive Lowering and Lifting Kits for SUV's / MUV's<br>**Major Collaborations**<br>Tied with Hindustan Liver Ltd. (Ice cream division)<br>**Flagship Company:** Bhogal Sons (Regd.)<br>**Main Markets Being Served**<br>**Domestic:** All over India<br>**Foreign:** UK, Germany, Holland, France, Belgium, Italy, Switzerland, Spain, Portugal, Mexico, New Zealand, Australia, Japan, USA, Canada |

# Eastman Industries Limited

## Incorporation and Integration

The concept of Eastman originated in 1971 by Mr. J. R. Singhal with initial investment of Rs 25000 with 6 employees. Initial products were rubber for the brake system in the bicycle. The first division was Eastman Rubber Industries at 437-Industrial Area 'B' Ludhiana. The initial turnover in the first year was l lac and forty two thousand rupees The simple entrepreneurial philosophies and integrated corporate policies have mobilized the company to achieve a present turnover of 30 million $.

Drawing strength from vast professional experience of its managers in this field, Eastman offers a wide range of products to meet the stringent needs of consumers. It is one of the fast movers on the global scene, supplying the world with quality bikes, components and accessories. It is responsive to market trends and serves business partners well with new product lines and healthy pricing.

Eastman industries Ltd. has been a pioneer in exports to Middle East, Europe and Latin America. It took two decades of rigorous efforts, besides keeping itself abreast with latest innovations world over to make it a leading name.

## About the Company

The present portfolio of Eastman consists of merchandising of bicycles, components and accessories as well as manufacturing of hand tools. The total turnover is US $30 million out of which 50% is from export market. Its main competitors are Hero, Avon, Atlas and TI cycles. The company is serving major OEMs in the domestic market. It is an ISO 9002 : 1998 certified company.

**Years to Remember for Eastman**

- 1978: The shipment of Eastman group bicycle brake shoes leaves for foreign shores.
- 1980: Argentina bikes move on the road equipped with Eastman bike parts.
- 1981-1986: Good business ties develop with a few other Latin American countries
- 1986 onwards: On to Europe, Middle East and Far East. Product adaptation and market research was initiated under World Bank project.
- 1997-98: Eastman receives National Export Award from the then Prime Minister of India.
- 2000: Eastman got ISO 9002 accreditation
- 2001: Quality in service ! Web based dynamic product catalog and customer servicing features introduced.
- 2002: Year of adding a few new products in the List.

**About the Chairman**

Mr. J. L. Singal born on Jan 3, 1946. 55 years old is a graduate having 28 years of experience in Small Scale Industry and Exports with a thrust area in Latin America countries. He is working as a managing director of Eastman Industries Ltd and Eastman Cast and Forge Ltd.

Mr. J. L. Singal has also held important positions in industry

- Vice Chairman, Punjab State Council – CII
- Former Chairman of Bicycle Parts & accessories of EEPC for All India
- Member – Punjab Export Promotion Board
- Member-Advisory Committee of Christian Medical College and Hospital, Ludhiana

- Treasurer-Shree Guru Nanak Dev committee with Deputy Commissioner of Ludhiana as President & Sh. S.P. Oswal as Vice President
- Member-Regional Advisory Committee of Custom Commisionrate, Amritsar

His wife Mrs. Darshana Singhal 50 years old is a graduate and working as a Director and his son Mr. Shekhar Singhal 25 years old is a commerce graduate and a MBA from IMT, Ghaziabad

**Mission Statement**

To make Eastman a preferred source of supply by providing the most appropriate products and services of the best possible quality, in the fastest possible manner, at the most reasonable prices

**Quality Policy**

To ensure that the customer considers Eastman Industries Ltd primary source for its requirements.

**Strategy**

- Continuous improvement in Quality System and quick redressal of customer complaint.
- Uniformity in specifications, OEM focused business presence in commercial fields and timely delivery to customers.
- To improve capabilities by regular training of work skills
- Self answerability of employees for effective communication
- To assist vendors in product development and inform them regularly

- To leverage Government policies for becoming better player
- Flawless Auditing

**Eastman Cast and Forge Limited**

It is a sixteen-year-old company, incorporated in the year 1986, with a manufacturing facility on sprawling 70,000 square feet covered area. The ECFC plant in Ludhiana manufactures a wide range of carbon steel and chrome vanadium Hand Tools.

An ISO 9002 certified facility to manufacture, EFCL started with an edge when it bagged prized O.E. accounts like Mahindra & Mahindra, Bajaj Auto – World's largest manufactures of scooters having collaboration with Kawasaki of Japan for motorcycles, Hero Honda limited, new Holland tractors – (India) a unit of world known Ford Tractors, HMT, Tafe, Swaraj Tractors& others. In a nutshell EFCL is fully equipped to satisfy all kinds of customers.
Besides OE suppliers, Eastman tools are widely accepted across the nation and in international markets. The company takes pride in declaring that it has also earned ***"German product safety standard"*** certification by TUV Rheinland another step forward on its path of continual improvement towards total customer satisfaction.

A great deal of customization, tailored packaging and professional services place Eastman in a selected brand of vendors for a host of buyers across the globe.

Its customers are all important OEM's and in experts Europe countries and few countries in Latin America are the thrust. It is an ISO 9002: 1998 recognized company and is planning to undertake ISO: 9001. it occupies the market share of 9%.

## Product Profile

Eastman Industries Limited is a manufacture exporter of a diversified range of bicycles, components and accessories, suitable to both conventional & contemporary bicycles. The company delivers complete bicycle, single speed and multispeed chain wheels, free wheels, axels, hubs, pedals, chains, frames and other parts & accessories

| S. No | Product | Brand | Year of Launch | Division |
|---|---|---|---|---|
| 1. | Rubber Spare (Bicycle) parts | Eastman | 1970 | Industrial Area, Ludhiana. |
| 2. | Bicycle Parts | Eastman | 1975 | Focal Point, Ludhiana |
| 3. | Hand Tools | Eastman | 1992 | G. T. Road, Ludhiana |

## Awards and Certifications

Eastman Industries Ltd has been recognized as Trading House (Exports) by Ministry of Commerce, Government of India.

They are honored with the National Export Award Trophy for the financial year 1997-98 presented by Hon'ble Shri Atal Bihari Vajpayee, the Prime Minister of India. Only 20 companies in India are honored at the National Level at each year.

Recently EIL received ITPO UAC Focus Award for 1999-2000. The company also earned "German Product safety standards" certifications by TUV Rhienland.

## Perspective

The success of EIL is attributed to my wife and to my parents.

The criticality of HRM is touching the heart of employees as HRM is the main area of success of business and in merchandising trade product is people, market is people and service is people.

Ludhiana will be able to have a phenomenon growth until we all in the Ludhiana industry mature ourselves and realize the grand base. When the competition sets in and each fiscal in the times to come will look to be a better year than present one. Now the emergence of Chinese good will lead some fair persons to probably go out of business and new generation will come in the business and whatever will be produced in Ludhiana will be out priced internationally. Chinese goods are going to find grip in Indian market because duties are going to go down further.

Indian firms have started a thinking process in Ludhiana only to remain competitive and they are going to face this challenge and have started afloat in the long run. The SSI sector will suffer the most because till now they have not realized the fact of SSI.

To tackle the challenge of globalization, Eastman is concentrating on Marketing Research and research in all aspects of business:

- Redefining the business processes.
- Cost cutting in operations
- Training employees on regular basis whether inside or outside.
- Sharp focus on each activity.

It has benefited Eastman reasonably well particularly in research aspects.

**Main Strengths**

- Experience in international trade.

- Causing commitment to customers/employers to the supplies of good and services.

After 10 years the group will have a phenomenal growth because Eastman is in tune with the global competition and trying to develop HR, which is to do a business today.

| **Snapshots** |
|---|
| **Year of Start**<br>1982<br>**Located at:**<br>Focal Point, Industrial Area, Ludhiana<br>**Main Products/Operations**<br>Manufacturer & Exports of Bicycle parts & Accessories<br>**Total Turnover**<br>30 million US $<br>**Domestic Turnover**<br>50% of total turnover<br>**Foreign Turnover**<br>50% of total turnover<br>**Certificates**<br>ISO: 9002, SGS Gold Seal<br>**Flagship Company**<br>Eastman Industries Ltd. |

# Hero Cycles Limited

The Indian bicycle industry came into existence when East India Company came to Calcutta in the year. It was there that the Englishmen brought bicycle technology to India. At that time, the parts were imported, assembled and then marketed in India. In 1953, the scenario changed entirely, when some of the noted companies like Hero and Avon were given the license to manufacture bicycles. After almost four decades, in the post 1991 scenario Indian industries are free to breath in the global environment. But at the same time this change has thrown up a number of challenges before the local industrial houses. In the presence of high tax rates, bureaucratic control and poor infrastructure the home industry finds it tough to stand upto global competition. Despite all these adversities, the cycle industry has grown to 14 million cycles a year and is growing at the rate of 15.8 percent per annum.

**Incorporation and Integration**

"Hero", the brand name symbolizing the steely ambition of the Munjal brothers, came into being in the year 1956. From a modest manufacturer of bicycle components in the early 1940's to the world's largest bicycle manufacturer today, the odyssey was fueled by one vision - to build long-lasting relationships with everyone, including workers, dealers and vendors. This philosophy has paid rich dividends through the years. Hero, a name synonymous to two wheelers in India, is today a multi-unit, multi-product, geographically diversified Group of companies. Through fully integrated operations, the Munjals roll their own steel, make critical components such as free wheels for their bicycles, and have the foresight to simultaneously diversify into myriad ventures, like product designing, IT enabled services, finance and insurance, just to name a few.

Throughout its success trail, the Hero Group and its members have displayed unwavering passion of setting higher standards for themselves and delivering simply the best to their customers.

The Hero Group philosophy is: "To provide excellent transportation to the common man at easily affordable prices and to provide total satisfaction in whatever sphere of activities it ventures into."

Thus apart from being customer-centric, the Hero Group also provides its employees with a fine quality of life and its business associates a total sense of belonging.

**"Engineering Satisfaction"** is the prime motive of the Hero Group and it has become a way of life and a part of the work culture in the Group. This is what drives the Group to seek newer vistas, adopt faster technology and create quality driven products to the utmost satisfaction of customers, partners, dealers and vendors.

Today the Hero Group has a number of accolades and achievements to its credit … yet consumer requirements and newer technologies provide fresh challenges every day, and at Hero the wheels of progress continue to turn ...

**Mission of the Hero Group**

- Maintaining leadership by keeping demanding customers satisfied with innovative products that are consistent in quality and reliability.
- By converting challenges into opportunities by initiating change.
- Improving the quality

Today Hero is the largest exporter of two-wheelers in India, besides being the fastest growing Indian two-wheeler company. The search for excellence knows no boundaries-global or otherwise. In 1983, it led Hero to form a joint venture (in technical and financial participation) with one of the world's largest automotive makers, Honda Motor Company Ltd. of Japan, for the manufacture of 100cc motorcycles in India.

A joint venture with Showa Manufacturing Co., Japan, for the production of front forks and shock absorbers for two-wheelers and four-wheelers followed. The Group also ventured into a technical consultancy agreement with Steyr Daimler Puch of Austria for the manufacture of the 65cc, Porsche-design mini-motorcycles. The latest addition to this is a technical collaboration agreement with National Bicycle Industries of Japan which has made Hero Cycles the only company in the country to export bicycles to Japan, a certification of Hero's stringent quality controls and state-of-the-art technology.

The Group has also been acquiring the services of foreign consultants and experts for identification and development of business opportunities and assistance in technical upgradation. The entire range of bicycle products of Gujarat Cycles Ltd., Baroda, was developed with German expertise and the entire software for bicycle parts was developed using Japanese know-how. Such technology assimilation through wide sourcing is a regular feature at Hero.

**Group Companies**

**Hero Honda Motors Limited**

Honda Motor Company of Japan and the Hero Group entered a joint venture to setup Hero Honda Motors Limited in 1984.Today Hero Honda has managed to achieve indigenisation of over 95 percent, a Honda record worldwide. Hero Honda is at present the largest-selling Indian motorcycle and the most fuel-efficient in its category. Hero Honda became the first company in the country to introduce four-stroke motorcycles and set the standards for fuel efficiency, pollution control and quality. It has a production capacity of million motorcycles which is expecting to be on the increasing trend in the coming years. Hero Honda is the market leader in motorcycles, with sales of over a million motorcycles and a strong market share of 47% during 2000-01. Its product range includes "Splendor" which is the largest selling motorcycle brand in the world with over 6.9 lacs vehicles sold in 2000-01. Passion, CBZ, CD100, CD-Dawn, Joy, Ambition. The Company focuses on providing "Value for Money" through its pricing strategies and after sales services. Hero Honda is now the leading two-wheeler Company in India.

**Hero Cycles**

Hero Cycles Limited was the first company of the Group and continues to be the flagship unit. •Starting with the modest figure of 25 bicycles per day in 1956 at Ludhiana, the Company extended its wings to establish its second unit in 1988 at Sahibabad in Uttar Pradesh. Today the combined production of both the units, at Ludhiana and Sahibabad is more than 19,500 bicycles a day.

The Hero Cycles wide product range caters to the entire spectrum of buyers and includes roadsters, racers and the latest all-terrain and city bicycles. The massive Hero Cycles plant at Ludhiana also houses the centralised rim-making facility for the entire range of Hero two-wheelers. Besides manufacturing all major components, it has in-house facilities for making pedals, handlebars, chain wheels, brakes and saddles.

In 2001, Hero Cycles launched various ranges of new products such as Hero Devil Dx, Hero Neon, Ranger Swing 21, Hero Buzz, Hero Missile, Hero Boss, Hero Terminator, Hero Salsa, Hero Limbo, Hero Lambada, Hero Jet, and the Powerbike. The Ranger Swing 21 is India's most advanced performance MTB, offering a 21-speed variant. Hero Buzz is India's first Y-frame bike.

Hero Cycles pioneered bicycle exports from India as early as 1963 and today exports bicycles and components to Europe, USA, Africa and the Middle East. While initial exports were restricted to Africa and the Middle East, today more than 50 percent of the bicycle exports meet the demands of markets in Europe and the US.

Hero Cycles Limited has been continuously upgrading technology and has even set up special units - like Gujarat Cycles Limited (now known as Munjal Auto Industries Limited), as a completed Export Oriented Unit (EOU), to meet international quality standards and demands

**Munjal Showa**

Munjal Showa Limited was established in 1985 in technical and financial collaboration with Showa Corporation, Japan - Leaders in the World of Shock Absorbers. The Company's state-of-the-art Shock Absorbers, Front Fork, Struts and Window Balancers/Gas Springs have become symbol of Quality and complete reliability for popular two-wheelers and four-wheelers. The ultra modern plant is situated in Gurgaon (Haryana). Shock Absorbers from Munjal Showa Limited can withstand more than two million cycle tests, which far exceeds ISI's stipulation of one million cycles.

Today Munjal Showa Limited is one of the largest suppliers of shock absorbers to major auto giants in India,

Japan, Germany, the United States and the United Kingdom, amongst other developed markets. The Company's products conform to the highest standards of quality, safety, comfort and dependability and are QS 9000, ISO 14001 and ISO 9001 compliant. The Company was conferred with the National Safety Award in 1992 and the British Safety Council's National Safety Award in 1996. "Better products through better technology" - is the maxim that guides the Munjal Showa team.

**Majestic Auto Limited**

Majestic Auto Limited is the country's leading manufacturer of mopeds. The Hero Majestic range of mopeds were introduced in the year 1978 and within a few years, Hero Majestic was a household name in the country. Hero Majestic Mopeds have also found great acceptance in the overseas markets, including countries in Africa, North & South America, Europe and the Far and Middle East and are homologated in Europe & USA.

Majestic Auto Limited is continuously working to upgrade the performance of their existing range of three different mopeds viz. Panther, Gizmo and Ankur, and to make them absolute environment friendly. The company also manufactures and exports Hero Allegro Exerbikes, Steppers and Joggers, the well-accepted market leaders in fitness equipment. The plant has a capacity of manufacturing 120,000 Mopeds annually. The Majestic range of mopeds is known to be sturdy, savage, surging and streamlined for long and winding, unkempt stretches of countrywide - an epitome of perfect ergonomics which adds class and comfort to it.

**Rockman Cycle**

Rockman Cycle Industries Limited was another Hero venture for self-reliance, founded at a time when there was an extreme scarcity of cycle chains in the bicycle-manufacturing units of the country.

Starting with 500 lengths of chains per day, the Company today manufactures about 25,000 single and multi-speed chains everyday, exporting about 25 percent of its total production. In 1964, the Company began the manufacture of bicycle hubs and today has a daily production of about 50,000 pieces.

**Highway Cycle Industries Limited**

Highway Cycle Industries Limited was established to manufacture high quality freewheels to meet the growing production demands of Hero Cycles Limited.

Initially the Company manufactured single-speed freewheels but in 1978, it began the production of multi-speed freewheels essentially to cater to the demands of foreign buyers.

Producing about 30,000 freewheels per day, the Company is a leader in its sphere and meets the strict quality specifications of markets in Italy, Germany, France and buyers in South America.

Presently, the Company exports 100 percent of its multi-speed and 30 percent of its single-speed freewheels.

**Munjal Castings**

Munjal Castings is engaged in the manufacturing of Die Castings of Aluminum and Zinc Based alloys in Pressure, Low Pressure and Gravity Die Casting processes.

The increasing demand for non-ferrous metal castings in bicycle and automotive segments led to the establishment of

Munjal Castings in the year 1980. Munjal Castings has 34 Pressure Die Casting Machines ranging from 80 ton to 1300 tons. The two 1300 ton and one 840 ton fully automatic short control machine have been imported from Buhler, Switzerland. There are 32 custom built Gravity Die Casting Machines and two low Pressure Die Casting machines. The company has recently added three CNC Milling machines from Deckel Maho, Germany.

**Sunbeam Auto Limited**

Sunbeam Auto Limited was established in 1986 to manufacture aluminum die-castings for the automotive industry. The setting up of the company was infact a giant step forward to offer quality die-casting components to the then emerging automobile sector.

Today, Sunbeam Auto Limited is the largest die-casting unit in Asia, setup on 30-acre sprawling complex in Gurgaon, on the National Highway 8, just 20kms from the International Airport of New Delhi

Sunbeam Auto Limited has acquired ISO 9002 certification from British Standards Institute, UK, in recognition of its commitment to total quality management. The Product range from Sunbeam Auto Limited comprises of: Crank Cases and Covers, Cylinder Blocks, Sliding Tubes, Hinges, Bottom, Cases, Transmission Cases, Rocker Arms, Trager Generator, Brake Levers, Motor Trager Links, Alternator Housing, Clutch Levers, Cylinder Heads & Covers, Cap Crank Bearings, Caliper Brakes, Hubs, Pistons, Seat Benches

Sunbeam Auto Limited has also set-up a state of the art piston manufacturing facility in technical collaboration with M/s Honda Foundry Company Limited of Japan, the pioneers in the world for manufacturing high-strength lightweight pistons used in light, powerful fuel-efficient engines. The Company today manufactures pistons of 40mm to 100mm dia for both the two-wheeler and four-wheeler segments. From its existing production capacity of 1.5 million pistons per annum, Sunbeam aims to double the capacity within the next two years.

**Hero Cold Rolling Division**

Hero Group's manufacturing activities rest on one basic ingredient - Cold Rolled Steel. Comprehending the significance of ensuring perfect quality of the basic raw material, the Group established its own cold rolling mill for steel processing in 1990. The was commissioned at Ludhiana in July 1991 with an initial investment of 320 million Rs and a production capacity of 50,000 MT per annum.

Hero Cycles CR Division was set up in consultation with MECON, Asia's largest engineering consultants, in technical collaboration with WEAN UNITED, USA. Over the years the Company has grown with an investment of 700 million Rs and possesses an installed capacity of 1,30,000 MT per annum.

Today the company serves many industries across the country and strives to meet customer requirements, expressed or implied, by maintaining a consistency in quality through continuous upgradation of technology and human endeavour.

**Metallic Forte**

The company has several firsts to its credit, including hydraulic auto gauge controls, computerized pass schedules, automatic slow down and a totally enclosed, semi-continuous pickling line, apart from effective anti-pollution and safety controls which were incorporated from the very beginning.

Hero Cycles Limited, CR Division has also entered into an agreement for technical assistance with Kawasaki Steel Corporation, Japan, for improvement in production yield, elimination of defects, reduction of customer returns and enhancement of maintenance operations against certain predetermined targets.

Hero CR Division is an ISO certified Company and is accelerating towards its aim of acquiring QS 9000 certification. The "People-Product Paradigm" ensures a motivated work force for maintaining highest standards of skill and attitudes.

Major alliances of the Hero Cycles Cold Rolling Division, that have helped it to steadily scale the heights are:

- M/S Metallurgical & Engineering Consultants (India) Limited (MECON)
- M/S Allied Consulting Engineers Pvt Limited
- M/S Multi Form Machinery Private Limited
- M/S The Tata Iron & Steel Company Limited
- M/S Essar Steel Limited
- M/S Steel Authority Of India Limited
- M/S Jindal Vijay Nagar Steel Limited

Cold Rolled steel from the Hero Cold Rolling Division is used to manufacture:

Automobile and automobile components, Bicycle and bicycle component, Pipes and tubes, Refrigerators, Furniture, Shutters, Bearings, Cable Tape, Transformers and Radiators, Electric Steel, Domestic appliances

Office automation products (Computer components, typewriters, Photostat machine, components etc)

**Hero Exports**

Established in 1993 as a Trading Company of the Group, Hero Exports has since been recognized by the Government of India as a Trading House and is currently exporting a wide range of products including Bicycle Components and Basmati and Non-Basmati Rice.

Hero Cycles Limited, the flagship unit of the Hero Group pioneered bicycle exports from India, as early as in 1963. While initial exports were restricted to Africa and the Middle East, today more than 50% of bicycle exports from the Group, meet the demands of American and European markets. This is primarily possible on account of appropriate product development and exacting quality standards.

The Hero Group has constantly upgarded technology and even set up special units like the Munjal Auto Industries Limited, formerly known as Gujarat Cycles Limited, to meet stringent international quality standards.

Hero Exports is also involved in the export of rice: Basmati & Non-Basmati Rice.With the brand name of Gulzar, Hero brings you the same 'Basmati' that graced the feasts of Kings. Each glossy, white grain has been graded and then matured to perfection - for the dish that is perfect.

**Munjal Auto Components (MAC),**

Munjal Auto Components (MAC), a QS 9000 certified company, has adopted "Near Net Shaped Technology" - the latest forging technology used the world over for Warm and Cold Forging. Near Net Shape, the term implies that the die so produced is as close to the final product as is possible, leading to marginal machining allowances and greater accuracy.

Advantages of Near Net Shape Forging comprise of:

High Quality Product

Reduction in Energy Cost
Tremendous saving of material
Excellent surface finish

The main product ranges comprise of:
Gear Blanks, Spline Shafts, Teeth Net Finish, Splines Net Finish, Dog Holes Net Finish and Lugs Net Finish . All production is carried out with strict adherence to the industry specific norms of quality and delivery.

Munjal Auto Components manufactures and markets components for the Auto sector as an Original Equipment Manufacturer (OEM) and also supplies the replacement market. The Company has a vision for the future and aims at leadership through excellent products. Munjal Auto Components envisions itself as suppliers of the latest international technology, and not just auto components.

**New Ventures in Group Companies**

**Hero Global Design**

Hero Global Design is the auto design subsidiary of the Hero Group. Hero Global Design intends to be a total auto design company that will provide both front end and back end designing for all kinds of automobiles, including two wheelers.

Hero Global Design offers engineering services in CAD/CAM/CAE related to New Product Development, Design, Engineering and Manufacturing. The delivery of these prototyping, concept, design and rendering services is based on a well-established development process, comprising of design reviews at various stages of development and validation of the products through in-house Tests and Quality Assurance.

The wide range of services offered by Hero Global Design include:

- 2D to 3D conversion/transition projects
- Development of industry specific CAD libraries
- Surface Modelling
- Solid Modelling for part design
- Sheet metal Design
- Assembly Modelling & Interference Checking
- Tool design and mold fill analysis
- Manufacturing (NC Programming, Post Processing)
- Reverse Engineering Projects
- Piping
- Wire Harness Design
- Analysis, Validation and Design Optimization Projects
- Work Group level PDM projects
- Development of technical publications or web documentation
- Prototyping

Hero Global Design has alliances with the following leaders in product design engineering:

| | |
|---|---|
| PTC: | Hero Global Design is the largest Certified Engineering Provider (CEP) alliance partner of PTC from India . |
| Porsche Design: | Hero Global Design is the exclusive representative of Porsche Design GesmbH (studio) in India. |
| Target Design: | Hero Global Design has a business agreement with Target Design, a leading industrial and automobile design company in Germany. |

The basic objective of the Company is to provide Italian design at Indian prices, e.g. an Italian designer would charge US$1 million for a complete vehicle design, which Hero Global Design would strive to provide at US$60 thousand.

**Munjal e-Systems**

Munjal e-Systems (a Hero Group member) aims to be the leading provider of integrated business solutions. It is specialize in Consultancy, Implementation and Support Services for Enterprise Resource Planning (ERP), Supply Chain Management (SCM) and Customer Relationship Management (CRM). We offer our solutions and services to Small & Medium organizations and enterprises across the country.

**Easy Bill Limited**

The company Easy Bill Limited headed by Mr. Rahul Munjal (CEO). is a venture of the Hero Group. The Easy Bill Limited has been promoted by the Hero Group to serve the needs of the Indian middle class. At Easy Bill Limited, convenience for the consumers is the key-word. The vision of Easy Bill Limited is to "Create a brand which offers CONSUMER CONVENIENCE in Bill Payment and reselling of communication services using e-transaction oriented products through a unique POS retail network."

The company will use the strengths of the Hero Group in retail management and collection of micro payments. The company has tied-up with mobile, electricity and telephone service providers to provide a complete package of one stop bill payment service to the customers. With the Easy Bill service, the customers do not have to go to different bill deposit counters to do the transactions. They do not have to stand in long queues, travel long distances to the counters and face a number of other problems associated with bill payments today. In total they do not have to fit in the low quality bill payment job in their busy schedules. With Easy Bill they get these services at the neighborhood friendly retail outlet.

The system employs advanced technology to provide credence to the scientifically designed service. Receipts are generated across the counter for both cash and cheque payments. The entire system is networked, facilitating the company executives keep a watchful eye so that the service quality is not compromised.

**About Mr. B.M. Lall, Chairman, Hero Group**

Mr Brijmohan Lall Munjal, patriarch of the US$1.8 billion Hero Group was born in 1923, in what is now Pakistan. After partition, the Munjal brothers started a small business of manufacturing bicycle components in Ludhiana in North India in the face of the bottlenecks of industrial infrastructure and investments. Mr Lall led a small time manufacturer of 60 cycles a day to become a manufacturing giant, which churns out not only 18,500 cycles per day but is also diversified into various domains. Undoubtedly, Mr Lall is a first generation business entrepreneur of the 1950s'.

Mr Lall has enriched the Hero Group with his vision of sound business governance and value driven management practices. His foresight has made the Hero Group a leader in its business. Mr Brijmohan Lall is a role model for Indian Industry in corporate governance and ethical and value-driven management practices. His principle-based leadership has led the Group companies to receive the best industrial governance and safety awards and acquire stringent value certifications.

**Products/Services**

| Company Name | Year of start | Main Products Operating | Location |
|---|---|---|---|
| Hero Cycles | 1956 | Cycles | Ludhiana |
| Rockman Cycle Industries Ltd | 1961 | Single & Multispeed Chains | Ludhiana |
| Highway Cycles | 1971 | Freewheels | Ludhiana |
| Munjal Showa Ltd. | 1985 | Shock Absorbers | Gurgaon |
| Hero Cycles Unit-II | 1988 | Cycles | Sahibabad |
| Gujarat Cycles Ltd. | 1988 | Auto parts | Baroda |
| Hero Cold Rolling Mills | 1990 | Steel Processing | Ludhiana |
| Hero Cycles Ltd. | 2000 | Cycles | Chennai |
| Hero Cycles Ltd. | 2000 | Cycles | Ludhiana |
| Hero Global Design | | Front end and back end designing of all kind of automobiles | -- |
| Munjal E - Systems | | Consultancy, Implementation and Support Services for Enterprise Resource Planning (ERP), Supply Chain Management (SCM) and Customer Relationship Management (CRM). | -- |
| Easy Bill Limited | | Bill Payment and reselling of communication services using e-transaction oriented products through a unique POS retail network | -- |

Mr Lall has received various accolades and awards for his immense contribution to the Indian industry. He was adjudged **Businessman of the Year in 1994** by a leading business magazine - Business India.

Mr Lall was amongst the first Indian industrialists to effectively implement backward integration and he is acknowledged as the trend setter in the area. Apart from the promotion of the Indian industry, he is the actively involved in many national associations such as CII, SIAM, ASSOCHAM and PHD and is a member of the Regional Board of the Reserve Bank of India. He is Honorary Fellow of the Indian Institute of Industrial Engineering.

In 1995, Mr Lall received the **National Award for outstanding contribution to the Development of Indian Small Scale Industry.** (NSIC award - presented by the President of India)

In 1999, the Business Baron recognized him as the "**Most Admired CEO.**"

The PHD Chamber of Commerce and Industry presented him with the **Distinguished Entrepreneurship Award in 1997**, in recognition of his outstanding exemplary entrepreneurship.

Xavier Labour Relations Institute (XLRI), a premier institution has conferred on him the honor of **Sir Jehangir Ghandy Medal for Industrial Peace in 2000.**

**Ernst and Young** has recognized him as the "**Entrepreneur of the year 2001.**"

Mr Lall has made an unfailing commitment of his time, energy and resources to strive for the upliftment of the communities and villages around the Group's manufacturing units. He has encouraged the setting up of numerous medical, educational and infrastructure facilities. Amongst his notable contributions to his adoptive city, Ludhiana, are the Ludhiana Stock Exchange, the Ludhiana Aviation Club - of which he is still the president - and the Dayanand Medical College and Hospital

**Snapshots**

**Year of start**
1956

**Located at:**
G.T. Road, Ludhiana

**Main Products/Operations**
Design and Manufacture of bicycles, associated components and sub-assemblies

**Total Turnover of the Group**
Rs. 9,500 crore appro.
Hero cycles Rs. 1015 crore
Hero Honda Motors Rs. 6,500 crore

**Domestic Turnover** 65%: **Foreign Turnover** 35%

**Certificates**
QMS as per ISO 9001:2000, EMS as per 14001:96

**New Ventures/Diversification**
Consultancy, Call Centre, Billing System, Computer Aided Designing

**Major Collaborations**

- National Bicycle Industries, Japan
- Honda Motors, Japan
- Showa Manufacturing, Japan
- Briggs & Stratton, USA
- First Ring, USA

**Flagship Company**
Hero Honda Motors Limited
Hero Cycles Limited

**Main Market Being Served**
**Domestic:** All Over India

**Foreign**
Europe, Middle East and Africa

**Famous Brands**

**Cycles:**
Hero Ranger, Li Angel, Kidd, Piranha, Devil, Hero Miss India, Active and Hero Buzz

**Mopeds:**
Hero Majestic, Hero Puch

**Motor Bikes:**
Hero Honda, CBZ

# Section 4: Steel Industry

- Indian Iron and Steel Industry
- Aarti Steels
- Upper India Steels

# Indian Iron and Steel Industry

The rapid development of steel capacity is indeed a logical corollary of any programme of rapid industrialization for a developing country. Steel is used as a basic material in the manufacture of metal products, machinery, transport equipment, textile and other machinery.

On the eve of independence in 1947 total capacity of iron and steel industry was of the order of 1.3 million tonnes- 1 million tonnes from Tata Iron and Steel Co. (TISCO) and 0.3 million tonnes from Indian Iron and Steel Co. (IISCO). By 1990-91, iron and steel industry had six integrated plants with an installed capacity of 10 million tonnes of steel ingots.

From the point of view of total investment, iron and steel industry is the most important industry, accounting for a total investment of Rs. 4,000 crore. Major portion of this investment is in the public sector plants. The industry provides direct employment to 2.5 lakh workers. The capital required for employing one worker works out to be Rs. 1,20,000. In this sense; it is highly capital-intensive industry. In spite of the tremendous importance given to the iron and steel industry and the heavy investment made, it is a pity that the country had to import increasingly large amount of steel - the value of imports of finished steel was Rs. 6,870 crore in 1996-97 and Rs. 3,570 crore in 2000- 01.

In recent years, Government of India have announced important changes in policy. Price and distribution controls. on iron and steel were removed from January 1992. This led to rise in prices of various items of steel. The imports of all items of steel are now freely allowed. Along with the deregulation of iron and steel, import duty on various items of steel were also reduced. This has had a moderating influence on market prices of steel.

**Production in Steel Industry**

(million tones)

| Year | Steel ingots | Finished steel |
|---|---|---|
| 1950-51 | 1.5 | 1.0 |
| 1970-71 | 6.1 | 4.6 |
| 1980-81 | 10.3 | 6.8 |
| 1990-91 | 13.7 | 13.5 |
| 2000-01 | 27.0 | 26.3 |
| 2002-03 | 31.4 | 29.5 |

Source: *Economic Survey,* 2002-03.

Government of India announced a new industrial policy in July 1991. Under the policy, the steel sector which includes mini steel plants, has been exempted from licensing subject to, however, locational stipulation. The Government envisages considerable additions to capacity in the steel sector specially from the sponge iron segment.

In recent years, the steel industry has been facing serious problems due to sluggish demand in steel consuming sectors, lack of investment in major infrastructure projects, cost escalations in inputs for iron and steel and increasing competition from aboard. The Government is taking necessary measures for revival of the industry. For instance, the Government set up a Task Force for the steel sector and on the recommendations of the this body, it has exempted seven inputs crucial in steel manufacturing from imposition of Special Additional Duty.

# Aarti Steels

## Incorporation and Integration

In 1977, Sohan Lal Mittal and Shiv Parshad Mittal incorporated Aarti Group with an initial investment of 25-35 lakh in the name of Aarti Steels Ltd. Before starting the Aarti Steels, Mittals were into cycle parts business. Unfortunately they incurred huge losses in all these companies so they shifted from the cycle parts business into steel business under the name " Aarti Group". They had four companies for the cycle parts: Behl Industries Pvt. Ltd., S.N. Gandhi & Sons, Deepak Enterprises and Sunflower. They had started the group with an approximate of 25-30 employees. Their initial product was Iron Rod through which they had an initial turnover of about 50-60 lakh. There Registered Office is at G.T Road, Miller Ganj, Ludhiana. Aarti Group achieved an annual turnover of U.S dollar 65 million in the year 2001-02 and has a workforce of over 2000 personnel.

## History of the Group

In 1979 the company started its first rolling mill and followed it up with a massive programme of vertical and horizontal integration to add various facilities in quick succession thereby commissioning Wire Rod Rolling Mill (1982-83), Induction Furnaces (1985-86), Oxygen Plant (1989), Steel Wire Drawing Unit (1991), Tyre Bead Wire Unit (1993) and Electric Arc Furnace (1995).

Aarti Steels Ltd. has got a mini steel plant with a capacity of 1.25 lakh tonnes per annum. The steel plant is the most modern composite plant having 30 M.T. EBT (Eccentric Bottom Taping), UHP, EAF (Electric Arc Furnace) with an equal capacity of Laddle Refining and 6/11 m radius three strand continuous casting and other balancing equipment. The R&D set up of the company is well equipped.

Aarti Steels manufacture wide range of products in Carbon, Spring Steel and Low Alloy Steels, which are used in automobile sector of Indian Economy. Constant upgradation of technology is always alive on the agenda of the company. Electromagnetic Stirring facilities at stage one of modernization have been recently installed for quality upgradation on continuous casting machine.26"feet Continuous Rolling Mill and Vacuum Degassing arrangements were installed in the year 2001.

The wire division of the company has also ventured into exports and expects good deals because of acclaimed quality and better service. ISO- 9002(is successfully implemented in all the group units. The group is also running its hospital besides theatre business at Ludhiana. To expand company's identity beyond steel, the company decided in 1994 to diversify into textile with the setting up of an 100% Export Oriented Unit (EOU), a Textile Division of Cotton Yarn at Ludhiana in the name of Aarti International Limited in implementation of the license from Government of India to set up Cotton Yarn Spinning Unit with an installed capacity of 50,000 spindles and 2000 rotors, company established the first Phase 28, 224.It has got ring frames both for combed and carded 100% cotton yarn with machine set up from Lakshmi Rieter India..Spindles unit for making both Combed and Carded in 100% Cotton with machine set up of Lakshmi Rieter India from Blow Room to Spinning and Schlaforst Autoconers for post spinning besides complete range of Zellweger Uster R & D Equipment and Xorella yarn conditioning plant from Switzerland and TFOs of Leewha Make Korea.

Aarti International Ltd. started civil construction from September 1995, which came into Commercial Production w.e.f November 18; 1996.It later on added another set of 28,080 spindles at same location, which came into commercial production w.e.f. November 18, 2000.

**Product Profile**

- Iron And Steel Products
- Cotton Yarn (100% EOU)
- Tyre Bead Wire
- Galvanized Wire
- Product Mix-Steel
- Product Mix-Wires

**Divisions of the Company**

| Sr. No: | Name of The Company | Year of Start | Main Products Operations | Location |
|---|---|---|---|---|
| 1. | Aarti Steels Ltd. | 1977 | Iron And Steel Products | Focal Point Ludhiana |
| 2. | Aarti International Ltd. | 1996 | Cotton Yarn (100% EOU) | Chandigarh Road, Ludhiana |
| 3 | Salig Ram Shiv Prasad | -- | Consignment Agency (TISCO) | Focal Point, Ludhiana |
| 4 | Aarti Palace | -- | Cinema | Ferozepur Road, Ludhiana |

**Quality Policy**

"We are committed to deliver products and services to the entire satisfaction of our customers through:

- Quality Management Systems
- Upgradation of technology as per process requirement
- Continuous improvement in process and product quality
- Principle of Each One-Teach One

- Team of Motivated Employees".

**Management's Perspective**

According to Aarti group success can be measured in terms of hard work, innovation, initiative and teamwork. The management-attributed success of the business on the theme of "Karam hi puja hai." There main competitive strength is that they work within the resources and don't believe in taking borrowings from outside. Using orthodox approach and not indulging into unethical practices is the weakness of the group and pointed out that they lagged behind, as they cannot deceive people. Further they haven't floated any public issue and are working with the internal sources of finance only.

Due to shortage of raw material there is little scope in Punjab to set up blast furnaces and can be set up in areas like Chattisgarh where raw material is cheap and readily available. Growth of industry depends on many factors like government policies and growth oriented incentives and India is definitely going to grow. The management viewed that the industry is not worried of threats from China but is expecting to face competition from the new technology of Blast Furnace projects, which converts iron into steel directly. Due to lack of iron and coalmines this new technology Blast Furnace is not commercially viable in Punjab. The ideal situation for these can be areas like Orissa & Chattisgarh. To face competition we have to be cost effective and maintain good quality. Globalization is both threat and opportunity for Indian firms if the quality of the product is good only then survival is possible. The main competitors of Aarti Steels Limited are Upper India Steel Ltd., Modern Steels Limited, Vardhman Special Steels.

The management also stressed on the need of the Information Technology because it helped in recording and keeping all the information efficiently. Though IT has helped a lot in the business but the company is not into IT ventures as such. Human resources are considered to be very important for any concern besides Marketing, Finance, and Production. Quality management is an indispensable part for the steel industry. At every step the organization needs good people to have good quality product.

The management believed that societal aspect of business should not be ignored and it is the top most responsibility of every concern to look after and take care of the society. Aarti group, as a whole, is trying to be socially responsible in the best possible way. They are running a charitable hospital "Deepak Hospital" located at Sarabha Nagar. Vaccination camps are organized every month in the hospital. In Nov. 2001, around 2400 people were vaccinated free of cost for "Hepatitis B."Aarti Steels was awarded "Rashtriya Samman Patra" from 1994-95 to 1998-99

| **Snapshots** |
|---|
| **Year of Start**<br>1977<br>**Located at:** Miller Ganj, Ludhiana<br>**Main Products/Operations**<br>Melting, Secondary Refining, Casting, Shaping, Tyre Bead, Wire Galvanized, Wire Patenting, Wet Drawing Machine, Product Mix-Steel, Product Mix-Wires, Cotton Yarn.<br>**Total Turnover**<br>Rs. 367 crore, Domestic Turnover Rs. 324 crore<br>Foreign Turnover, Rs. 43 crore<br>**Certifications**<br>ISO 9002 (Det Norske Veritas Quality System Certificate)<br>**Main Markets:** Domestic<br>Foreign: Srilanka. Taiwan. China. Singapore. Bangladesh. Turkey, Korea, Egypt. Belgium, Malaysia, Russia |

# Upper India Steels

### Background/Historical Perspective

Upper India Steel (UIS) is not a story of a Mini Steel Plant. It is a vision to pioneer a collective human effort with one goal in mind, *"TO BE THE BEST"*. Since the first batch of ingots rolled out over three decades on April 13$^{th}$ 1965 technical development being prime of concern, UIS expanded its capacity periodically from its meagre 6000 TPA to its ever growing current capacity of 200000 TPA.

UIS has always sought to continuously adapt itself to changing environment customer needs and new evolving technologies. With a view to meet the growing demand for high quality steel from specific customer – users, it is progressively developing and upgrading its plant machinery through the installation of modern equipment for meeting "Customer's Changing Needs." As a result, it has achieved remarkable progress within a period of thirty-five years from a small turnover of Rs. 0.946 Cr. in 1965-66 to a turnover of Rs. 120 Cr. by the end of 1999-2000 financial year.

### Incorporation and Integration

Upper India Steel Manufacturing & Engineering Company was founded in year 1965. The company is spread over an area of 36 acres with lush green lawns. The high standards, both in expertise and result oriented endeavours, have sustained a successful history of producing high quality products from its very inspection. UIS represents the country's commitment to progress through self-sufficiency, professional experience, and utilization of proven expertise and adoption of welfare environment in order to produce a wide range of high quality steels in India. UIS excels in producing Spring Steel, Forging Quality Steel catering primarily to the OEM's in the automotive sector. In the Tool Segment, UIS is the largest producer of which is exported finally the world over, earning foreign exchange for the country. With a zero strike rate UIS boasts of an exceptional, attitudinal, approach to the management at all levels. Constant exchange of ideas and welfare schemes keep the physical, emotional and psychological parameters at their best. UIS employs hundreds of persons belonging to different faiths and religions. The company is a shinning example of *unity in diversity*.

At a mammoth cost, anti air pollution equipment with Japanese technology has been installed to ensure a dust free environment.

UIS has an advanced Steel Melting Shop with system standardisation of the highest degree enabling it to cast a wide range of high quality steels cost effectively. UIS has numerous rolling mills interwoven together, enabling it to roll a wide array of sections simultaneously, at short lead times, and working towards the JIT concept.

The constant Research & Development at UIS ensures its ensures its endeavour for the finest quality products. This perhaps why UIS may be amongst the only Indian outfit to fully adopt the Zero Defect culture. Moving on this path the company have achieved an important milestone by implementing International Quality System Standard ISO 9002.

UIS has made forays into the international markets in the File Steel sector of which it is the largest manufacturer in the country. UIS is a regular exporter to Spain, Mexico and Columbia. Various functions of UIS comprising of purchase, inventory, sales, finance and personnel are knitted together with state of the art information flow systems, using local area networks.

**Markets: Foreign Presence and Domestic Presence**
**The main markets served by UIS are:**

- Domestic Market:

1. **OEM's (Original equipment manufacturers):**
   a. **Automobile manufacturers**
   b. **Vendors of automobile manufacturers.**
2. **Replacement Markets.**
3. **Engineering / Tools Industry.**

- International Market:

UIS exports File Steel to Mexico, Columbia and Spain for Chisel work, Special Steel Flats to Nepal and Saudi Arabia. UIS is also making indirect exports to USA, UK, Europe, Australia, Gulf Countries and Bangladesh etc. through Export Agencies / Traders / Manufacturers.

**Future Plans of UIS**

The future plans of UIS are to add up:

- 22" Fully automatic rolling mill.
- Cold drawing facility.
- Vacuum Degassing facility.

**Products / Services**

UIS represents the country's commitment to progress through self-sufficiency professional experience, utilization of proven expertise and adoption of welfare environment in order to produce a wide range of high quality steel in India.

UIS excels in producing Spring Steel, Forging Quality Steels catering to the OEM's in automotive sector. In tools segment UIS is the largest producer of File Steel nation-wide most of which is exported finally the world over.

**Various Kinds of Steel Manufactured by the UIS**

- Carbon Steel

- Carbon – Manganese
- Alloy Steel
- Semi / Free Cutting Steel
- Boron Steel
- Spring Steel (Silico Manganese and Chrome Vanadium Moly Steel)
- File Steel
- Cold Forging Quality Steel

**Awards and Certification**

- AD Merkblatt W.O/TRD 100 from RWTUV, Germany
- ISO 9001:2000 RWTUV, Germany
- Engineers India Limited, India.
- Central Boiler Board, India as a "Well Known Foundry". (IBR)
- Indian Oil Corporation Ltd, India.
- Bharat Heavy Electricals Ltd. India.
- Bharat Earth Movers Ltd. India
- Audco India Ltd.

**Competitors of UIS**

The major competitors of USI are:

1. Sunflag Iron and Steel Co., Nagpur
2. Modern Steels, Mandi Gobindgarh
3. Vardhman Special Steels, Ludhiana
4. Nahar, Ludhiana

| Snapshots |
|---|
| **Year of Start**<br>1965<br>**Located at:**<br>Shandari Kalan, G.T. Road, Ludhiana<br>**Main Products**<br>Steel<br>**Total Turnover**<br>Rs. 125 crore (approx.)<br>**Domestic Turnover**<br>60%<br>**Foreign Turnover**<br>40%<br>**Certificates**<br>ISO: 9002<br>**Flagship Company**<br>Upper India Steel<br>**International Market**<br>Mexico, Columbia and Spain for Chisel work, Special Steel Flats to Nepal and Saudi Arabia. USA, UK, Europe, Australia, Gulf Countries and Bangladesh<br>**Future Plan of UIS**<br>Plant expansion and introduction of new technologies |

## Section 5: Textile, Yarn and Hosiery

- Indian Textile, Yarn and Hosiery Industry
- Duke India
- JCT
- Malwa Industries
- Nahar Industries
- OCM
- Vardhman Spinnings and General Mills

# Indian Textile, Yarn and Hosiery Industry

People no longer buy clothes only to keep their body warm or cool. They buy them also because of the way the clothes make them feel masculine, feminine, rugged, different, sophisticated, young and glamorous. Buying clothes has become an emotional experience. Textile business is now selling excitement rather than cloth. The first textile mill in India was started in 1854 under the name of "Bombay spinning and weaving company". During 1871-75, 17 new mills were established. In 1971, there were 668 mills in the portfolio of Indian textile industry. At the end of March 1989, there were 1054 mills in the country (771 spinning and 283 composite mills) with 126 spindles and over 2 lakh looms. At present Indian Textile Industry accounts for 20% of total industrial production. The industry currently provides direct employment to 15 million people and is the second largest employer in the country after Indian Railways. At the end of March 1994 there were 1,175 mills in the country (906 spinning mills and 269 composite mills) with 28 million spindles and 1.6 lakh looms. There were 132 closed mills by the end of March 1994.

The structure of the textile industry is extremely complex with the modern, sophisticated and highly mechanized mill sector on the one hand and the hand-spinning and hand-weaving (handloom) Sector on the other; in between falls the decentralized small scale powerloom sector. If we include all the three sectors, tit cotton and synthetic textile industry in India is the largest industry in the country, accounting for about 20 percent of the industrial output, providing employment to over 20 million persons and contributing around 33 percent of the total export earnings.

The Indian textile industry is predominantly cotton based with 65 per cent of the fabric production in the country being accounted for by cotton. Production of raw cotton varies from year to year depending upon rainfall and weather conditions, and price fluctuations in raw cotton affect the industry. Production of yarn is almost entirely in the organised sector and over the years, it has been showing a steadily rising trend - as for example, from 1600 million kg in 1988-89 to over 3,480 million kg in 2003-04. The fabric-production has also recorded an increasing trend over the years - from 20,600 million metres in 1989-90 to 46,008 million metres in 2002-03. In the production of fabrics, the decentralized sector accounts roughly 95 per cent and the mill sector has approximately 5 per cent share only.

**Direction of Exports of Ready-made Garments**

US $ million

| Country | 1987-98 | 2002-03 |
|---|---|---|
| USA | 427.0 | 1705.2 |
| UK | 156.1 | 300.4 |
| Germany | 194.7 | 415.7 |
| France | 88.7 | 346.5 |
| CIS | 153.2 | 159.4 |
| Canada | 38.1 | 192.5 |
| Italy | 75.7 | 157.6 |
| Japan | 26.8 | 79.5 |
| Netherlands | 55.0 | 168.0 |
| UAE | 13.7 | 468.5 |
| Others | 174.6 | 964.5 |

Source: *Economic Survey*, 2002-03

**New Textile Policy, 2000**

On November 2, 2000, the Government of India announced the New Textile Policy to make India a global player in textiles and readymade garments by raising the industry's exports from $ 11 billion to $ 50 billion by 2010. Out of this, the share of ready-made garments will be $ 25 billion. The Government has decided to dereserve the garment industry from the SSI category so as to make the industry internationally more competitive. Till now, the garment sector was under SSI reservation with an investment Ceiling of Rs. 3 crore and the maximum limit of foreign direct investment of 24 percent.

Two more important modification have been introduced. Firstly, FDI limit of 24% has been removed and foreign companies will able to make 100% investment through Foreign Investment Promotion Board (FIPB) route. Secondly, 50% export obligation on firms in which foreign equity is allowed, has been removed.

# Duke India

## Incorporation and Integration

"Duke" – a brand of today's apparel industry, took birth in 60's. With a very modest beginning and long term vision the company entered deep into the business world and developed a successful corporate track record with a variety of fashion products. In 1966, Jain brothers began their journey in the garment business with T-shirts only but today Duke has a modern equipped plant for production of T-Shirts, Polo Shirts, Sweat Shirts, Track Suits, Lowers, Bermudas, Jackets, Bush Coats, Wind Cheater Shirts, Trousers, Denims, Shorts, Pullovers, Thermal Wear, Inner wear in the fashion hub of Ludhiana. Duke was adjudged as "India's No.1 Selling T-Shirt Brand" by ORG-MARG in their latest survey.

## Background

The Duke saga commenced about four decades ago, in Ludhiana, the fashion hub of Punjab. Today Duke embraces a complete vertically integrated garment, manufacturing plant, with knitting, dyeing, processing, finishing, mercerizing, compacting, embroidery and printing under one roof. Production facilities are located in India and Nepal.

## Journey of the Company

Mr. Komal Kumar Jain, the driving force behind the success of Duke, in late 70's had a vision to foresee new emerging trends in the Indian apparel market. At that time, there was no manufacturer of quality T-shirt in India and Mr. Jain with an experience of over a decade in the knitwear industry targeted T-shirt market aggressively. In 1980 Mr. Jain started manufacturing T-shirts under DUKE brand name and targeted the Punjab and adjoining markets initially. The international quality of the T-shirt coupled with aggressive marketing and highly reasonable prices, instantly made' duke' a brand to be reckoned with and then after there was no looking back for Duke and Mr. Komal Jain as well.

Duke Fashions(India) Ltd pioneered the T-shirt culture, and gradually established several new trends in Knitted garments and fabric research, in 1998, thermal wear was introduced for the first time in India under the brand name of NEVA by Mr. Nirmal Jain, younger brother of the founder. Another constituent of Duke saga VENUS Garments is headed by Mr. Anil Jain the youngest of the brothers. The group also consists of Duke Fabrics and Glaze Garments.

Today, Mr. Kuntal Jain, son of the founder, is steering the flagship brand in the new millennium. Thanks to his dynamic programs, Duke Group is acknowledging today as the undisputed leader with a turnover of Rs. 125 crore. Over 8,00,000 garments are produced every months by 3000 skilled and technical personnel.

**Family Flashback**

Mr. Komal Jain, Chairman of the company, who belongs to Ambala, started his career at very young age when destiny put him on the hard test of the life after untimely demise of his father Late Shri Dharam Parkash Jain in 1960s. Late Mr. Jain had three sons. Being the eldest son, at the age of 16 years, he had to start fighting for his livelihood. Mr. Jain shifted from Ambala to Ludhiana in 1962 and entered into the garment business. At that particular time, the goods were supplied to Kolkatta market only. After having an exposure of the market, Mr. Jain took an initiative and started his entrepreneurial career in 1966 along with his brothers Mr. Nirmal Kumar Jain and Mr. Anil Kumar Jain.

**Sister concerns**

Mr. Komal Kumar Jain, the driving force behind the success of Duke, is heading DUKE group comprising of:

- Duke Fashions India Ltd
- Neva Garments Ltd
- Venus Garments Ltd
- Glaze Garments Pvt. Ltd
- Duke Fabrics Pvt. Ltd
- Duke Nepal Ltd.

Presently, Jain brothers have successfully created an empire of fashion garments with 6 group companies having 3000 employees and a turnover of Rs.125 crore.

**Philosophy of the Group**

The group's corporate philosophy is based on the following principles:

- Credibility, integrity and honesty
- Straight onward business dealings
- Work as a worship
- Spirit of social service and human respect

**Products**

The product range of Duke consists of Plains, Stripes, Designer T- Shirts in various sizes and versatile styles & elegant colours. Shirts in checks & stripes, Jackets, Bermudas, Shorts, Lowers, Sweat shirts, Creyons - Kidswear and many more.

Today, Duke is the only national T-Shirt brand which offers a unique blend of international quality at reasonable prices. In addition to this, the stitching designs, contemporary styles and attractive eye-catching colours make Duke T-Shirt stand apart from other T-Shirt brands available in the market. Be it a party , hunting youth or young corporate executive or an upwardly mobile man, Duke has plenty for everybody in its portfolio. Duke has over 200 different styles & designs in unlimited colour combinations to cater to the various segments of the market in every season. Company's creative team of designers is capable of forecasting styles, colours& predicting specially created blends which is suitable for Indian climatic conditions and match the international standards..

**Total Quality Control**

In order to have a total control over quality of its products, Duke has its own, Knitting, Dyeing, Mercerizing, Finishing, Compacting, Garments Printing, Embroidery and Garments making all an imported machines. Right and fabric to Garment Printing, Embroidery and garments making all on imported machines. Right from yarn to fabric and fabric to Garment making there are series of quality checks. The in-house Quality Assurance

Team ensures the high quality of every garments. Only best garments are offered to the market after stringent quality checking tests. The company has received most coveted ISO 9001-2000 certificate by DNV Netherlands the largest certification body in India.

**Marketing Network**

The next 4 to 5 years witnessed the transformation of Duke into a national T-Shirt brand and by the end of 1985, Duke had almost covered all the important markets across the country. Presently, it hosts a marketing network consisting of over 2000 Multi Branded Outlets (MBO's) all over India in addition to 12 Specialty Stores in various cities. This massive network is touched by their own sales team. Duke is also available at stores in middle east & Sri Lanka. as well.

## Awards and Rewards

Duke Fashions(India) Limited has received the most coveted IS) 9001-2000 Certificate from DNV, the largest certification body in India, for practicing TQM in all units.

ORG-MARG, the largest market intelligence service in Asia, has proclaimed Duke T-shirts as the number one selling brand in India.

Mr. Komal Kumar Jain, Founder, was awarded the prestigious Udyog Patra by the Institute of Trade & Industries for his contributions towards economic growth. DFU publications has felicitated Duke with the "Inside Fashion" award, for excelling in retail.

## Future Plans

The company is already manufacturing T-Shirts, Jogging Suits, Sweat Shirts, Shorts, Lowers, Bermudas etc. This year Company has launched Jackets for winter season and in summers plans are for shirts and trousers. The company has big plans for advertising to be seen through most of the medias, The Company is expanding the marketing network opening up new specialty stores and launching Duke brand in the international market.

| Snapshots |
|---|
| **Company Name**<br>Duke Group of Companies<br>**Located at:**<br>G.T. Road, Near Jalandhar bypass, Ludhiana<br>**Name of the Chief**<br>Komal Kumar Jain<br>**Year of Start**<br>1966<br>**Main Products/Operations**<br>T-Shirts, Polo Shirts, Sweat Shirts, Track Suits, Lowers, Bermudas, Jackets, Bush Coats, Wind Cheater Shirts, Trousers, Denims, Shorts, Pullovers, Thermal Wear, Innerwear<br>**Domestic Market**<br>All Over India<br>**Foreign Market**<br>Middle East & Sri Lanka<br>**Total Turnover**<br>Rs. 125 crore<br>**Domestic Turnover**<br>Rs. 71 crore<br>**Foreign Turnover**<br>Rs. 54 crore<br>**Certifications**<br>ISO 9001:2000, DNV Certificate For Quality<br>**Group Companies**<br>Duke Fashions India Limited<br>Neva Garments Limited<br>Venus Garments India Limited<br>Glaze Garments Pvt. Limited<br>Duke Fabrics Pvt. Limited<br>Duke Nepal Limited<br>**Future Plans**<br>Expansion of Marketing Network |

# JCT

## Incorporation and Integration

The story of JCT goes back to the 1920's when Lala Karam Chand Thapar began his "tryst with destiny" with a coal agency. His aspirations and far-sightedness lead him from this coal agency to become the owner of a coalmine given up as "Sick" by the British. He nurtured this unit back to profitability and within a short span of time had a chain of coalmines, which attained national importance.

His attraction to "sick" units made him acquire interests in diverse fields such as paper& Pulp, Engineering, Electricals, Chemicals, Edible oils, Textiles, Construction & Shipping. These companies, known today in the industry as Ballarpur Industries Ltd, Crompton Greaves Ltd, Greaves Cotton Ltd, JCT Ltd, JCT electronics Ltd, Bharat Starch & Chemicals, Thapar Intrafor, KCT Bros, Indian City Properties Ltd. etc. have come to be called **The Thapar Group**

Lalaji's interest specifically in the Textile industry began very back in 1946 with the setting up of Jagatjit Cotton Textile Mills (known as JCT Ltd. today), situated in Phagwara (Punjab). He later took over a sick textile unit by the name of Shri Sadul Textile Mills at Sriganganagar (Rajasthan), nursed it back to health, and subsequently merged it with JCT.

## Journey so far

The JCT group has diversified into different production activities like Filament Yarn, Fibers, Steel, Electronic, and Export and Agro products. JCT has come a long way since its inception, and now has a turnover of over Rs. 1,000 crore and a work force strength exceeding 15,000 employees.

JCT Ltd. at Phagwara went into commercial production in the year 1951. The name of *JCT* was so given because Maharaja of Kapurthala *Late Sh. Jagatjit Singh* laid the foundation stone of the mill. In the beginning, JCT manufactured cotton varieties of medium range, gradually introducing superfine cotton fabrics, thereby earning a name in the field of textiles. JCT has made a reputed name in synthetic market by producing plain and fancy suitings. The exports of cotton and cotton/polyester varieties is done to Russia, USA, Latin America, Europe, Mauritius, Bangladesh, Sri Lanka, Middle East etc, these exports help JCT to earn huge valuable foreign exchange for the nation.

Working environment and Society

The textile Division at Phagwara employs more than 7000 workers and gives indirect employment to lakhs of people. It has a consistent record of excellent relations with the workmen, which is mainly on account of following the modern concept of workers participation in management. It is also contributing to the physical health of society by way of promotion of sports in the country and has given many international players in the game of Football. Its Football team has won many prestigious tournaments and brought laurels to the state of Punjab.

In its welfare activities JCT has a most modern school where free education is imparted to employees' children up to X class, this school is now being upgraded to impart education up to +2. JCT's growth is phenomenal. Its annual turnover, which was Rs.1.8 crore in the year 1951, has already crossed Rs.300 crore in respect of company's Textile Division. The company is making rapid strides towards further growth.

**Quality Concerns**

JCT is synonymous with quality. With stringent quality controls at every stage of the production process, it is no wonder that the textile division of JCT is the first in the Industry to be accredited with ISO 9002 certification.

JCT Limited, a blue-chip company of THAPAR GROUP, incorporated in the year 1946 in Phagwara, is one of the largest composite textile unit in Northern India based in Punjab, one of the major cotton producing states of India. JCT Ltd. has a capacity of producing over 3 million meters of finest cotton and blended fabrics every month for domestic markets with an annual turnover of around $ 100 million.

**Mission Statement and Quality Policy**

- To consolidate and develop core business areas namely Textiles and Synthetic Fibers.
- To retain our position amongst the leading composite Textile Mills of India, and to remain within the top two groups of companies in the Synthetic Fibers industry.
- To expand and diversify into allied product areas. To simultaneously increase global presence. To develop international markets with domestic markets to achieve rapid growth.
- We at JCT, commit ourselves to strive for excellence and innovation in every report, process and service so that we have a clear competitive edge and our customers are enthusiastically satisfied. Our thoughts and actions, forever, will be characterised by our customers in focus, both internal and external.
- We will pursue initiatives that demonstrate excellent performance in all w at we do. This is done with dedicated participation of each individual and

teamwork of all our people to improve continuously and create a self-sustaining positive work environment.

- JCT resolve to represent quality, integrity, reliability and excellence to its customers, suppliers, society and above all to ourselves.

The modernisation at various stages has resulted in state-of-the-art production facilities. In spinning, the technology included Schlafhorst Auto Coro and Auto Coners. Laxmi Rieters Ring Spindles

**Recent Developments**

The policy of the management to reinvest its profit year after year led the Mills to rapid growth into one of the leading textile mills in the country. In 2000-2001, JCT went in for modernization of both the textile units and invested about Rs. 200 crore for modernization of Phagwara unit. This unit is now one of the most modern units with the state-of-art technology, which includes:

- HVI Cotton Testing Equipment, Crosrol Blow rooms and Cards with Schalaforhst Open End Machine, Sulzer Weaving Machines and Emerizing Machine from Sucker Muller.
- It also includes a lab with modern testing equipment necessary for maintaining quality.
- It has also a full-fledged Research & Development Cell which is recognized by the Govt. Of India.
- It has also a pre-treatment Range and continuous dyeing Machine from Benninger/Monforts which, perhaps, is the first of its kind in Northern India.
- The second phase of modernization which is in the pipeline, envisages installation of high speed shuttles and looms with balancing machinery to manufacture high priced and superfine quality of fabrics to cater to

the requirement of overseas market and also the domestic urban sector.

- Capabilities:

1. HVI system (Cotton Testing)
2. Open end preparatory
3. Open End spinning
4. Carding and Ring spinning
5. Auto Corners:
6. Weaving Machines
7. Finishing Machines
8. CAD System

**Group Companies/Sister Concerns/Divisions**

The Thapar Group includes:

- Ballarpur Industries Ltd.
- JCT Ltd.
- Crompton Greaves Ltd.
- Greaves Cotton & Company Ltd.

These companies have gone beyond their initial industrial interest and pioneered a wide range of products and services through their subsidiaries. The Thapar group's spectacular growth in a span of over 80 years is the result of two factors: a clear philosophy that governs mission of business across all levels of hierarchy and an openness of mind to share global technologies with those who are willing, determined and confident.

The Thapar Group's manufacturing values ensure associations only with the world's best and most capable corporation. The collaborations' list consists of giants like DU-Pont, Zimmer AG, Hitachi Ltd., OKI Electronicals, Westinghouse, David Brown, Ruston & Hornsby, Hawker Siddsley, Siemens Ag and Brush Electronicals.

The Group owes its success to a well-known attitude of doing business, globally and nationally. An attitude that involves effective changes in terms of both technologies and infrastructure and ability to adopt changing economic scenario and warm management philosophy that always put people first.

**Products/Services**

- JCT Ltd. is apart of Thapar Group of India
- The group has widespread operations all over India and Abroad comprising of over 54 companies and 84 manufacturing plants.
- Products/Services

1. Paper
2. Electrical
3. Telecommunication
4. Starch
5. Chemicals
6. Biotechnology
7. Engineering
8. Electronics
9. Textiles
10. Man made fibers
11. Glass
12. Computer hardware

- Indian operations

1. Polyester staple fiber
2. Composite textile plant
3. Steel wires
4. Composite textile plant
5. Picture tubes.

- Exports

1. UK & USA

2. South east Asia
3. Middle east
4. Bangladesh
5. Sri Lanka & Mauritius

**Stock Listings**

Presently the equity shares of the company are listed at the following stock exchanges:

- The stock exchange Mumbai (BSE)
- The Ludhiana Stock exchange Association Ltd (LSE)
- The Delhi Stock Exchange Association Limited (DSE)
- The Calcutta Stock Exchange Association Limited (CSE)

With the extensive connectivity of the BSE, investors have access to dealings in the equity shares of the company all over the country.

The bulk of the trading in the equity shares of the company takes place on the BSE only. The trading on the other Company takes place on the BSE only. The trading on the other stock exchanges is almost nil. Companies have also made an application with the national Stock Exchange (NSE) for listing of its shares with them. Earlier when the said Stock Exchange used to allow trading even of unlisted shares, the equity shares of company was being traded in a big volume.

**Diversification**

The Thapar Group's Flagship on a voyage that never seems to an end. The right measure of dynamics and strategic diversification has made JCT the flagship Company of Thapar Group. Today, JCT ranks amongst the largest companies in the corporate India.

JCT Ltd. has always carried with the spirit to diversify and the vision to succeed. This is manifestive in JCT'S successful forays into diverse fields. Beyond textile, JCT'S operations include filament yarn (Nylon and Polyester), steel wires, electronics, fibers and overseas operations- making it a multi-product, multi-technology group which is market driven and fuelled with high standard of performance and work ethics.

The JCT Group as it stands today is a professional enterprise with modern management thinking, advanced technology, committed work force, the right global connections and a positive risk taking attitude that sets the corporation apart as a leader.

| Snapshots |
|---|
| **Name of the Company**<br>Jagatjit Cotton Textile<br>**Year of Establishment**<br>1946<br>**Located at:**<br>G.T. Road, Phagwara, Distt. Ludhiana<br>**Main Products**<br>Textile, filament yarn (Nylon and Polyester), steel wires, electronics, fibers and overseas operations<br>**Total turnover**<br>Over Rs 275 crore (approximately) Domestic, Foreign<br>**Major collaboration**<br>DU-Pont, Zimmer AG, Hitachi Ltd., OKI Electronicals, Westinghouse, David Brown, Ruston & Hornsby, Hawker Siddsley, Siemens Ag and Brush Electronicals<br>**Flagship companies:** JCT Ltd., Phagwara<br>**Main domestic market:** Through out India<br>**Foreign Market:** Russia, USA, Europe, Sri Lanka, Mauritius, Middle East |

# Malwa Industries

**Incorporation and Integration**

Oswal family is known for its magnificent contribution towards textile industry of India. The family splits resulted into the generation of different group named as:

| | |
|---|---|
| Malwa Group | Vidya Sagar Oswal & Jangi Lal Oswal |
| Nahar Group | Vidya Sagar Oswal & Jawahar Lal Oswal |
| Vardhman | Rattan Chand & S.P. Oswal |
| Oswal Spinning | Lachman Das Oswal & Ashok Oswal |
| Shreyans | Rattan Chand & D.K. Oswal |

If there is one thing that distinguishes the Oswals from the country's other business family, it is only gut – feel. This has kept them afloat even after six successive splits. 85 years ago, an 11-year-old boy left his village in search of livelihood. Over a period of time he created a business empire of over Rs.2000 crore. Lala Vidya Sagar Oswal (96) was studying in the 4$^{th}$ standard when he lost his father to plague, which had spread in the area at that time. He was the eldest son in the family. He decided to move out to Ludhiana.

There he started an arthiya shop and then a provisions store. However, he suffered losses in both ventures. Ultimately he took up a job on a monthly salary of Rs. 10 with Faqir Chand, a leading hosiery manufacturer of his time, with an assurance that he would be allowed to learn the technicalities of the job. The entrepreneur in him was always alive and vibrant and he picked up the nuances of the trade. His mother helped him by selling all her jewellery. He installed a machine and started manufacturing socks. The business kept on growing, and in a span of a few years he installed 10 more machines.

The VSO Group is committed to its belief in the basics. From humble beginnings, way back in 1931, to today, the Group has always engaged in industrial activities that relate to the basic necessities of life, manufacturing knit wears, cotton, yarn, vegetable oils, vanaspati, sugar, paper & Denim. The commitment is even reflected in future ventures-agro-based industries and the infrastructure sector.

**Group Companies**

- Malwa Cotton Spinning
- Punjab Wool combers Ltd
- Malwa Industries Ltd
- Oswal Knit India
- Mukerian paper Mills
- Oswal Sugars Ltd.

**Malwa Cotton Spinning**

Popularly called Malwa is among the top ten textile mills of Indian sub continent. The first unit was incorporated in the year 1976 in Barnala District Sangrur, in the state of Punjab. And the second came into being in the year 1988 at Paonta Sahib, District Sirmour, in the state of Himachal Pradesh.

Headed by Shri Jangi Lal Oswal Chairman cum Managing Director, Malwa Cotton Spinning Mills Ltd. has benefited greatly under his expert supervision and valuable experience.

He has pumped new life into the industry by supplementing the units with very efficient machinery which proved to be not only economically viable but also improved on quality and range of yarn being produced.

The mills are equipped with hitech state of art machineries from world renowned textile machinery manufacturers like Reiter, Trutzler, Crossrol, Schloforst and savio. All the above process machines are also equipped with latest on line quality control equipments combined with computerised information system. W

World wide recognized accepted high reliability Uster quality control equipments form the core of company's R&D and constant monitoring quality control department. An extremely dedicated, skilful work -force of 5000 workers including highly experienced textile professionals, is the driving force that ultimately yields products as unique as their efforts to bring it about. In-house training maintains the upkeep of the staff with technologies, abroad. The team, headed by dynamic chairman, Mr. Jangi Lal Oswal is committed to meet the challenges of Global textile exacting standards. Malwa Yarn is well sought by domestic & international markets. The products are widely demanded, the world over.

**Punjab Woolcombers Ltd.**

Envisaging a vast potential in wool, Punjab Woolcombers Ltd. was conceived and incorporated in the year 1977. It rapidly grew to become the India's finest wool combing unit and the largest manufacturer of 'Wool Mark' woollen worsted hosiery yarn. Set over sprawling 9.25 acre plant in the business centre of Ludhiana in the State of Punjab, it has grown from strength to strength to boast of the finest equipment, technology and skilled personnel that is on the job to produce high quality wool , symbolic of Punjab Woolcombers Ltd.

At the plant, wool combing, dyeing of fibres/yarns, worsted spinning, woollen spinning and manufacturing of other textile goods is carried out.

About 3 million pounds of combed wool is produced here annually. State - of the - art equipment hums at the plant, heralding quality standards which have found recognition of world class wool by the International Wool Secretariat (IWS) for its woollen worsted yarn and also recognized by the Australian Wool Corporation.

Diversification and expansion has led to the project to manufacture Fine Lambs wool Yarn. A new woollen spinning unit has been established for this particular purpose. Constantly on the lookout for any changes the Research teams are guiding the company in to the future. Ready to adapt and accommodate changes has been the building block around which technology has triumphed and ensured that only the finest wool is produced and delivered to the customer. Consistency is the key which has kept Punjab Woolcombers Ltd. growing and made it possible for it to achieve many distinction. With an attitude that balances technology, precision and quality control, Punjab Woolcombers Limited is set to chart a success that is as different and determined as The VSO Group.

**Malwa Industries Ltd.**

Part of Malwa Group, based in Northern India with sales and offices all over India and overseas, Malwa Industries excel in the field of spinning high quality large multi variety of cotton and synthetic yarn and also manufacture world class Sweaters under the brand name Casablanca and is licensee of " Pringle of Scotland".

The Denim plant is strategically located close to the heart of finest cotton growing areas in Northern India. The plant is fully integrated with State of the Art machinery from Switzerland, USA, Belgium and Japan to give its customers the Real Classical Indigo Denim, made with the best Rope

Dyed Technology under an Eco-Friendly Environment. With the aim to meet both the physical and visual standards, the company has the flexibility to meet the trends in all aspect of design, appearance and other developments which is expected by today's fashion conscious market.

The machinery and the facilities are equally complemented with highly motivated and skilled workforce, which works round the clock to deliver a world-class product. The aim is to produce variants of Denim in number of weights, widths and roll lengths as desired by the customers. The target is to suit the needs of every Garments Manufacturer, large or small, to give the optimum levels in performance from cutting room to customer satisfaction.

To ensure the optimum performance in garment manufacturing, to reduce cost and reach the best fabric utilisation levels, the company tries to give its customers, a fabric which has undergone rigorous Internationally recognised System of Quality Assurance at each stage of production. Thereby reducing:

- Wastage
- Rejection

**Plant and Equipment: Malwa Cotton**

The production capacity of the Barnala unit is 30 tones per day and the Paonta Sahib unit spins out 38 tones per day. The product is versatile and finds use in many different ways in the textile and clothing industry of which it forms the essential ingredient.

Spinning out from the unit is wide range of yarns made from Cotton, Acrylic, Polyester, Viscose and other synthetic fibres, Cotton yarns produced is both carded and combed, then there is Acrylic yarn, polyester Viscose yarn and other blends in dyed and Grey.

The high quality of the product has carved a place for itself in the export market where all kinds of cotton yarns, synthetic yarns and their blends are exported. Export growths have been phenomenal and predict the future trends. Malwa Cotton Spinning Mills Ltd. have been marked from the beginning to spin a success story all their own.

The experienced cotton selectors of the company are spread over the cotton belt of Punjab. Control on quality of Cotton is exercised to keep it contamination free right from picking stage.

Cotton is ginned in company's modern Ginning Unit comprising of both Saw and Roller Gin. Each bale passes out of Ginning Factory after it meets Malwa's Quality Standards. All the contamination free bales produced in the Ginning Factory meets Uster HVI900 Grade. Cotton is processed in mills of the company under controlled conditions created by sophisticated State of Art, Humidity and Textile Air Engineering system provided by Luwa Humidification System. Each process confirms to stringent quality norms specified by Textile Research Associations of India.

**Quality: Malwa Cotton**

Quality of the product is constantly monitored at various stages of yarn manufacturing. Savio winders of the company are equipped with third generation contamination control Uster cleaners & coupled with Air Splicers

ESPERO VOLUFIL CONE TO CONE BULKING :

First time in India, the Company has imported world class cone to cone bulking (continuous shrinking and bulking) a winding machine VOLUFIL, model ESPERO from Savio, Italy for the shrinking of acrylic yarn, Hb and blends, and wool and blend set yarn. The Machine is derived from the latest technological development of contiums shrinking system, which ensures the complete shrinking through out the yarn which acquires an extremely regular structure and shows excellent volume and roundness. This machine is equipped with electronic yarn clears and mobile splicer. The packages produced by this machine have optimal density metering and uniformity.

With a 66KV sub station in the plants backed by own electric generation sets assures the continuous production at the plants

Wearing a light Cotton Shirt, a snug sweatshirt or a soft lambs wool sweater gives an individual, a specific feeling of physical well being. Such comfort depends essentially on the quality of the yarn used. The units of Malwa Cotton with its spreaded wings Oswal Knit India, Malwa Processing House and Punjab Woolcombers Ltd. are equipped with the most sophisticated third generation equipments of Zellweger Uster, the world market leader in textile electronics which enables Malwa industry to manufacture optimum quality and competitive products from fiber to yarn. The company has all the testing and monitoring systems used in raw material inspection, in process production phases and final yarn.

**Raw Material**

Dedicated, committed and involved cotton selectors of the company at different stations headed by experienced supervisors and Vice President spares no pain in the selection of Kapas or Raw cotton available in the market. Kapas is ginned in company's own well-established Saw and Roller Ginning Factory at Fazilka.

Before ginning, utmost care is taken to weed out all foreign matters like jute thread, coloured polypropylene foils, contaminated fiber, turfs, pieces of coloured threads and fabrics, ropes, feathers etc, by our experienced workers. Selected samples of individual lots are further tested at HVI 900 Spin Lab System. On the basis of quality characteristics, the better graded samples lots are given green signal for procurement. Ginned lots are once again tested and graded at the works for the various characteristics and put into designated godowns. Before taking into mix and finally feeding into blow-room line, each and every bale of different types is opened and sorted out for all remaining foreign matters by our functionally and actively well trained competent manpower to get the very desired quality of yarn.

It is company's aim to match the quality of yarn and services to the requirement of its customers. The Company has developed its reputation owing to its efforts to supply desired quality and timely delivery of yarn to both domestic and international customers, Constant up gradation of the quality of yarn is also being carried out .

**Awards and Certifications**

In recognition of company's export performance; Govt. of India has awarded the status of "Export House", an award conferred to selective textile mills.

Thus knotless, flawless & high quality yarn confirming to uster standards is produced. Acrylic fiber is procured from world-renowned manufacturers and Acrylic cotton yarn & high bulk Acrylic yarn are produced. Dye house facility at company's works enables it to produce dyed yarn of exact shades.

Malwa Cotton also produces polyester yarn, polyester cotton yarn, viscose yarn, dyed viscose yarn and viscose cotton yarn. Raw materials like polyester, viscose are procured from reputed manufacturers.

Malwa Cotton has bagged ISO 9002 certification the highest mark of recognition on the international scale. This is an achievement not by accident but as a result of constant endeavour and commitment to all round excellence and total customers satisfaction both in India and Overseas.

**Products/Services: Malwa Cotton**

{PRIVATE} With 1,40,000 spindles spread over Punjab and Himachal Pradesh, it gives the production of

| | |
|---|---|
| {PRIVATE}Cotton Yarn | 45 tonnes/day |
| Acrylic Yarn | 25 tonnes/day |
| Polyester Viscose Yarn | 10 tonnes/day |

**Product Range of the Company: Punjab Woolcombers**

| | |
|---|---|
| 100% Pure Wool | Woolmark, for hosiery |
| 60% Pure Wool 40% Acrylic | For Hosiery |
| 100% Acrylic | For Hosiery |
| 100% Acrylic | For Hosiery For Wearing |
| 70% Polyester, 30% Wool | For Weaving |
| Lambs Wool Yarn | |
| 90:10 Wool : Nylon | For Hosiery |
| ShetlandYarn | |
| 70:30, Wool:Nylon | For Hosiery |

**Product Range: Malwa Industries**

1. Basic OE x OE Indigo "Casablanca"
2. Basic Ring "Pringle"
3. Lycra Stretch "Body Wrap"
4. Indigo Cords "Magical Moods"
5. Silky Chino " Comforts"
6. Coloured Weft "Deadly Duo"

**Foreign Presence: Malwa Cotton**

The company is engaged in exports of all kind of yarn for the last 7 Years. Products are well accepted in Asia, Europe, Africa & American continents.

Worldwide Export Market includes:

| Asian Market | European Market | African Market |
|---|---|---|
| Japan | Germany | South Africa |
| China | U.K. | Egypt |
| Korea | Russia | Kenya |
| U.A.E. | Spain | Mauritius |
| Hong Kong | Italy | Nigeria |
| Singapore | Switzerland | Sudan |
| Cyprus | Belgium | Tanzania |
| Israel | Cuba | |
| Malaysia | Greece | |
| Taiwan | Portugal | |
| Turkey | Slovenia | |
| Vietnam | Sweden | |
| Bangladesh | | |

Malwa Cotton Spinning Mills handles design, production, marketing and sales at Ludhiana and yarn manufacturing at Barnala (Punjab) and Paonta Sahib (H.P.) units.

**Market and International Operations:**
**Punjab Woolcombers**

Punjab Woolcombers is currently exporting to the following countries: Dubai, Saudi Arabia, Pakistan, Kenya, Algeria, Canada, Tanzania, Mauritius, Nepal and Bangladesh.

| **Snapshots** |
|---|
| **Name of the Company**<br>Malwa Group of Industries<br>**Year of Establishment**<br>1931<br>**Located at:**<br>Industrial Area, Ludhiana<br>**Founder and Owners**<br>Vidya Sagar Oswal and Jangi Lal Oswal<br>**Turnover**<br>Rs 2,000 crore (approximately)<br>**Products**<br>Yarn, Polyster, Wool<br>**Domestic Market:** Through out India<br>**Foreign Market:** Asia, Europe, and Africa<br>**Famous brands**<br>Pringle, Casabalanca |

# Nahar Group of Industries

**Incorporation and Integration**

The Nahar Group, one of the leading business groups of India came into existence in 1949 with the initial efforts of three Oswal brothers, Shri Vidya Sagar Oswal, Shri Lachman Das and Shri Rattan Chand Oswal. They started a hosiery factory to manufacture socks only. It was the dynamism, vision, hard work, farsightedness and co-operativeness of Mr. Vidya Sagar Oswal that small hosiery factory in the days of II world war bagged a contract from military. This was the zoom-up point for the Oswal brothers. On the 23rd June 1949, the Oswal hosiery factory split into:

1. Oswal Woollen Mills
2. Oswal Spinning & Weaving Mills Ltd.

Mrs. Vidya Sagar Oswal and Mr. Rattan Chand Oswal managed the OWM and Mr. Lachman Das Oswal headed Oswal Spinning & Weaving Mills Ltd.

The initial capacity was 800 spindles. Mr. Vidya Sagar Oswal gave a mission to the company. It was to target three basis needs of mankind viz. Roti-Kapda-Makaan.

In 1956 the spindle capacity was increased to 2000 and then in 1960, a hosiery unit was attached to OWML and in 1965, the spinning capacity was raised to 12000 spindles. By 1966, the export market was taped and during the process Russia was targeted.

Today as they step into the new millennium, those nascent days of 800 spindle start-up become a distant memory as the Nahar Group surges ahead to establish itself as a reputed Industrial Conglomerate with a wide-ranging Portfolio - cotton and woollen yarns, fabric processing, hosiery garments, knitwear's, sweaters, steel, soaps, sugars, infrastructure development, information technology.

Though in many areas group has achieved market leadership but because of tough competition it is pulled back to refocus, restructure and reading its corporate blueprint to establish a new and appropriate equation with the new market forces. This really was the essence of their positive vision 2000 thrust. It encompassed global aspiration and consolidates brand equity for the domestic markets. Regarding the first, the groups aggressive and market survey forays have helped zoom the export sensex, contributing to over one third of the present turnover of the group. Focusing on the second market driven brand extension relating to their high profile and top line '**MONTE CARLO**' has met with the resounding success, '**CANTERBURY**' another brand too is not far behind. Both however are associated wit the 'Woollen Sweaters and Jerseys'.

However, beyond there professional portfolio most concrete reflections are there for all to see - Jawahar Lal Oswal Public charitable Trust which runs free dispensáries in remote areas to fulfil the medical needs of the under-privileged and Mohan Dai Oswal Memorial Hospital, promoted by Oswal Mills.

This group turnover has reached the new peak at Rs. 1800 crore with foreign exchange earning of Rs. 600 crore. The world is the market, presently group products are centre of attraction in textile and yarn market of USA, UK, Germany, Russia, Japan, New

Zealand, Holland, Thailand, Hong Kong, Singapore, Mauritius, Dubai, South Africa, Israel, Bangladesh etc.

The group companies have been awarded ISO 9002 certification by the bureau of Indian standards. As on the date, the Nahar Group is the second largest spinning group of the country and has an aggregate spindle of more than four lakh. The group has a clear goal-becoming India's largest spinning group as well as exporter of yarn.

**Company Profile**

The following companies are under the Nahar Group:

- Oswal Woollen Mills Ltd.
- Nahar Spinning Mills Ltd.
- Nahar Exports Ltd.
- Nahar Fibers Ltd.
- Nahar Fabrics Ltd.
- Oswal Cotton Mills Ltd.
- Nahar International Ltd.
- Nahar Industrial Enterprises Ltd.
- Nahar Industrial infrastructure corporation Ltd.
- Nahar Sugar and Allied Industries Ltd.

**Oswal Woollen Mills Limited**

OWM was established in 1949. The CMD of OWML is Mr. J.L. Oswal. It is located at Ludhiana. The company is manufacturing all types of blended worsted yarn, Lamb's wool yarn for knitting and weaving, blankets, lohis, shawls and branded garments such as Monte Carlo and Canterbury etc. Company has a turnover of more than Rs. 220 crore. Today with over 17200 in terms of total spindlage and manufacturing high value - added items like designers knitwear, the front-runner soars ahead. OWM remains committed towards moving with the times and changing with the needs of the market forces that defines the new millennium, in their ultimate objectives of providing quality, value-addition and range for the customer.

**Nahar Spinning Mills Ltd.**

This company was incorporated in 1980 as a 100% Export Oriented Unit (E.O.U.). The company is an ISO 9002 certificate holder company. The MD of the company is Mr. Dinesh Oswal. It is engaged in manufacturing all types of cotton, acrylic and blended yarn, as well as knitted fabrics and garments. It has a full-fledged Dying Unit also.

**Nahar Exports Ltd.**

The company is headed by Mr. Dinesh Oswal. It is located in Ludhiana, Sangrur and Lalroo. Established in November 1988, the company is also an ISO 9002 certification holder with manufacturing of 100% cotton and polyester/cotton yarns. Company has 100% EOU. Nahar Exports has 5 plants with a spindlage capacity of 145000 spindles, manufacturing a wide range of premium quality and value - added yarns and exporting to enthusiastic customers in the Europe, Hong Kong, Singapore, Mauritius and South East Asian Countries.

**Nahar Fibres Ltd.**

The company was added to Group's fleet in 1989. It is an ISO 9002 certification holder company. It is manufacturing 100% acrylic, melage, 100% cotton yarns. Company has capacity of 55000 spindles.

**Nahar Fabrics Ltd.**

The company was established in July 1982. It is manufacturer and exporter of cotton/polyester-blended fabrics, satin for bedspreads, twills, drills and fine poplin for shirting. The works of the company is located at Lalroo near Chandigarh and other main operations at Ludhiana. Presently, the company is having turnover of Rs. 394 crore.

**Oswal Cotton Mills Ltd.**

Established in 1999, as a process and finishing house for cotton and cotton blend fabric for use in shirting and bottom wears. it is located at Lalroo near Chandigarh. It has installed capacity of 360,000 spindles. Further plans of the Group include manufacturing of Shirting/Trousers with branded name and the same shall be sold in both the domestic and the international market.

**Nahar International Ltd.**

Mr. Kamal Oswal is the MD of this company. It was incorporated as Punjab Con Cast Steel. It is located at Ludhiana, Bhiwandi (Rajasthan), Lalroo (Punjab). It is manufacturing round, square and flat various type of steel as well as acrylic cotton yarns in dyed and grey forms. It has capacity of 1,00,000 spindles.

**Nahar Industrial Enterprises Ltd.**

The company was incorporated in September 1983 and is headed by Mr. Kamal Oswal. It is located at Raikot, Mundian (Ludhiana), Lalroo near Chandigarh. The company has two divisions namely, oil and soap division and the Textile Division. The company is also engaged is manufacturing of 100% cotton yarn company has spindlage capacity of about 38000 spindles.

**Nahar Industrial Infrastructure Corporation**

It was incorporated in August 1994 for the purpose of development of Industrial Parks/Industrial Estates. It is located at Lalroo near Chandigarh. The park will have an area of 2500 acres out of which 600 acres have already been required. The park would be having infrastructural facilities like a captive power plant, effluent treatment plant, water supply, telecommunication, conference centre etc. Thus it will become not only a landmark achievement for Nahar Group, but also an asset for India to be proud of.

**Nahar Sugar and Allied Industries Ltd.**

This company was incorporated in 1993. It is headed by Mr. Kamal Oswal. It is located at Amloh near Khanna. It is an integrated sugar complex to produce white crystal sugar. It has an installed capacity of 2500 TCD to 3500 TCD. Further plans are to increase capacity to 5000 TCD.

**Achievement of Nahar Group**

The groups' continuous excellence in exports has been recognized by the EXPORT PROMOTION COUNCILS as well as the GOVT. OF INDIA by best owing several exports awards and trophies.

To whom a few:

- 1989 and 1990 first Gold Trophy is Global Exports and first Silver Trophy in Hosiery Exports.

- 1989-90 to 1993-94 export award consecutively for 5 years for export of Woollen Hosiery Garments.
- 1993 International award of excellent performance in Exports.
- 1998-99 Silver Trophy for Second highest Export Performance.
- ISO 9002 certification awarded by the bureau of Indian Standards.

**Quality Policy**

The quality policy of OSWL is that they are committed to provide total customer satisfaction by not only meeting but exceeding the agree customer requirements.

**Quality Objectives**

- To implement and ensure compliance to ISO-9002 quality system at all time and practice of Total Quality Management.
- To provide training to all personnel involved in quality related activities.
- To promote personal development of employees, leadership skills and team building.
- Optimum utilization of resources.
- To closely monitor to adhere to customer needs and delivery schedule.
- Employees shall implement and adhere to policy as applicable in their respective areas.

**Chairman's Perspective**

According to Mr. Jawahar Lal Oswal hard effort and ability of entrepreneurship, timely decision and attainment of highest level of transparency and accountability in its operations is the foundation of success of his group. Beside entrepreneurship he personally put human resources management No.1 in all the functioning areas and levels. In his views without human resource development we cannot succeed in any area or section like marketing, finance and production. Human resources are a driving force that always propel toward progress, prosperity and success. He personally feels that no industrialist at present can rise to success without having better policy of human resource development and their finest utilization.

While talking about the future of Punjab industry especially with the emergence of low cost competition from the firms of other countries he said that there is no threat to industry in Punjab. Apprehensions of such challenges cannot be ruled and for that industrialists in Punjab have to upgrade their industrial unit with latest technology so as to compete with cost as well as quality. According to him so far as the technical knowledge is concerned we are no way behind from other developing countries and we can face challenges of globalization provide the government liberalize the rules, bring down the import duty and other direct cess and try to eliminate the unexpected burden faced by industrialists.

While talking about social responsibility he said that we believe in ensuring high quality of goods according to standard stipulated by government under international standard organization (ISO). He said that we are fully aware of social responsibility for not creating any kind of pollution whether it is noise, water or air. We are careful not to allow exploitation of human resources by having policy not to employ workers below 18 years of age. Again he stress that we are also very cautious to provide hygiene and healthy working place and atmosphere.

While talking about his future plans he said that expansion in all his units is being carried out and which is always an on going process. Nobody can predict regarding coming years. However, having a positive attitude towards business as well as life we can assume that within the coming years our business will be flourished with the true efforts, hard work and we would achieve No. 1 position in spinning and textile.

**Snapshots**

**Year of Start**
1930, then Group Split took place in 1993
**Located at:**
G.T. Road, Ludhiana
**Main Products/Operations**
Yarn, steel, hosiery, acids, sugar and allied products, trousers, T-shirts, jackets
**Total Turnover**
Rs. 2,000 crore
**Domestic Turnover**
Rs.1,600 crore
**Export Turnover**
Rs. 400 crore
**Certificates**
ISO 9002, Best Exhibited Product Award from IWS Best Export House Award
**Stock Exchange Listing**
Ludhiana Stock Exchange
**Main Domestic Market**
All Over India
**Main Export Markets**
Europe, Hong Kong, Taiwan, Mauritius and South-East Asian countries

# OCM Woollen MILLS

**Incorporation and Integration**

OCM Woollen Mills, popularly known as OCM, is a unit of Birla VXL Ltd, which is a part of country's premier industrial house, the Birla Group. It was established in Amritsar in 1924 by a British Company for the manufacture of high quality hand-knotted carpets for the supply to its subsidiary company, the East India Carpet Limited. OCM carpets have enjoyed the highest goodwill for their fine quality and vibrant designs both in the home and foreign market and that is from where it got its name OCM, Oriental Carpet Manufacturing.

In 1972, the British Company divested its holding and Mr. S.K. Birla belonging to the renowned business family of India, assumed its control and since then OCM never looked back and progressed further and further with its modernization-cum-expansions plans. Today, the production capacity of OCM is about 90 Lakh meters. This has been made possible by the consistent thrust of the company in adapting itself to the changing trends and environment both at home and abroad, and by committing to its customers with its strong and valuable relationship.

Today, OCM has become a synonym for quality suitings. In fact, OCM is the first worsted mil in India to get the prestigious ISO 9001 certification. It has already been a recipient of several prestigious Export Awards and Trophies during the last few years. The company has its edge not only in the home market but is also exporting to several, countries like Canada, USA, Middle East and others its innovative world and wool blended fabrics. Hence, all department of OCM ranging from designing to finishing work congenial for producing the just right kind of the fabric which has a right feel, fall and drape and maintains its ironed look through out the day.

OCM is one of the India's most modern and composite worsted and woollen Mills. It has the facility to execute all stages of production, spinning, weaving, processing, dyeing and final finishing. For the proper working of the organization and for proper handling of the machines, training is imparted to workers, superiors and managerial staff. Though the form of training can be different, it can be orientation training/on the job training or promotional training.

**Profile of the Company**

**Birla VXL: The Company**

Birla VXL is a part of S.K. Birla Group and manufactures fabrics for suitings under the world famous brand names of OCM and Digjam

The two textile mills of Birla VXL are:

- OCM Woollen Mills, Amritsar, Punjab
- Digjam Woollen Mills, Jamnagar, Gujarat

OCM and Digjam are two of the most highly respected brands in the Indian market. Between them they command a market share of 26% and reach every nook and corner of India through a chain of over 4000 retailers. The manufacturing capacity of the plants has been recently increased from approximately 8 million meters to 14 million meters. By the year 2005 A.D. the group look up to around 25 million meters per annum. OCM will then as an individual unit be ranked as on amongst the top seven factories in the world.

On its sprawling 40-acre site, OCM has achieved a new generation 'technological edge' which incorporates the latest imported machines and contemporary processes. In fact,

OCM has distinct advantage of having under a single roof, the facility for every process – right from the fiber to the finished fabric.

**Quality Control**

The products of the group carry the ISO 9001 and the Woolmark certifications. A forerunner in adopting new and efficient methods and technologies, OCM has the rare distinction of being the first worsted composite mill in India to achieve both the ISO 9001 certification as well as implement an ERP solution.

A completely vertically integrated plant, OCM has in house production facilities to convert tops to finished fabrics through and using state-of-the art machinery. All the materials pass through stringent checks at every stage and help in delivering outstanding quality.

**Marketing**

OCM has a formidable market presence and into the minds of discerning consumers has, today become synonymous with quality suitings. The company's marketing arm lays strong emphasis on distribution. The 1,800 strong dealer network – one of the largest in India – sends regular feedback on the brand, market trends and market needs.

**Foreign Collaborations/Tie-Ups**

Taking full opportunity of the changed economic policies of the country it has entered into tie ups with a few foreign giants, to gain from the synergy. Recently, Birla VXL entered into tie-up with HAGGARS, an American Company for the ready-made supply in the domestic market, and a joint venture with a renowned French firm,

DORMEUIL for presenting the Indian consumer with wide and diverse range of finest English and European associating fabric into currently available in the Indian Market. Hence with the common pool of expertise of design, style and technical know-how the company hopes to provide the market with an exclusive range of suiting fabrics with a nice blend of traditional and innovation for retaining the OCM synonimity with leadership.

**Operations of Different Departments**

**Plant Capacity:** At present, the Weaving capacity of OCM is 11 million meters per year, which is projected to increase to 18 million meters at full maturity. Spinning capacity is 5300 tonnes per year. This feeds the in -house requirements as well as supplying yarn to the export and domestic markets OCM employs 571 executives and 2384 Workers.

**Dyeing:** Dyeing consistency is maintained, with the help of a spectrophotometer - a computerized colour matching system, that ensures consistency of quality and uniformity of every batch.

**Spinning:** Ring frames with 12,000 spindles from Zinser (Germany) convert the tops into various fine counts of yarn. The spindles have now been increased to 38,000. The counts produced range from 2/25's right up to 2/100's.

**Weaving:** OCM uses 250 computerized, high-speed, shuttleless Dornier and Sulzer looms.

**Finishing:** Using some of the most sophisticated equipment in the world, OCM turns out fabric that is unmatched in fall, feel and drape.

**OCM Catalogue**

OCM unveils a collection that reflects the latest trends across the international ranks, choosing your fabrics, was never so easy or as enjoyable.

- Tweeds
- The Gold Collection
- The Cool Gold Collection
- Wedding Collection
- Regular Suitings
- Jackets
- Trousers

**Competitors of the company**

**For Terri wool market its competitors are**

- Raymonds
- Dinesh
- Reid & Taylor

**For Terrine market its competitors are**

- JCT
- Grasim,
- Siyarams

**Ranking among competitors**

- Raymonds
- OCM
- Reid & Taylor

**Achievements**

Over the last few year Birla VXL limited has grown by leaps and bounds. The major stress has been on exports. Today Birla VXL are shipped to over 40 countries the world over. Shipment of worsted wool, suiting fabrics and ready to wear garments along have increased from US $6 million to nearly US $30 million in just 2 years. The major destinations are Europe, the USA and Middle East

| **Snapshots** |
|---|
| **Year of Establishment** |
| 1972 |
| **Located at:** |
| Amritsar |
| **Name of the Chairman** |
| Shri S.K. Birla |
| **Main Products/Operations** |
| Tweeds, Gold Collection, Cool Gold Collection, Wedding Collection, Regular Suitings, Jackets, Trousers |
| **Popular Brands** |
| OCM & DIGJAM |
| **Total Turnover** |
| Rs. 500-550 crore approx. |
| Export Turnover Rs. 135-165 crore approx. |
| **Foreign Collaborations** |
| HAGGARS, an American Company |
| DORMEUIL, French firm |
| **Domestic Markets** All India |
| **Foreign Markets** |
| Canada, USA, Middle East, Australia, Britain & Germany. |

# Vardhman Spinnings and General Mills

**Incorporation and Integration**

The Vardhman Group is one of the largest Textile houses in the country with a turnover of about Rs 1900 crore and employs around 20,000 people. The group has sizeable presence in spinning, weaving, sewing threads, textile processing, acrylic fiber manufacturing and alloy steels.

**About Shri S.P. Oswal**

Mr. S.P. Oswal heads the Vardhman group. Born on 8th April, 1942 at Ludhiana, he joined the family business in 1966 when the group turnover was Rs. 1.5 crore with spinning capacity of 12,000 spindles.

Mr. Oswal did his schooling and Bachelors in commerce at Ludhiana. He obtained Masters in Commerce from Punjab University in 1966.

At present Mr. Oswal is acting as chairman of Vardhman Spinning & General Mills, Ludhiana. He is also acting as executive chairman of Mahavir Spinning Mills Ltd., Ludhiana, chairman and managing director of Vardhman Polytex Ltd., Ludhiana, chairman of Vardhman Agencies Ltd., Bharuch and chairman of VMT Spinning Company Ltd., Baddi.

Apart from these positions he is also a member of Punjab Pollution Control Board, Patiala, Member of National Council, Confederation of Indian Industry (CII) and Chairman of Punjab State Council, Northern region, CII, and member of committee of Administration, TEXPROCIL.

He also has been founder president and director of Ludhiana Stock Exchange Association, Ludhiana, and President Northern India Textile Mills Association. Mr. Oswal also takes keen interest in field of education. He has been a member of Board of Management, Punjab Agricultural University, Ludhiana and Member, Board of Governors, Punjab Technical University, Jalandhar.

Mr. Oswal has one daughter, Ms. Suchita, who is acting as executive director of the group. She is married to Mr. Sachit Jain and he is also acting as the executive director of the group.

**Company Profile**

The Vardhman Group started its corporate journey with installed capacity of 6000 spindles in 1965 under the Flagship Company Vardhman Spinning & General Mills limited at Ludhiana. Over the years the group has expanded its spinning capacities besides adding new business. The group has also diversified yarn processing, weaving, sewing thread, fabric processing, acrylic fiber manufacturing and special and alloy steel.

Vardhman is a leading group in India having interest in textiles and 'special steel' manufacturing. The group has expanded manifold since its inception. The group has 18 operational plants with installed spinning capacity of about 5,00,000. Spindles, 216 shuttle less looms and about 45 tonnes per day dyeing capacity, capable of Processing variety of raw materials available worldwide.

The uniqueness of the Vardhman group lies in the fact that not only has it excelled in all its endeavours but has also established a firm footing through its deep rooted culture that imparts the group an unassailable strength and confidence to face the future.

Vardhman Group consists of integrated facilities of spinning, weaving and Finishing with half a million spindles, weaving capacity of 208 looms and fabric finishing capacity of 30 million metres per annum.

**Sewing Threads**

In 1982 Vardhman entered the sewing thread market as a forward integration project. With 53,000 spindles capacity at Hoshiarpur, Vardhman threads are the second largest selling brand in the country.

Another integration has been Vardhman's entry into weaving. Grey fabric- weaving division at Baddi has already made its mark as a quality producer in the home market

**Journey....**

From a small beginning with 6000 spindles in 1965, the group has come a long way to emerge as the largest yarn spinner in the country with a capacity of over half a million spindles. The product range has also expanded from 100% cotton yarns to the largest range of grey and dyed cotton, blended and synthetic yarn. Group has total of twenty manufacturing units spread all over India. Sh. S.P. Oswal, Chairman who is a gold medallist in Master of Commerce, heads the group. He is supported by Professionals/Unit heads and Corporate team. Corporate Office of the Group is situated at Ludhiana where most of the business decisions including Sales/Purchase/Finance/Projects/HRD/ Secretarial are taken. A team of Professionals is there in Corporate Office to support Chairman for carrying out group operations.

**The 1960s**

The decade of sixties saw the birth of today's one of the largest textile-manufacturing group. Lala Rattan Chand Oswal at Ludhiana founded Vardhman Spinning and General Mills Ltd on 7th December 1962. The unit was incorporated on 27th December 1962.VSGML started commercial production of cotton yarn with 6,000 spindles in November 1965.

**The 1970s**

Seventies saw the small mill growing into a large conglomerate. In 1975 the unit was granted industrial license for 50,000 spindles. In 1977-78 the unit diversified into Acrylic yarn spinning by becoming the 1st textile mill in the country to spin acrylic yarn on modified cotton spindles. In the same year 15,000 spindles were diversified into the production of synthetic and blended yarns. It also introduced "Hand knitting Yarns" for the first time, which became its premium product. This year also witnessed a major diversification in the production programme of VSGM by shifting to manufacture of industrial yarns. In 1980, first dye house of the group was commissioned for in-house dyeing capacity of yarn and fabric.

**The 1980s**

Start of the eighties was not so good as the industrial unrest caused closure of factory for 3 months from 14th April 1982 to 19th July 1982. In 1984-85, the latest generation G-5 ring frame was installed in Unit-II .In 1985-86, VSGML started exporting cotton yarn to Bulgaria and exports were spread to Western Europe and other parts of the world. In 1987-88, Quality circle movement took birth in VSGML with the inception of Quality Circle "Aradhana" in the dye house. In the last year of this decade, VSGML was awarded with the IBPL Energy Conservation Award.

**The 1990s**

This decade saw Vardhman emerging as the largest textile producer and exporter of the country. Vardhman received numerous awards in this decade. VSGML was accorded the status of "Recognized Export House" by the government of India on 20$^{th}$ September 1990, on the basis of major export from the unit. Vardhman was awarded the "TEXPROCIL" bronze trophy for excellence in exports in 1992-93. In 1993, VSGML became the first textile mill in the country and the first industrial unit in Punjab to be awarded the prestigious ISO 9002 certification. Shri S.P. Oswal was awarded Exports Excellence Award by the then President of India, Shri S.D. Sharma on 17$^{th}$ December 1994.The production of dyed yarn product, "Daffodil" commenced in 1994.

The year 1995 saw a major change in the group as the unit was bifurcated into two parts, namely Unit-I involved in manufacture and sale of spun yarn and Unit-II, engaged in dyeing of yarn and related activities on 6$^{th}$ May 1995.

The founder of the Vardhman group, Lala Rattan Chand Oswal passed away on the night of 5$^{th}$/6$^{th}$ January 1998.

In the year 1998-99, Spinning-2 started the production of polyester sewing thread for the first time. In the last year of the century, 2000, "CUDDLES" India's first ready to knit pack for others was launched by Miss India 2000, Gul Apang, on 14$^{th}$ September 2000. "Bunte Bunte Kismat Chamke", a contest for the hand knitting yarn customers was also launched in the same year.

**New Millennium**

In the new millennium, Vardhman launched ERP (Enterprise Resource Planning) in March 2001.

**Mission**

"Vardhman aims to be a world class textile organization, producing diverse range of products for the global textile market. Vardhman seeks to achieve customer delight through excellence in manufacturing and customer service based on creative combination of state-of-the art technology and human resources. Vardhman is committed to be responsible corporate citizen."

**Group Companies**

Today the Vardhman Group comprises of three listed and three unlisted companies & two joint ventures –

**Listed Companies**

1. Vardhman Spinning And General Mills Ltd.
2. Vardhman Polytex Ltd.
3. Mahavir Spinning Mills Ltd.

**Unlisted Companies**

4. Vardhman Threads Ltd.

**Joint Ventures**

5. Vardhman Marubeni Threads Spinning Co. Ltd.
6. Vardhman Acrylics Limited

All the three Unlisted Companies are subsidiaries of MSML and were started as Joint Venture with Foreign Partners. As on date VMT & VAL are still Joint Venture Companies where as the group has already bought back the shares in VTL, and VTL has now become a 100% subsidiary of MSML.

**Companies at a Glance**

**Vardhman Spinning & General Mills Limited (VSGML)**

This flagship company of the Group, was set up in 1962 by the Oswal's, with a capacity of 6000 spindles for manufacturing of cotton yarn at Ludhiana, Punjab. The unit commenced production in 1965. The company has, over the years, expanded the spinning capacity at Ludhiana to reach at present level of installed capacity of 61708 spindles. This unit also has a Dyeing capacity of 18tpd.

In the year 1973 company put up a Mini-steel plant at Faridabad in the name of ***Oswal Steels***. Later on in the year 1994-95 company sold out this Steel Unit with a capacity of 25,000 MT per annum of Rolled products to another Group Company, namely M/s Mahavir Spinning Mills Limited. In order to diversify its operation geographically, in 1989, the company decided to set up a new spinning unit under the name and style of "Auro Spinning Mills" with a capacity of 25,200 spindles in village Baddi, Tehsil Nalagarh, Distt. Solan, in the state of Himachal Pradesh. The unit became fully operational in 1991. Over the years, the spindleage has increased to 67560 spindles.

VSGML also set up a Weaving Unit at Baddi in March 1992, for manufacture of cotton grey cloth with installed capacity of 72 Looms. Over the years, the number of looms has been increased to 208.

The Company has also set up a dye house at Baddi in technical collaboration with NIHON SANMO, Japan, in 1995 for fibre.yarn dyeing capacity of 18 tpd. Over the years, the capacity has been expanded for yarn dyeing to 8tpd, and for fibre dyeing to 22 tpd. The company set up new 100% Export Oriented Unit (EOU) of 25000 spindles. The unit was commissioned in March 1998. The present capacity of the unit is 27040 spindles. The company has set up 'Fabric Process House" in the name and style of "AURO TEXTILES" at Baddi with technology from Topai Sanyo, Japan, with final capacity of 30 million metres. The unit was commissioned in 1999.

**Mahavir Spinning Mills Limited (MSML)**

Mahavir Spinning Mills Limited (MSML) was promoted by M/s Vardhman Spinning & General Mills Limited (VSGM). The company was incorporated in October 1973.

In 1975, the company set up a spinning mill with an installed capacity of 25,000 spindles for manufacturing cotton, synthetic and blended yarns at Distt. Hoshiarpur, in Punjab. The capacity of Hoshiarpur Unit has been steadily increased and is presently at 56,000 spindles.

In 1981, the Company set up a new spinning unit with an installed capacity of 25,000 spindles by the name of Arihant Spinning Mills for manufacturing cotton and acrylic yarns at Malerkotla, Distt. Sangrur, Punjab. Over the years the Company undertook capacity additions and presently has a capacity of 1,11,892 spindles.

In the same year, i.e., 1981, the Company diversified its product line by setting up facilities for manufacturing of sewing thread with an installed capacity of 4.5 tonnes per day (TPD) at Hoshiarpur, Punjab. The capacity of the aforesaid sewing thread unit has been gradually expanded to 17TPD.

On April 1, 1988, Mohta Industries Ltd., a sick company, was merged with Mahavir Spinning Mills Ltd. As approved by the Board for Industrial and Financial Reconstruction (BIFR). Mohta Industries Ltd., at the time of merger, had a division known as Mohta Alloys & Steel Works, a mini steel plant at Ludhiana. This division is now a part of Mahavir Spinning Mills Ltd. The company has renamed the mini steel plant from Mohta Alloys & Steel Works to Vardhman Special Steels. The company has also set up a Rolling Mill with an installed capacity of 40,000 TPA, in its Ludhiana Steel Unit for manufacture of a wide range of alloy steel/rolled products. The rolling mill has become operational in 1995. The present capacity of SMS is 135000 MT per annum and of rolling products is 65,000 MT per annum.

In the year 1994-95 Company also acquired a Steel Unit of another Group Company, namely M/s Vardhman Spinning & General Mills Limited, which had a rolling Mills facility at Faridabad in the name of Oswal Steels with a capacity of 25,000 MT per annum. This steel division at Faridabad has been non-operational since November 2000.

In 1992, the Company set up a 100% Export Oriented Unit (EOU) for manufacture of cotton yarns with an installed capacity of 25200 spindles under the name and style of Anant Spinning Mills at Mandideep, Distt. Raisen in Madhya Pradesh. Over the years the company undertook different expansion schemes and presently has capacity of 74496 spindles.

The company, in 1994-95, set up a gassed mercerized unit at Hoshiarpur, Punjab in technical collaboration with Kyungbang Ltd., South Korea with a capacity of 1.7 tpd. The capacity of the aforesaid unit has been gradually expanded to about 7.00 TPD.

In the year 1999-2000 the company undertook an expansion of Sewing Thread business by installation of Unit-II at Ludhiana with a capacity of 5 TPD to be implemented in two phases. The first phase with a capacity of 2.5 TPD has commenced production in January 2001.

**Vardhman Polytex Limited**

VPL was originally promoted in the joint sector by Mohta Industries Limited (MIL) and Punjab State Industrial Development Corporation Limited (PSIDC), & was incorporated in the name of Punjab Mohta Polytex Ltd (PMPL) in August 1980. The spinning unit of the company at Bhatinda, Punjab, started commercial production in 1984 with an installed capacity of 9504 spindles and 504 rotors. In April, 1988 MIL which had been registered with Board for

Industrial and Financial Reconstruction (BIFR) as a sick Company, was merged with Mahavir Spinning Mills Limited (MSML), as a consequence VPL also came under the fold of the Vardhman Group. With the acquisition of PSDIC's shareholding by MSML, VPL became a subsidiary of MSML with effect from June 1989. The name of the company was changed from Punjab Mohta Polytex Ltd to Vardhman Polytex Ltd in August 1991. At the time of merger, MIL had a division known as Mohta Alloys & Steel Works, a mini steel plant at Ludhiana. The division is now a part of MSML.

Vardhman Polytex Limited came out with Right-cum-public issue of Fully Convertible Debentures in February 1993, the conversion of which was due in October 1993. After the said conversion, the Company ceased to be a subsidiary Company of MSML. The capacity of this Unit has been gradually increased to 49472 spindles.

VPL, in 1990 – 91, added a new Worsted Spinning Unit at Ludhiana, under the name of Anshupati Textile, with a capacity of 4800 spindles to manufacture acrylic yarn of various counts. The capacity of the plant stands increased to 8000 spindles. The Company commissioned a DTA unit at Baddi under the name & style of Arisht Spg. Mills with a capacity of 25000 spindles in 1996 – 97 Presently the installed capacity of the aforesaid unit is 41472 spindles. Further, the Company commissioned a 100% Export Oriented Unit (EOU), under the name of Arisht Spinning Mills (100% EOU) at Baddi in 1997 – 98 with an installed capacity of 24288 spindles.

**Vardhman Threads Limited**

In the year 1993-94 Mahavir Spinning Mills Limited entered into a Joint Venture Agreement with one of the world's best manufacturer of Industrial Synthetic Threads, M/s Barbour Campbell Group Limited of Ireland. A joint venture company named Barbour Vardhman Threads (Pvt.) Ltd. was incorporated and a plant to manufacture industrial synthetic threads was set up Baddi with an installed capacity of Industrial Sewing Threads of 1TPD. The Company started its commercial production in April 1995. Its products have specialized application for Shoe and Leather Industries. During the year 1992 – 2000 the management & control of M/s Barbour Campbell Group Limited was taken over by a competitor company, viz Coats Viyella Inc. which made the continuation of Joint Venture practically difficult. Accordingly, in the same year MSML entered into a Disengagement Agreement whereby it bought out the entire stake of 'Barbour Group' in the Company and the JVA stood terminated w.e.f March 2000, thus making the company a 100% subsidiary of MSML. Upon the approval of the members, the company continued its activities under the new name ***"Vardhman Threads Limited".***

**VMT Spinning Company Limited**

Mahavir Spinning Mills Ltd. in the year 1994 – 95 entered into a Joint Venture Agreement with M/s. Marubeni Corporation and Toho Rayon Company Limited of Japan for setting up of 100% Export Oriented Unit to Manufacture Cotton Yarn. Production Facility was established at Baddi in Himachal Pradesh by the name of VMT Spinning Company Limited (100% EOU) with an installed capacity of 25000 spindles. This Company has started its commercial production in September 1996. The capacity of the aforesaid unit has been gradually expanded to 28320 spindles.

## Data Regarding Various Group Companies at a Glance

| Name Of The Company | Year Of Start | Main Prducts(S)/ Operations) | Location |
|---|---|---|---|
| Vardhman Spinning and General Mills Ltd. | 1965 | Spun Yarn, Fibre Dyeing, Yarn Dyeing, Woven Fabric and Fabric Processing | Ludhiana, Punjab |
| Auro Spinning | 1990 | Cotton, Blended, Fibre Dyed and Fine Count | Baddi, H.P |
| Auro Weaving | 1992 | Grey Woven Cotton and Blended Yarns Fabric | Baddi, H.P |
| VSGM100%EOU | 1997 | Cotton Yarns | Baddi, H.P |
| Auro Dyeing Mills | 1995 | Fibre Dyeing and Yarn Dyeing | Baddi, H.P |
| Auto Textiles | 2000 | Fabric Processing | Baddi H.P |
| Vardhman Spinning and Weaving Unit- II | Under raising | Yarn Dyeing | Ludhiana, Punjab |
| Mahavir Spinning Mills | 1973 | Spun Yarn, Sewing Thread, Gassed Mercerization, Steel Melting and Rolled Products | Hoshiarpur, Punjab |
| Arihant Spinning Mills | 1981 | Cotton Yarns, Cotton, Blended, Acrylic, Melange, Fine Count | Malerkotla, Punjab |
| Anant Spinning Mills | 1992 | Cotton Yarn | Mandidee P |
| Arihant Mills | | Cotton, Blended, Melange, Fine Counts | Bhopal, M.P |
| Vardhman Polytex Ltd | 1980 | Spun Yarns | Bathinda. Punjab |
| Anshupati Textile Mills | 1990-91 | Acrylic Yarns | Ludhiana, Punjab |

### Vardhman Acrylics Limited

In the year 1994-95 Mahavir Spinning Mills Ltd. signed a Technical Collaboration Agreement with M/s Kawasaki Heavy Industries Limited and Marubeni Corporation for the transfer of technical know-how from the M/s Japan Exlan Company Limited (acrylic fibre manufacturer) for setting up an Acrylic Fibre Project for manufacture of 16500 TPA. Pursuant to Joint Venture Agreement entered by the Company, the Acrylic Fibre Project was set up at Jagadia, Bharuh by the name and style of Vardhman Acrylics

Limited (Subsidiary of Mahavir Spg. Mills Limited). This subsidiary of MSML started its commercial production in March 1999. the present installed capacity of the Company is 16500 MT (TPA).

**Quality Certifications**

Vardhman is earning laurels by exporting yarns and fabric of international quality to several countries in the west, Africa and the Far East earning valuable foreign currency for the country. Vardhman is the first company among textile industry to receive the ISO 9002/ISO 1400-quality awards in India.

**Products/Services Profile**

**Yarns:** The group is the largest spinning group of the country with a spindlage of about 5.5 lakh spindles. The group has Twelve production plants located in the states of Punjab, Himachal Pradesh and Madhya Pradesh. In many of the yarn market segments Vardhman holds the position of market leader, besides being large and reliable supplier in the country. Vardhman is also the largest exporter of yarn from India. The group yarn exports amount to over USD 100 million covering the most quality conscious markets in the world. The to talk export of the cotton yarn of the group is about 7% of total export of cotton yarn from the country.

**Sewing Thread:** Vardhman entered the sewing thread business in 1982 as a forward integration of its yarn business. The group had to struggle for survival being pitted against the large multinational organizations. Today with approx. 21 MT per day sewing thread manufacturing capacity in its plant at Hoshiarpur, Ludhiana and Baddi. Vardhman threads have emerged as second largest selling sewing thread brand in the country, next only to Madura Coats Ltd.

**Weaving:** Continuing its onward march on the value curve, Vardhaman group entered weaving business in 1992 with a capacity of 7 million meter per annum. The capacity has been subsequently expanded to 24 million meter per annum. The group has already made a mark as quality producer of grey poplin / shirting / suiting in the home market and has also entered the highly competitive export market. The group is now exporting a fairly large volume of its production.

**Processed Fabric:** In its quest for further value addition Vardhman started fabric processing in 1999.Vardhman established a modern fabric process house in 1999 with a capacity of 30 million meters per annum. Vardhman fabric is dedicated to meet customer demand for top quality finished fabric through product innovation, world-class quality, state of art technology and excellence in service.

**Fibre:** In 1999, the group set up an Acrylic staple fibre plant at Bharuch in Gujarat in collaboration with Marubeni and Japan Exian of Japan. The plant has annual capacity of 165000 mt per annum.

**Steel:** The steel business was set up in 1973 as diversification with a capacity of 35000 mt per annum. Later on group acquired a steel plant from Mohta group of industries in 1988 and converted this loss making unit into a profitable business in first of operation with the group. Subsequently, the steel mill has been modernized and expanded to a capacity of 100000mt per annum. Catering to high technology quality conscious alloy steel segment, the unit has a reputation of being a dependable source of supply of special and alloy steel to Indian/ International standards.

**Vardhman Product Mix**

- Fabric 9%
- Yarn 65%

- Sewing Thread 12%
- Fibre 8%
- Steel 6%

**Group Business and Capacities**

Spinning 526000 Spindles
Weaving208 Air-Jet Looms
Sewing Threads 22 Tonnes/Day
Yarn/Fibre Dyeing 45 Tonnes/Day
Steel Sms 100000 Tonnes/P.A.

**Foreign / Domestic Market**

| S.no | Name of the firm | Capacity | Market |
|---|---|---|---|
| 1 | Vardhman Spinning And General Mills, Lothian | 61,708 Spindles | Domestic |
| 2 | Anshupati Textile Mills, Ludhiana | 8,000 Spindles | Domestic |
| 3 | Mahavir Spinning Mills, Hoshiarpur | 56,000 Spindles | Domestic |
| 4 | Vardhman Polytex Ltd., Bathinda | 49,472 Spindles | Domestic |
| 5 | Arihant Spinning Mills, Malerkotla | 1,11,892 Spindles | Domestic |
| 6 | Auro Spinning, Baddi | 67,560 Spindles | Domestic |
| 7 | Asm, Baddi | 24,288 Spindles | Exports |
| 8 | Arisht Spinning Mills, Baddi | 41,472 Spindles | Domestic |
| 9 | Vmt, Baddi | 28,320 Spindles | Exports |
| 10 | Vsgm 100% Eou, Baddi | 27,040 Spindles | Exports |
| 11 | Arihant Spinning Mills, Malerkotla | 21,000 Spindles | Exports |
| 12 | Anant Mills, Mandideep | 74,496 Spindles | Exports |
| 13 | Auro Dyeing, Baddi | 30 TPD | |
| 14 | Auro Weaving Mills | 208 LOOMS | |
| 15 | Auro Textiles, Baddi | 30 Million mtrs /yr | |
| 16 | Vardhman Special Steels, Ludhiana | 1,00,000 MTA – Billets<br>40,000 MTA – Rolling | |
| 17 | Vardhman Special Steels, Faridabad | Closed as on date | |
| 18 | Gassed & Mercerised Unit, Hoshiarpur | 7 TPD | |
| 19 | Msml, Lothian | 2.5 TPD | |

**Manufacturing Units**

- Hoshiarpur
- Malerkotla

- Bathinda
- Baddibaruch
- Mandideep

**Distribution Centres**

Ludhiana, Chandigarh, Delhi, Kanpur, Indore, Ahemdabad, Mumbai, Patna, Kolkata, Bangalore, Chennai, Tirupur,

**Collaborations**

In today's world each and every company needs to work in collaboration with some other company and take advantage of the synergy. Vardhman has also collaborated with the world leaders. The various companies with which Vardhman has collaborated are:

**Marubeni and Toho Rayon of Japan for VMT Spinning Co. Ltd.:** In its growth program through strategic alliances, Vardhman has streamed its VMT Spinning Co. Ltd. With Toho Rayon, Japan, a pioneer in spinning technology and Marubeni, the worlds largest house in order to service the global market.

**Nihon-Sanmo Dyeing Ltd., Japan for the Fibre/Yarn dyeing house:** To keep pace with the changing expectations of users, industries and consumers, Vardhman has collaborated with the Nihon-Sanmo Dyeing Ltd., Japan, and the world leaders in dyeing technology, to provide the know-how for its fibre/yarn-dyeing house.

**Kyung Bang Limited, South Korea for gas mercerized dyeing:** To match the ever-growing needs of the garment manufacturing industry, value addition has been done to the gas mercerized yarn. Vardhman invited technical know-how regarding the dyeing process from Kyung Bang Ltd., South Korea.

**Marubeni Corporation and Exlon of Japan for Acrylic Fibre Plant:** For the Vardhman's 300-crore Acrylic

Fibre Plant, Vardhman has collaborated with the Marubeni Corporation and Exlon of Japan, world famous producer of Acrylic staple fibre, with the best wet spinning technology in the world.

**Tokai Senko, Japan:** Vardhman has collaborated with Tokai Senko of Japan for technical know how of process house. The production capacity would be 50,000 meters per day of processed fabric.

**A & E, USA:** A license agreement for production and marketing of A & E's products in India has recently been signed. This is expected to form the basis of further business between the two companies.

**Awards and Certifications**

The group has so far received 22 awards for excellence in exports from various organizations like TEXPROCIL, FIEO, Punjab Deptt. of Industry. The group has bagged gold trophy from Texprocil six times for being the largest exporter in categories like Yarn and Woven fabric.

| Group Company | No. of Awards Won |
|---|---|
| VSGM | 14<br>5 Gold Trophies from Texprocil<br>4 times Best Exporter award from Punjab Department of Industry and FIEO |
| MSML | 7<br>Gold Trophy from Texprocil and outstanding export performance award from FIEO. |
| Anant | Gold Trophy |

IS 14002/ISO 9002

Certification

**Diversification**

The first major diversification came in 1973 with the setting up of Oswal steels (later named as Vardhman Special Steels) at Faridabad, to manufacture special and alloy steel with an initial capacity of 50,000 metric tons, along with matching rolling mills and equipped with modern chemical, metallurgical and mechanical laboratories to produce special and alloy steels.

In 1986, it added another steel unit, also named Vardhman Special Steels at Faridabad. At present the group has combined steel melting capacity of 1,25,000 tpa and rolling mills capacity of 65,000 tpa. / 20,000 meters per day.

**Snapshots**

**Year of Start**
1962

**Located at:**
Chandigarh Road, Ludhiana

**Main Products/Operations**
Cotton, Blended, Acrylic, Hand Knitting Yarn Production, Yarn Dyeing And Specialty Steel Production

**Total Turnover**
Rs. 2138 crore
Domestic Turnover 55%; Foreign Turnover 45%

**Certifications**
ISO 9002

**Flagship Company**
VSGM, Ludhiana.

**Main Markets Being Served**
Domestic: All Over India.
Foreign: Asia, Middle East, Africa and Europe.

# Section 6: Tyre and Tube Industry

- Indian Tyre and Tube Industry
- Hindustan Cycles and Tubes
- Metro Tyres
- Ralson India

# Indian Tyre and Tube Industry

The world tyre industry is worth around US $ 70 billion. The industry is marked by a presence of around half a dozen major players, who together occupy 70% of the world market share. The worldwide tyre industry is likely to witness more restructuring efforts after the deal between Goodyear and Sumitomo of Japan. Analysts are speculating that there will be only six to seven major players across the world. The big three of industry i.e. Michelin, bridgestone and Goodyear (before its alliance with Sumitomo) each had annual sales of US$ 12 billion. Inevitable, the alliance has increased the competitive pressure on second tier majors, notable Continental of Germany, Pirelli of Italy and Yokohama of Japan. They would also have togo on the acquisition route in order to survive. These structural developments are taking place against a background of continuing overcapacity in the industry, estimated at around 30% and slow growth in Latin America and the Asia-Pacific region in the wake of their financial crisis.

Major part of the world sales of car and truck tyres is to the replacement market. The replacement market is self-perpetuating and has inbuilt growth despite short-term setbacks from time to time. As the worldwide automotive sales are rising by a marginal 2% per annum, sales to the replacement segment will continue to dominate.

As far as Indian tyre industry is concerned, it is touching a volume of Rs. 98000 crore. In India, the growth of tyre industry depends upon the performance of agricultural and industrial sector. While the tyre industry is mainly dominated by the organized sector, the unorganized sector holds way in bicycle tyres. In many ways, the Indian tyre industry reflects trends in the global tyre market where capacities are concentrated in the hands of a few large players like Goodyear, Michelin, Pirelli, Bridgestone and Continental. Almost 80% of the tyre market in India is controlled by the six large players leading to allegations of cartelisation in the past.

The major players in the organized tyre segment consist of MRF, Apollo Tyres, Ceat and JK Tyres, which account for 63% of the organized tyre market. The other key players include Modi Rubber, Kesoram Industries and Goodyear India, with 11 per cent, 7 percent and 6% share respectively. Dunlop, Falcon, Tyre Corporation of India Limited, TVS – Srichakra, Metro Tyres and Bal Krishna Tyres are some of the other players in the industry. MRF, the largest tyre manufacturer in the country, has strong brand equity. While it rules supreme in the industry, other players have created niche markets of their own.

**Challenges Ahead**

Capacity utilization of the industry at present is 62%. Companies, which have a stronger presence in the truck and bus tyres, segment: Apollo, Modi, Ceat and JK enjoy higher market share in value term, though in volume terms (measured in numbers) their share is much smaller. We may expect that the tyre industry will have more than one concern to deal with in the medium to long term. In the recent past, more than one foreign tyre major has evinced interest in entering the Indian market, which is a pointer to the fact that the industry will remain on the growth path in the near future. The tyre industry has rightly targeted at increasing the rate of radicalization in the country to cater to the changing needs of the automobile industry and the export market. The industry, in turn, expects the government to support it by legislating a favourable tariff environment.

Looking ahead a lot is need to be done and, perhaps, the need of the hour is a concerted strategy involving both the industry and the government to face the challenges lying ahead.

# Hindustan Cycles and Tubes

## Incorporation and Integration

Lala Jagjit Rai Maini, a lawyer, a graduate from Lahore University, laid the foundation stone of Hindustan Tyres Ltd. in 1968-69 with an initial capital of around Rs. 15 lakh. He started his business as an importer of Cycle tyres and Dunlop tyres from Robinhood Cycles, Lancashire, England.

Mr. B.C. Maini born on 10th Nov. 1944, who is now the Chairman & Managing Director of the company, joined his father, Lala Jagjit Rai Maini for business in 1968-69 just after the Matriculation. Mr. Somnath Maini, younger son of Lala Jagjit Rai Maini who is presently working as a Director of the company, is a diploma holder in rubber technology. Mr. Vijay Maini, chartered accountant, son of Mr. B.C. Maini joined his father in year 1987–88.

In 1969-70, they started the production of bicycle tyres and tubes with the team effort of 150 employees at first unit located at Industrial area-A, Ludhiana. Initially the turnover was Rs. 28-29 lakh per annum in 1969-70.In 1972, the second unit of Hindustan Tyres Co. at Kanganwal Road, Ludhiana started functioning.

DIVISIONS

Hindustan Tyre Co. (Unit-I) → Initial Investment of Rs. 15 Lacs (appx)

Hindustan Tyre Co. (Unit-II) → Initial Investment of Rs. 40 Lacs (appx)

**Present Investment in both units is Rs. 700 lacs.**

Hindustan Cycle and Tube Ltd. manufactures cycle tyres and tubes, and is also dealing with auto tyres and tubes. The present total turnover of the group is Rs140 crore, out of which exports are about Rs.7-8 crore, and domestic markets have a share of the remaining Rs132 crore.

The group has two units, Unit–I is located at Industrial area-A, Ludhiana and Unit–II is at Kanganwal Road Ludhiana. The present level of investment in both the units is nearly Rs. 7 crore.

| S. No. | Name of the Unit | Year of start | Main product & initial investment | Location |
|---|---|---|---|---|
| 1. | Unit No. 1 | 1968-69 | Standard cycle tyres/tubes, Rs.15 lakh approx. | G-3, Textile Colony, Industrial Area-A, Ludhiana |
| 2. | Unit No. 2 | 1972 | Auto tyres &tubes & fancy tyres, | Kanganwal Road, Ludhiana |

## Company Profile

The group has 34 sale outlets in India, and is also dealing with Hero and Atlas, for supplying cycle tyre as original equipment manufacturer. The group is also exporting to countries like Egypt, South America, Turkey, Iran, Syria, etc. The main competitors of the group are Ralson Tyres, Metro tyres and Govind Rubber. The market share is 16% in cycle tyres. The group has no stock exchange listing. It plans to start manufacturing tubeless tyres for scooters shortly.

## Mission

"Faith in bright future and hence continued expansion in areas which we know the best."

Here 'continued expansion' and 'bright future' signifies development of latest design of tyres, and to have a good R&D base so as to meet the technological or the design changes in the current business world.

**Awards and Certifications**

In 2000, the company obtained ISO 9002: 1994 certification from International Certification Ltd. New Zealand. The company received ISO - 9001 certification in May 2002.

**Product Profile**

- Standard Cycle Tyres
- Auto Tyres
- Auto Tyre for Three Wheeler
- Cycle Tubes
- Nylon Cycle Tyres
- Fancy Short Size Cycle Tyre

**Bicycle Tyres**

**Type**

Heavy Duty, Nylon

**Brand**

Bheem, Arjun, Mahashakti, Dhamaka,

**Type**

Heavy Duty, Cotton

**Brand**

Black Panther, Tiger, Super, Janta,

**Type**

Bicycle, Nylon

**Brand**

7 Star

**Type**

Semi Heavy Duty

**Brand**

Honda, Sumo, Safari, Punjab Mail, Good Air, Lucky Star, Shaktimaan, Raja,

**Type**

Short Size

**Brand**

Simta, Glider, Beach, NDC, Balloon

**Cycle Tube Brands**

Tiger, Arjun, Toofani Taqat, Dollar

**Auto Tyre Brands**

Plus Power, Rock, Glider, Rally, Sultan, Shaktimaan, Kissan, Sumo, Tiger, Panther, Arjun, Shakti, Commando

**Chairman's Perspective**

In the present scenario, where every company is meeting the delight of the customer by providing good quality products, whether in FMCG, electronics, durables, services, etc. Hindustan Cycles & tubes Ltd. is also in the same lane as its mission depicts to have continued expansion by taking into account the latest development in the tyre industry.

The company is focusing on its personnel as it believes that team-work is most important in every department of the company.

The company believes that awards are not important for them, they just want to satisfy the customer, which could be counted as the major achievement of the company. The success of the company can be attributed to Marketing Department because it is only marketing department which exploits the weaknesses of the competitor and produce quality and durable products.

But not to forget, HRM is an important functional area. As the capabilities of the management and senior officials is reflected in the company's working envi-ronment, so HRM plays very crucial role for the group.

**Challenges Ahead and Future Plans**

The company proposes to set up a new unit for manufacturing Radial Auto Tyres in the near future. The view of the MD was that the cycle trade is a low paid, and burden of export of the cycle tyre is on India so the production reserved for export will increase to 20% in future.

The competitive strength of the company lies in the economies of scale, and well-equipped R&D. The unit is being run with minimum of overheads and has the lowest interest burden in the whole tyre industry. The main competitive advantage for exports is the lower labour as compared to cost any other country, even in China and Argentina, the labour cost is about $20 day. In India the major competitive weakness in any business is that long commitment is not possible as policies in India change very frequently.

The markets with high potential in India are of U.P., Madurai and Chennai, whereas in exports Egypt (according to volume), and Latin America and Europe (according to profits), offer the greatest potential. Turnover of cycle tyres/tubes is Rs.120 crore and of auto tyres/tubes is about Rs.20 crores.

The complete range of bicycle and auto tyres/tubes is available with Hindustan Tyre Company. The cost of production according to them is less and there are two shifts of twelve hours each. Rejection rate is also very low.

The Indian market is very large and is still not saturated, so they offer prospects of growth for every company. Developed countries have stopped manufacturing cycle tyres

/tubes so India has opportunity to export in bulk to such countries. Now the exports markets can be explored more thoroughly through web sites, which was not possible 20 years ago.

Information technology has played a major role now, one can locate the customer in half an hour without any wastage of resources. Hindustan Tyres Ltd. fulfils its social responsible by offering ample opportunities for employment of young managers. Secondly, it provides for a pollution-free environment, by launching time-to-time devices or technologies. Management education, today, should lay stress on all-round development of students, not only in academics but also in other fields.

The cycle industry is growing and the future of Hindustan Tyres & Tubes is bright, taking into account the globalization of the whole world.

**Snapshots**

**Year of Start**
1968-69
**Located at:**
G.T. Road, Ludhiana
**Main Products/Operations**
Auto Tyres/Tubes, Cycle Tyres/Tubes
**Total Turnover**
Rs.140 crore
Domestic Turnover Rs.130-132 crore,
Export Turnover Rs.7-8 crore
**Percentage of Different Products in Turnovers**
About 80% Bicycles/Tubes
& About 20% Auto Tyres/Tubes
**Certificates**
ISI and ISO 9002
**Flagship Company**
Hindustan Cycles and Tubes Ltd.
**Main Domestic Market**
All Over India
**Main Export Markets**
Egypt, South America, Iran, Syria

# Metro Tyres

## Incorporation and Integration

From a humble beginning in 1968, with 20-25 employees, and a turnover of Rs. 20-50 lakh, Metro Tyres made steady progress to establish itself as a market leader for bicycle tyres & tubes in India and achieved a turnover of Rs 300 crore. As a result of steady increase in production of quality products, the company ventured overseas and developed a niche for itself in the international market as well. The company also kept itself abreast with latest technologies and developed Nylon tyres through its own R & D efforts.

MTL was incorporated on 18/1/1974 under the Indian Companies Act, 1956, as a private limited company with the main object to manufacture cycle tyres & tubes, and pioneered the shift of the cycle tyre industry to the northern part of the country. Today this industry has flourished to such an extent that more than 70% of the total demand of cycle tyres and tubes of the country is met by manufacturers based in Ludhiana. The company is being effectively managed since inception and has always stressed on stringent quality standards. The products are well accepted in the national as well as international markets.

## About the Entrepreneur

Sardar Mann Singh, 74 yrs old, started his career in trading of tyres and tubes at Kanpur in the sixties. In 1967-68 he got the idea to become an entrepreneur, as at that time there was acute shortage of tyres & tubes in the market. At that time tyres & tubes were sold at ration depots. Sardar Mann Singh took it as an opportunity and started manufacturing tyres & tubes.

Mr. Rummy Chabbra, 40, and Mr. Navneet Chabbra, 35, Sons of Sardar Mann Singh are both graduates and married. Both of them are deeply involved in the family business and are making concrete efforts to make their business grow in the face of general recession that is being faced by Industry.

**Units in Ludhiana**

MTL has four units in Ludhiana

- Unit 1: 503, Industrial Area B, Ludhiana.
- Unit 2: B-27, Focal Point, Ludhiana.
- Unit 3: Jugiana, GT Road, Ludhiana.
- Unit 4: B-46, Focal Point, Ludhiana.

**Journey...**

In the year 1983, the company diversified into the manufacture of tyres & tubes for scooter, motor cycles, LCVs, Animal Driven Vehicles and Tractors, under the brand name of '**Metro**'. These products have also been well accepted in the market.

| S. No. | Product | Branch | Launch | Unit |
|---|---|---|---|---|
| 1. | Cycle Tyres | Metro | 1968 | 503, Industrial Area B-Ludhiana |
| 2. | Cycle Tubes | Metro | 1970 | 503, Industrial Area B- Ludhiana |
| 3. | Cycle chains | Metro | 1983 | 503, Industrial Area B, Ludhiana |
| 4. | Bicycle nylon/cotton tyres | Metro | 1987 | B-27, Focal point, Ludhiana |

In the year 1999, an off-take agreement was signed with Continental AG, Germany, for the manufacture of bicycle tyres & tubes under the '**Continental**' brand. To implement this project, an ultra modern plant with state of the art machinery was set up. This plant employs the latest technology for the manufacture of bicycle tyres & tubes.

**Quality Policy of the Group**

Following is the quality policy for the company for which they strive for:

"We (Metro Tyres Ltd.) will strive to achieve prosperity & customer satisfaction through continuous improvement in the product quality, competitive pricing and timely delivery."

**Quality Objectives of the Group**

- Upgrading product processes and technology.
- Training employees to achieve continuous improvement in their work areas.
- Building and improving quality through process control.
- Increasing the production capacity to achieve the targets.

**Products/Services**

**Cycle Tyres:** Bicycle tyres are made from natural as well as synthetic rubber & are of two types: cotton & nylon.

**Cycle Tubes:** Bicycle tubes are moulded from either Natural rubber or Butyl rubber

**Bicycle Chains:** Bicycle chains can be supplied in any number of links or in rolls of 150 meters. Each chain is packed in a Metro box, and 50 boxes are packed in a master carton. A 150 meters chain, wound on a metal spool, is packed in a strong wooden case.

**Tyres for Auto Segment**

- Moped
- Motorcycle

- Scooter
- Three Wheelers
- Hand Carts
- Jeep
- Tractors

**Vision**

The success of the business is attributed to the leadership qualities and hard work put in by the management and employees of the group. 'Vision' has become an important aspect of today's business scenario. It has been the 'Vision', which has led MTL to become what it is today. MTL attributes its success to the hard work of its Human Resource.

**Most Precious Assets**

Metro's most precious asset is its professionally trained and dedicated human resource. HRM is the most important aspect of any organization's working. Relation with employees had become the most vital aspect, as employees were the lifeblood of any organization

**Strengths**

The strengths of the group are Quality, Brand, CRM, Supply Chain Management and Zero Defects.

**Awards and Certifications**

Metro Tyres & Tubes and home appliances of the company have also been granted 'ISO 9002' certification by the Bureau of Indian Standards. Incidentally, it was the first company in the industry to achieve this distinction.

**Diversification and Expansion**

Ortem Fans, New Delhi

The company has diversified into the field of home appliances such as electric fans, electric irons, sewing machines, etc, under the brand name "**ORTEM**". Keeping the customer foremost in mind and for the convenience of buyers, the company established a full-fledged "Export Division" at New Delhi. The export division has the capability for entertaining & servicing enquiries relating not only to the company products, but also for non-company commodities and engineering goods.

**ORTEM FANS** – Brand Ceiling Fans are being manufactured at Noida. This unit is being managed by Rummy Chabbra

| **Snapshots** |
|---|
| **Company Name**<br>Metro Tyres Limited<br>**Started in**<br>1968<br>**Located at:**<br>Metro Road, Ludhiana<br>**Current number of employees,** 4500<br>**Products**<br>Bicycle tyres & tubes, bicycle chains, automobile tyres & tubes<br>**Export Destinations**<br>Germany, Europe, Middle East<br>**Buy Back Arrangement**<br>AG Continental Germany<br>**Sales Offices**<br>76 throughout India in the name of Metro Sales. Dealer network of 15000 all over India.<br>**Total turnover**<br>Rs 318 crore; **Export Turnover,** 18% of total turnover<br>**Domestic Turnover,** 82% of total turnover |

# Ralson India

**Introduction**

The global village exists. Whether we like it or not- whether we want it that way or not- we are in an age of practically instant communication from anywhere to everywhere. The successful corporations of this century will be those who make a decision to join the global business battle and get in touch with what the best practice global companies are doing right now. The orientation of the global economy has shifted from production to marketing.

The post 1991 scenario in which the Indian industries are free to breathe in the global environment, has posed a number of challenges before the local industrial houses. In the presence of high tax rates, bureaucratic control and poor infrastructure the home industry finds it tough to stand the global competition. It holds good for the Indian Cycle industry, which is facing intense price competition from the Chinese cycle. This in turn affects the local tyre and tubes manufacturing companies.

Indian bicycle industry started when East India Company had come to Calcutta. It was at that time that the English people brought cycle and cycle tyres/tubes technology to India. At that time, the spare parts were imported and assembled and marketed in India. In 1953, the scenario entirely changed. When some of the noted companies like Hero and Avon were given the license to manufacture the bicycles.

Today the cycle industry has grown to 10 million cycles a year and is growing at a rate of 11 percent. This in tern has a backward linkage with the tyre manufacturing industry.

**Incorporation and Integration**

Ralson India Limited, Ludhiana started way back in the year 1974 by Sh. S.P. Pahwa. Along with his brother Late Sh. O.P. Pahwa, he made the first successful attempt to indigenously manufacture the bicycle tyres in India. With the passage of time Ralson grew at an outstanding pace. It not only led the domestic tyre market but also got a break through in international markets like south Asia, Latin America, Africa and Middle East. Today Ralson(India) Ltd. Headed by Mr. Sanjeev Pahwa, the present managing director of the company. He is a highly focused person who stresses on quality work and has a passion for perfection.

**Company Profile**

The strength of Ralson lies in its 4000 strong and skilled work-force striving zealously to meet their targets . Ralson is the first and only ISO 9002 company in the cycle tyre segment in India. It produces cycle tyres and tubes of international standards.

Ralson's daily production is approximately 11,000 tyres /tubes sets. Such strengths give Ralson an unmatched capability to offer the largest and most comprehensive range of cycle tyre profiles and sizes in India. There are a large number of companies producing cycle tyres namely, Usha, Hindustan, Bedrock, Swahneys, Krishna, etc. From all these companies Ralson (India) Ltd. Clearly stands out in quality. The proactive R&D wing of Ralson gives it unmatched capability to custom make tyres, tubes and components for the home and overseas buyers. It also offers an inbuilt guarantee of timely supplies. Perhaps this is why all prominent Indian bicycle manufacturers, namely, Hero, Avon, Atlas and BSA prefer Ralson tyres and tubes as original equipment in their bicycles. Ralson has a network of 27 branches across the country.

**Journey .....**

- Started with Accessories in 1971
- Started manufacturing of tyres in 1974
- Started manufacturing of hubs in 1974
- Started manufacturing of tubes with jointed tubes in 1982
- Started manufacturing of nylon tyres in 1983
- Started manufacturing of cycle nylon in 1990
- Started manufacturing of bicycle tubes in 1996
- Launch of super-shakti tyres in 2000
- Launch of R-777 in 2001.

**Group Companies**

Mr. O.P. Pahwa & Mr. S.P. Pahwa started Ralson. Mr. O.P. Pahwa handled the operations of Ralson(India) Limited, Ludhiana until 1991. After his death his son Sanjeev Pahwa became Managing Director of the company.

- Ralson Born in 1974
- Separation in 1991
  - ❖ Ralson (India) Limited
  - ❖ Ralson Enterprises Limited

Both of them have defined their territories in which they will market their products. Ralson(India) Limited has confined its area of operations to eastern and central India, Goa and Nepal. Whereas Ralson Enterprises Limited operates in western, northern and southern India. When the separated companies have to sell their product in their own areas/territories they do it under the name of Ralson (India) Limited. But when the Ludhiana unit has to sell its' product in the territory of Bhopal unit, the product is sold under the name of Ralson Enterprises Limited. When the Bhopal unit has to sell its' product in the territory of Ludhiana unit it uses the name Nosler Enterprises Limited to avoid unhealthy competition.

**Quality Policy**

At Ralson (India) Limited people are committed to achieve and sustain market leadership through satisfaction of customer's need by continuous improvement in quality. Delivery and Value for money of their product namely tyres and tubes.

The group proposes to achieve the quality policy by:

- Manufacturing products as per satisfaction and standards agreed with the customers
- Continuously improving the quality of material, proce-sses and products.
- Maintaining and continuously upgrading the quality management system.
- Ensuring active involvement of employees at all levels.
- Creating a safe healthy and pollution free working environment.

**Philosophy and Performance**

The success of the business is attributed to Sh. Sant P. Pahwa and Sh. (late) O.P. Pahwa who had started the business in the year 1974. The initial production of the company was approximately 300 tyres per day. Today, the production has risen to 105000 tyres per day, 25000 hubs and 4000 workers. The annual turnover of the company is more than 350 crore. The company believes in providing the best quality at reasonable price.

The company believes that human resources are the most critical element in an organization. The success of any functional department depends on how efficiently the human resources of that department work. That is why Ralson takes care of each and every need of its workforce and employees. The work environment of the company is highly congenial and acts as a motivational factor to improve the performance.

**Important brands**

Important brands of tyres and tubes manufactured by Ralson

**Tyres**

R-777, Super-Shakti, Diamond Supreme, Himalaya, Ruf-tuf, 7 Star, Nylon Grip, Super Master, Punjab Tiger

**Tubes**

Chetak, Diamond Supreme, Punjab Tiger, Gem, Super-Shakti, Butyl Tubes

**Awards/Certifications**

- It was first to get R&D recognition from department of Science & Technology, Govt. of India.
- First company to introduce nylon tyres in India.
- First company to make cycle tubes confirming to ISI.
- For three years in succession the Chemical and Allied products Standards Promotion Council of India has conferred upon Ralson the CAPEXIL awards for highest export of bicycle tyres and tubes.
- For the consecutive 4 years Ralson has got Compexel award in exports from Export Promotion Council. It has got ISO 9002 certification on tyres and tubes from ISI.

**Technology Handshake**

Ralson has fully computerized and automated it's operations. They are making use of SAP & ERP in their business. The company's management believes in adoption of the changing technology to keep itself ahead of others in this competitive era.

**Towards Society**

The management of Ralson never misses an opportunity to serve the society. From time to time various camps are being organized by the company to uplift the health and hygiene in the society. Service to the society is one of the most important objective of the company.

| **Snapshots** |
|---|
| **Year of start**<br>1974<br>**Located at:**<br>G.T. Road, Ludhiana<br>**Main Products/Operations**<br>Bicycle Tyres & Tubes, Cycle mudguards, freewheels, Bells, Seats<br>**Total Turnover**<br>US $ 88 million (as per website)<br>Domestic Turnover: 20%<br>Foreign Turnover: 80%<br>**Certifications ISO 9002**<br>CAPEXIL<br>**New Ventures**<br>Auto Tyres at Doraha<br>**Flagship company**<br>Ralson India<br>**Main markets being served**<br>Domestic: All over India<br>**Foreign**<br>Branches in the various countries of Africa, Gulf, Latin America and South Asia. |

## Section 7: Other Industries

- Indian Edible Oil Industry
- Indian Telecommunication Industry
- Indian Sports Industry
- India Pharmaceutical Industry
- Indian Paper Industry
- Amrit Vanaspati (Food)
- Bharti (Telecommunications)
- FC Sondhi and Company (Sports Goods)
- FMI (Measurement Tapes)
- International Tractors
- Leader Valves (Machinery Parts)
- Raxbaxy Laboratories (Pharmaceuticals)
- Shreyans (Paper and Textiles)

# Indian Edible Oil Industry

The oilseeds/vegetable oil industry is perhaps the most dynamic segment of India's food processing sector with a significant contribution to the economy in terms of investment, employment and income. Also, it ranks among the world's largest, in the company of the U.S., China and Brazil. The wide range of crops and their derivatives are used for cooking oil, direct consumption, and animal feed and industrial application.

The Indian oilseeds-based sector, growing at a healthy 6-8 per cent per annum, boasts an annual turnover of Rs. 70.000 crore and a robust import/export trade valued at Rs. 12,000 crore. India is the world's largest importer of vegetable oils and an exporter of oil meals (mainly extractions of soyabean, rapeseed), castor oil, sesame seed and select groundnut kernels. The processing industry is a bewildering medley of products, processes and technologies. There are an estimated 15,000 oil mills with a total capacity (for primary crushing of oilseeds) of 36 million tonnes; nearly 800 solvent extraction plants with combined capacity of over million tonnes; over 600 refining units capable of refining close to 10 million tonnes of crude oils; and 230 Vanaspati factories with installed capacity of over 3 million tonnes.

**Challenges**

Oilseeds/vegetable oils have an inherently low level of profitability. The opportunity here is not to add new capacity but to consolidate the industry, building greater efficiency through scale. Success in this industry requires substantial skills and investment. As a result, for most businesses, the challenge is not so much how to enter the industry as how to exit. With the exception perhaps of refineries, much of the domestic industry's fortunes are dependent on indigenous oilseeds production. Despite being an important commercial crop grown in about 25-26 million hectares in two seasons, oilseeds cultivation in the country faces several challenges including lack of technology application, cultivation in small and marginal lands that too under rain-fed conditions, low level of input usage and traditional agronomic practices. However, as indigenous oilseeds output, and in turn vegetable oil production, has been trailing consumption growth, imports have become a necessity. Currently, imports are confined to edible oils. Oilseed imports are seen unviable because of phyto-sanitary regulations and customs duty.

**Issues to be Addressed**

Some of the key issues impacting the oilseeds/vegetable oil industry relate to production, processing, marketing, consumption, import, export, quality, technology, fiscal and monetary aspects, among others.

The domestic industry will have to capture value by building supply chain efficiencies. Establishing backward linkages is the way forward for the industry. Contract farming of oilseeds will mean assured supplies of raw material. The Government has to balance the interests (often conflicting) of 100-crore consumers, millions of farmers and the industry.

Today, the vegetable oils sector is at the crossroads. Neither the policy makers nor the industry representatives have a clear vision of the future direction. The overall objective of a long-tern perspective plan for strengthening the sector should be one of building global competitiveness and WTO – Compatibility.

# Indian Telecommunication Industry

For the Rs.50,000 crore telecom services industry, 2002-2003 will go down as a defining year on several fronts. With the cellular industry adding a million customers every month, it can easily be called the year of the cellular. After years of under-realised growth potential since 1995, finally, the Indian cellular industry is posed at an inflection point for growth of a kind not witnessed in the past. But all this has been achieved by the industry against daunting odds.

**Cellular Take-off**

The cellular segment is charged up as never before. Adding nearly 6.4 million subscribers in a year, clocking a growth rate off over 80 percent for the third year in a row and stepping on the pedal of new subscriber additions, the future seems fairly bright for cellular players. In 2002-03 alone, the cellular segment recorded by growth rate of 97 percent over the previous year, ending with a subscriber base of 12.7 million. The industry has consistently registered growth rates of over 15 percent in each quarter since March 2002, touching 20 percent and above in recent quarters. As of Sep 2003, the top three players in the cellular sweep stakes were the Bharti Group, BSNL, and Hutchison Group. Together the accounted for nearly 65% of the subscriber base and with the recent addition of 3.15 million of new subscribers the top three companies had a 73 percent share in the industry. The distribution of the subscriber base across metros and circles A, B and C does not throw up any surprises. As of Sep 2003, the metros had a share of 33.4 percent. Circles A, B and C accounted for 35.9 percent, 26.5 percent and 4.2 percent respectively. But there are differences in the strategies of the top three players.

## Trends in Telecom Service Industry

**Mobile Services:** The cellular subscriber base swelled to 12.7 million in 2002-2003, recording a 97 percent growth over the previous year. Between July-Sep 2003, the industry added over 1 million subscribers on an average compared to 0.8 million in the previous quarter. As expected this trend continually accelerating.

**Limited Mobility:** The entry of limited mobility service providers under the basic service license has transformed the dynamics of the market place. By end Sep 2003, this service had toted up 4.7 million subscribers. Out of this Reliance Infocom dominated with a subscriber base of 4.2 million which have growing substantially

**Tariffs:** Cellular traffic have been heading south over the past three years. But the consumers were truly spoilt for choice with the onset of five to six players in each circle. And that triggered an all-mighty price war, the effects of which are still being felt on the tariff schemes.

**Long Distance:** The long distance rates – both international and domestic – fell by over 50 percent in the past year. The long distance tariffs, which were subsidising the low domestic tariffs all along disappeared in a single stroke.

**Basic Services:** The basic services subscriber base has grown by only 8 percent in 2002-2003 over the previous year. In the first quarter of 2003-2004, basic services actually lost subscribers. But managed to record modest growth of less than 1 percent in July-Sep quarter and still battle is on for the survival. The cellular industry beat the basic services hands down, with little comparison between the two.

**Consolidation:** Consolidation with in the cellular industry, which had gathered momentum in 2000 with the emergence of three dominant groups: bharti, Hutch and IDEA (a joint venture of Birlas, Tatas and AT&T). has since slowed down. With intra-circle mergers being allowed recently by the govt. it is likely to set the stage for the next big round of consolidation in 2004 and 2005.

**Rural Telephony:** The record of the private basic operators in meeting rural telephone/village public telephone obligations has hardly been encouraging. With the exception of BSNL, hardly any private basic operator has met its rural telephony obligation significant way.

# Indian Sports Industry

The sports goods industry of India has its roots in Sialkot, Pakistan. When India was partitioned in 1947, many of Sialkot's skilled Hindu craftsmen migrated across the border into Punjab, settling in Jalandhar, where the Indian sports goods industry is now based.1 The Indian sports goods industry has expanded to include the areas of Meerut, (Uttar Pradesh) and Gurgaon, (Haryana). Most of India's sports goods are exported to the United Kingdom, The United States of America, Germany, France and Australia. There are 364 registered sports goods exporters with the Sports Goods Export Promotion Council (SGEPC) alone. According to a report published in The Hindu, the annual export turnover of this industry is over Rs. 206 crore. The industry is mainly concentrated in Meerut and Jalandhar.

The sports goods industry in India has witnessed a phenomenal growth over the past five decades and now occupies a place of prominence in the Indian economy in view of its massive potential for employment, growth and export. There has been an increasing emphasis on its planned development, aimed at optimal utilisation of resources for maximising the returns, particularly from exports. The export of sports goods has gained momentum particularly in the last decade and achieved an impressive growth reaching an export figure of Rs.217.51 crore (US$ 61.27 million) during 1996-97.

The countries where Indian sports goods are imported are the United Kingdom, Australia, the United States of America, Italy, Germany, South Africa, France, New Zealand, Netherlands and several Asian countries. The Indian sports goods industry manufactures 318 items. However, major items that are exported are inflatable balls, hockey sticks and balls, cricket bats and balls, boxing equipment, fishing equipment, indoor games like carom and chess boards and different kinds of protective equipment.

The Indian sports goods industry is a highly labour intensive industry which provides employment to the weaker sections of society and also employs a large number of women. The total number of persons working in the entire sports goods industry is about 30,000.5

The manufacture of sports goods operates at five levels in India. First, there are the suppliers of foreign clients. These are the bigger companies which are geared mostly to the export market. Secondly, there are hundreds of smaller units and small factories which employ about 10-12 workers. These units mainly produce for the domestic market. Thirdly, there are the 'middlemen' or 'contractors', who are given subcontract orders and generally operate in the production of hand-stitched inflatable balls. They collect the semi-finished products from the factories and distribute them among the households in order to get the work completed. The fourth level comprises of individual home-based workers, who rely on the middlemen to deliver them their work. Finally, there are the service industries that supply all kinds of raw materials, which are required in order to manufacture sports goods.

# Indian Pharmaceutical Industry

The Indian pharmaceutical industry, though small in size compared to several heavy industries, is highly visible to the public, the media, and governmental and non-governmental organization. For one thing, its products and their performance affect the healthcare of the population and consequently the country's economic development. The parameters of growth and performance that have made the industry recognized global leaders are well known. For example, its turnover is estimated at $5.5 billion (Rs. 25,000 crore) and with an annual growth rate at constant prices of 809 percent is expected to reach $25 billion by 2010. Exports in 2002-2003 were around 50 percent of the domestic market making the industry a net exporter. Drug prices in India are some of the lowest in the world and India have one of the largest inventories of highly skilled pharmaceutical professionals. It has potential to take a leadership position in the promotion of its traditional systems of medicine among the global community.

In spite of such an impressive performance, India accounts for less than 1.5 percent of the global pharmaceutical market in value terms. Even in terms of production volume. It produces not more than 8 percent of the world's output. Modern drugs reach only 40 percent or less of the Indian population mainly in the urban and semi-urban areas and the per capita annual consumption of drugs is as low as $3.5.

Obviously the potential for growth in the domestic market itself is enormous and considering the rapid strides made in export markets in the last few years, the estimate of $25 billion by 2010 seems reasonable. In order to achieve this, large investments are required in a number of areas such as R&D, contract production, clinical services and contract research by Indian and International companies operating in India. The industry is gradually shifting towards high-margin, high value, new generation therapeutic segments like cardio-vascular. Neuro-psychiatry, anti-diabetes and life style diseases among others. There are about 300 manufacturing and formulation units in the organized sector accounting for nearly 75 percent of the total sales.

The dominance of the multinational companies has steadily declined over the years and their share has dropped from 70% in 1971 to 35 percent while Indian companies have increased their market share to nearly 65 %. The industry plays a vital role in the economy. It employs nearly 29 lakh persons and there are over 20,000 units engaged in pharmaceutical business with total production around $6.5 billion (inclusive of exports).

**Export Performance of Pharma Industry**

Indian Pharma exports have substantially increased in recent years. Over a decade, exports grew at a CAGR of over 26 percent. Today Indian Pharma exports exceed imports. More than 500 bulk drug molecules are supplied by India to the world markets. With its core competence in bulk drug manufacture and strengths in formulation development and manufacture, the Indian industry is well poised to become a major player in the global generics industry. Nearly 60 major brands with global sales of over $60 billions are going off patent over the next ten years.

**Post-2005 Scenario**

Post-2005, there will be a need to shift from process research to basic research and companies that make a headstart in this area are the ones that will reap rich dividends. With the introduction of product patents in 2005, Indian firms will need to focus on product innovation. Exclusive marketing rights and product patents will provide the strategic impetus for companies to invest in product research.

Other significant factors that will impact the market could be the emergence of corporatisation in healthcare growth of health insurance, deeper rural penetration, development of strong OTC market and marginalization manufacturing, process development, business development and supply chain management will be the ones that succeed. The key success factors in the immediate future will be ability to restructure product pipelines and launch new products, develop new molecules and increase there area of therapeutic coverage in high-end, high growth, anew generation segments. Stronger focus on explores will require world-class manufacturing facilities that conform to stringent international regulations.

## Indian Paper Industry

The first paper mill was set up in India more than 100 years ago. The industry operated under a protective tariff since 1925. Attracted by high profits under the protective tariff umbrella, many new paper mills were set up. During the period of planned development, the paper industry made rapid progress, India's forests providing abundant raw materials for its smooth working. Production rose from 3.5 lakh tonnes in 1960-61 to 42 lakh tonnes in 2002-03. The production of newsprint rose from 0.4 lakh tonnes to 5.6 lakh tonnes between 1961 and 2003-04.

**Growth of Paper Industry in India**

(in lakh tonnes)

| | Paper and paper board | | Newsprint |
|---|---|---|---|
| Year | Installed Capacity | Production | Production |
| 1950-51 | - | 1.1 | |
| 1970-71 | 9 | 7.6 | 0.4 |
| 1997-98 | 31 | 31.0 | 4.6 |

Source: *Economic Survey*, 2002-03.

There are at present 340 units producing paper and paperboard in the private sector with installed capacity of 31 lakh tonnes - it was as high as 42 lakh tonnes in the previous year. These units are of diverse size, type and magnitude. There are about 30 large integrated mills, well organized and well equipped and there are about 270 small units, which are too small and too moderately equipped. Actually, the last decade witnessed a phenomenal growth in the small paper sector (a small paper mill has installed capacity of 24,000 tonnes per annum), actively promoted by the Government. As a result, the small sector now accounts for 50 per cent of the installed capacity and of production of paper in the country.

### Rapid Growth of Small Units

In the early 1970s, when the country was faced with a paper famine, the Government came to appreciate the role of small paper units because of the short gestation period, the use of cheap second hand machinery readily available in foreign countries, the use of non-conventional raw materials such as rice-wheat straw, bagasse, jute stalks and waste paper. The small units could be set up in any part of the country and would have an important role to play in backward areas: -The Government gave necessary fillip and encouragement to technocrats and entrepreneurs to venture into the paper industry and the investment funds came easily from the public sector financial institutions such as the IDBI, IFCI and the ICI. The small paper units went into production and averted the paper crisis and also the need to import paper and paperboard and thus have helped the country to save Rs. 300 crore of foreign exchange annually. To some extent, the small units were uneconomic; their costs were high and their quality WBS low. In order to ensure that these mills exist along with large paper mills, the Government gave various excise concessions and reliefs from time to time. And, as mentioned earlier, the small paper mills have grown so rapidly that they account for 50 per cent of the installed capacity as well as of annual production.

### Future Prospects of the Paper industry

The industry should be helped to optimise capacity utilisation through renovation and modernisation of existing large mills. In this connection, the prices fixed by the Government for various types of paper were unrealistic and did not provide for reasonable returns on capital. As a result the industry was hard put to plough back funds for expansion and modernisation. With the removal of price and distribution controls on white printing paper in 1988, paper industry (especially large units) was able to get remunerative prices.

One of the most serious problems facing the paper industry is the rapid depletion of fibrous raw materials. Bamboo continues to be the mainstay although some success has been achieved in the use of mixed hardwoods, bagasse and other agricultural residue. As bamboo cultivation is becoming uneconomical, reliance has to be placed on unconventional raw materials such as hardwood. Paper mills may have to undertake plantation forestry in their surrounding areas.

In recent years, the production of paper and paperboard has recorded moderate but steady progress. India is now self-sufficient in the production of most varieties of paper and paperboard. Only certain varieties of paper are being imported. However, a majority of paper mills still use outdated technology/machinery.

To help the industry, the Government has taken various measures which include: excise rebate to small units, abolition of customs duty on the import of paper grade pulp and wood chips, removal of statutory control over production, price and distribution of white printing paper and providing infrastructural support by way of increased allocation of coal and wagons. In addition, the concept of broad banding has been extended to paper and pulp products whereby the firms will have the freedom to manufacture any variety of paper within the overall limit of licensed capacity.

# Amrit Vanaspati (Food)

**History of Company**

1940 - The Company was incorporated at Ghaziabad. The main object of the Company manufactures vegetable oil products and paper. The company's products are sold under the trade names "Golden Arrow", "Rajhans" and "Cotex".

1974 - The Company started Engineering division to fabricate plant and machinery for vanaspati, refined oil, solvent extracted oil and other minor items.

1979 - The Company holds all the 36,000 No. of equity shares issued by the New Prahalad Mills Ltd., Mumbai. The name of this subsidiary was changed to Amrit International Ltd., with effect from 19th March.

1981 - Paper Unit Production was started in June. Two of the coal-fired boilers were converted into rice husk fired boilers.

1984 - Production further improved. A new generating set of 1450 KVA was installed to meet the shortfall in power supply. The Company undertook to expand its capacity from 10,000 TPA to 24,000 TPA

1985 - The cost of production further went up due to an order of the Government to the industry to have their entire production tested by ISI. The paper production went up despite strike by workers for about one month and stiff competition from small and large scale units which resulted in a fall in the prices of finished products.

1986 - Due to judicious changes in the oil purchase policy of the company, the profitability of the units was well protected. The paper unit suffered a setback due to increase in cost of inputs and depressed market conditions.

1987 - The working of the both the vanaspati units was satisfactory despite a further rise in oil prices. The

Government increased the quota of imported oil to vanaspati industry to 70% with effect from 1st April, which improved the availability of raw material.

1989 - The overall performance showed marked improvement, which was reflected in growth of turnover by 17% over the previous year. The performance of both the vanaspati units was satisfactory despite highly uncertain and difficult trading conditions and severe pressure on margins.

1990 - Production of vanaspati and refined oil declined due to disturbed law and order situation in the North and North Eastern part of the country, frequent policy changes leading to uncertainty about raw material supply, and suspension of operations at the Ghaziabad factory for about two months for undertaking major repairs in plant and machinery.

1993 - `Ginni Gold' refined sunflower oil, `Ginni' and `Banasari' performed well and Marigold the table margarine introduced in the previous year was extended rationally during the year.

**Incorporation and Integration**

India is a vast country. The population is increasing very rapidly after independence. Since 80 years India is facing the crisis of food grains and edible oils. The food front is improved with a bumper harvest. But in edible oil it is still a big crisis in India, particularly Northern and eastern zone of the country. In south zone coconut is the coursc of edible oil.

To meet up this edible oil crisis, about 60 year ago, the Amrit Company came into existence and with grace of Late Shri Laxmi Narayan Bajaj a great industrialist and with the good guidance of Shri N.K. Bajaj and full cooperation of management the name of the company is sow spreading throughout the world and now it is one of the leading Vanaspati, refined oil and specially products manufacturing companies in northern India and first company in India in the industry to be accredited with ISO 9001 certifications. The main companies of Amrit Group are

- Amrit Vanaspati Company Limited, Rajpura
- Amrit Enterprises Limited, Abohar
- Amrit Paper, Saila Khurd

Amrit Vanaspati, Rajpura was setup in the year 1969-70. Mr. T.P. Khaitan was the founder of the unit with a manufacturing capacity of 100 mt per day of Vanaspati. Later on in the year 1982-83, the plant is situated at Rajpura-Chandigarh Highway. The unit is spread over 42 acres of land. The raw oil particularly, the cottonseed, rice brand are available in the vicinity of Rajpura. Being at an advantageous position, It is in close proximity of Punjab, Haryana and Rajasthan for sales of finished products thereby resulting into savings on account of freight and other expenses in purchase of oils and sale of finished goods. It is my great pleasure to mention that the group has an annual turnover of Rs. 550 crore and also it has about 35% market share in northern India.

**N.K. Bajaj**
Chairman
Amrit Group of Companies
**J.K. Khaitan**
Managing Director
ABCL, Hoshiarpur
**Pawan Khaitan**
Managing
Director
ABCL, Rajpura

**Profile of the Company**

Mission Statement of the company

"To produce and sell goods and services to achieve the highest return on sale in the industry to the total satisfaction of the customers, employees and shareholders in that order"

**Production Capacity**

The unit at Rajpura started with a manufacturing capacity of 100 mt per day of Vanaspati. Later on in the year 1982-83, the capacity was increased to 125 mt per day. In year 1985-86 a separate facility to produce refined oils was setup with a capacity of 60 MT per day. At present the unit is manufacturing around 170 mt of Vanaspati per day mainly in small pack under the brand Gagan, a well known and accepted brand of the market. Apart from this it has 40 mt per day production capacity plant at Amrit Bakery Shortening (ABS) and 10 MT per day production capacity plant of margarine under the brand name "Marigold".

The company is also having its oils mill with installed capacity of 100 mt per day and solvent. Today the unit has a installed capacity of 7000 mt per month against 3000 mt per month in its first year of operations. In year 1980, the company undertook a major diversification program and setup a paper unity at 10,000 TPA capacity at Sailakhurd in Punjab The popular brands of the company are Gagan, Ginni & Marigold. The company has been ranked amongst the 100 companies of India.

**Product Range**

**Vanaspati**

- Sunehri Teer
- Gagan

**Refined Oil**

- Ginni

**Shortenings**

- Amrit (for biscuits, cakes & breads)
- Amrit ( for puff products)
- Gaganlite (all purpose cooking shortening)

**Margarines & Spreads**

- Marigold

**Paper**

**Divisions of the Group**

**Edible Oils and Fats:** The production of vanaspati & refined oil aggregated to 64157 tonnes in 2002 as against 62300 tonnes in 2001. The overall performance of the edible oils segment was adversely affected during the year 2002 due to various problems affecting the industry.

**Paper:** The production of paper during the year under review was 36646 tonnes in 2002 as against 30534 tonnes in 2001. The paper market has been relatively stable since the last year. The intense pressure from the pollution authorities necessitated the management to look at various other option of outsourcing the production for growth.

**Dairy Products:** The capacity utilization of Amrit food division continues to be low though going up gradually from year to year. Efforts are being made to process the milk for other institutional buyers such as Mother Dairy & others.

**Sale and Distribution Network**

The company has a strong strength of around 700 dealers, 45 depots, 5 C&F points & over 2 lakh retail outlets

ABCL is catering to the states of Punjab, Haryana, Jammu & Kashmir, Rajasthan, West Bengal, Parts of MP, North Eastern States and UTs. On an average ABCL market share in these states baring West Bengal & North Eastern states, is roughly around 60%. The sales turnover at Rajpura Unit is around 325 crore.

## Quality Certification

It is the only company in edible oils to have ISO 9001 certification. Most of the ABC brands have been honoured with Monde selection occasions. The quality of GINNI GOLD refined Sun Flower oil has been recognized to be of international standards by Monde selection and has awarded this product in Paris. The company has also awarded silver medal to Marigold Table Margarine in Paris.

## Diversification/New Ventures

The stupendous growth of the company has been possible because ABCL has continuously endeavoured to bring new products with uncompromising quality to the Indian consumers. It was here at ABCL that revolutionary products such as Marigold, table margarine, and merritreat were developed. Thus ABCL is continuously trying to produce new products to meet the valid needs of consumers. During 1980s the company undertook a major diversification program and setup a paper unit at 10,00 TPA capacity Sahilkhurd, Distt Hoshiarpur in Punjab.

## Some Special Features of the Company

- The company has developed its own technology base in all its operations. The R&D centres have been setup in all the manufacturing units which carry out research work in several areas including process developments towards efficiency improvements, quality improvements, capacity optimization, waste reduction etc.

- The company has derived benefits of product diversification, cost reduction & better quality as a result of the above efforts.
- The company is continuing with its endeavour to raise awareness level of the staff about the seriousness of the energy conservation.
- ABCL has carried out various modernizations up gradation schemes in the past to increase the capacity of its plants and improve operational efficiency etc.
- With a high capacity utilization, strong marketing team, R&D, strong distribution network, the company has plans of expansion.
- To facilitate trading in equity shares of the company in dematerialized form ABCL has entered into agreement with central depositor services (India) Limited.
- The company has implemented ERP software and has adopted SAP R/3

| Board of Directors | |
|---|---|
| **Name** | **Designation** |
| Mr. J K Khaitan | Managing Director |
| Mr. A K Bajaj | Managing Director |
| Mr. Praveen Kumar | Nominee Director |
| Mr. G N Mehra | Independent Director |
| Mr. H S Goenka | Independent Director |
| Mr. Atam Parkash | Director |
| Mr. Naresh Kumar Bajaj | Chairman and Managing director |
| Mr. T M Sen | Director |
| Mr. D G Chaudhury | Nominee Director |

| **Snapshots** |
|---|
| **Start of the operations of Group**<br>1940<br>**Located at:**<br>G.T. Road, Rajpura, Punjab<br>**Year of Establishment of Rajpura Plant**<br>1969-70<br>**Name of the Chairman**<br>Shri N.K. Bajaj<br>**Name of the Chief Executive**<br>A.K. Bajaj<br>**Main Products/Operations**<br>Vanaspati, Refined Oil, Margarines & Spreads, Paper<br>**Popular Brands,** Gagan, Ginni, Marigold<br>**Total Turnover**<br>Rs. 600 crore<br>**Regd. & Corporate Office**<br>Amrit Nagar, G T Road Ghaziabad - 201009<br>Uttar Pradesh<br>**Listings**<br>• Delhi Stock Exchange<br>• Mumbai Stock Exchange<br>• Madras Stock Exchange<br>• Uttar Pradesh Stock Exchange<br>**Diversifications/New Venture**<br>Paper Products<br>**Markets**<br>Punjab, Haryana, Jammu & Kashmir, Rajasthan, West Bengal, Parts of MP, North Eastern states and UTs |

# Bharti (Telecommunications)

## Incorporation and Integration

### About the Founder

A graduate from Punjab University, Mr. Sunil Bharti Mittal started his first business venture at 18 years of age in the manufacturing sector in 1976 in Ludhiana with a capital of Rs. 20,000. This was beginning of "Bharti Empire". His first foray was in the small-scale sector. Being in Ludhiana, the choice was limited and he tried his hand first at manufacturing crankshaft, cycle parts and then spinning. A small stainless steel plant for both cold rolling and hot rolling was setup. However, these businesses were then opted out of.

Finding the need for a bigger canvas, Sunil moved to New Delhi 1978. With no big industrial family lineage to fall back on, trading seemed to the best option. In 1980, he started importing portable generators. By 1982-83 he was the largest importer of generators from Honda Motor Co. & Suzuki Motor Company. However wanting a corporate break, Mittal entered the pharmaceutical sector. A joint venture United Pharma was formed with New Delhi based businessman R.K. Gupta to manufacture capsules. The company today known as Bharti Healthcare, is still a part of the group and is looked after by elder brother Rakesh Bharti Mittal. The move to telecom sector did not happen till 1983, until the Indian government banned the import of generators. This meant shutting shop overnight, leaving Mittals with nothing to do. Sunil Mittal took six months off and looked for a business that he could get into. A visit to trade fair in Taiwan introduced him to push button telephones. A tie up with Taiwan company Kingltel followed and Bharti started importing Key Telephone Systems (KTS) into the country.

From 1983, telecom became an obsession for Mr. Sunil Bharti Mittal. The privatization of telecom sector in 1984 started the group's foray into the telecom terminal side. Its first milestone was the licence to manufacture telephones. In 1985 the company entered a joint venture with Siemens for telephone terminals in India.

For the next six years with a focused approach, Bharti got more involved with Siemens systems and started scaling up. Though there were many opportunities in between – Switching equipments, SDS etc. Mittal's missed them because they were lacking some resources. However, the decision was to stay in the telecom terminal side of the business and gradually extended to the telephone, fax machine and the entire gamut of telecom products. With the opening of telecom sector to value-added services in 1992, actual growth of the company started.

**Journey......**

**1985**

*Bharti Telecom Limited* (BTL) incorporated and entered into a technical tie up with Siemens AG of Germany for manufacture of electronic push button telephones.

**1987**

Ludhiana Factory of BTL commenced production of electronic push button telephones with annual capacity of 200,000 sets. (Installed capacity of approximately 10,00,000 sets).

**1989**

BTL tied up with Takacom Corporation, Japan & Lucky Goldstar Corporation of South Korea for manufacture of telephone answering machines & cordless telephones.

**1991**

BTL entered into an OEM Contract with Premier Telecom, a wholly owned subsidiary of Sprint Corporation of USA (a Fortune 500 Company) for manufacture and export of telephone sets. & Second factory of BTL set up at Gurgaon near Delhi, primarily to manufacture telephone sets for export to Sprint Corporation, USA.

**1992**

*Bharti Cellular Limited* (BCL) formed to offer cellular services under the brand name AirTel.

**1993**

BTL is Awarded ISO 9002 Accreditation for Gurgaon factory. BTL provided technical assistance for manufacture of Electronic Push Button Telephones in Uganda

**1994**

BTL's Ludhiana factory also awarded ISO 9002 accreditation. BTL entered into a strategic alliance with Casio, Japan for assembly and marketing of Casio Radio Pagers in India. BTL entered into an OEM contract with CONAIR, USA for manufacture and export of telephone sets. BCL awarded a license to operate cellular services in Delhi.

**1995**

Formed *Siemens Telecom Limited* – a joint venture with Siemens Limited to market telephone terminals under SIEMENS and BEETEL brand names. Acquired *Goa Telecommunications & Systems Ltd.,* an existing profit making company to manufacture Wireless Transmission Equipment. Formed *Bharti Telenet Limited* (BTNL), a consortium with Telecom Italia, Italy (then STET) to bid for basic & cellular services in terms of nationwide tenders. BTNL awarded License to operate cellular services in Himachal Pradesh. BCL launched GSM cellular services in Delhi.

**1995**

Bharti Tele-Ventures Limited incorporated on July 7, 1995. Bharti Cellular launched mobile services *'AirTel'* in Delhi Formed *Siemens Telecom Limited* – a joint venture with Siemens Limited to market telephone terminals under SIEMENS and BEETEL brand names. Acquired *Goa Telecommunications & Systems Ltd.,* an existing profit making company to manufacture Wireless Transmission Equipment. Formed *Bharti Telenet Limited* (BTNL), a consortium with Telecom Italia, Italy (then STET) to bid for basic & cellular services in terms of nationwide tenders. BTNL awarded License to operate cellular services in Himachal Pradesh. BCL launched GSM cellular services in Delhi.

**1996**

Bharti Telenet launched mobile services in Himachal Pradesh

**1997**

Bharti Telenet obtained a license for providing fixed-line services in Madhya Pradesh circle Bharti Telecom formed a joint venture, Bharti BT , for providing VSAT services

**1998**

Bharti Telecom formed a joint venture, Bharti BT Internet for providing Internet services. First Indian private fixed-line services launched in Indore in the Madhya Pradesh circle on June 4, 1998 by Bharti Telenet thereby ending fixed-line services monopoly of DoT (now BSNL)

**1999**

Warburg Pincus (through its investment company Brentwood Investment Holdings Limited) acquired equity interest in Bharti Tele-Ventures. Bharti Tele-Ventures acquired an effective equity interest in Bharti Mobile (formerly JT Mobiles), the mobile services provider in Karnataka and Andhra Pradesh circles

**2000**

New York Life Insurance Fund, or NYLIF, acquired a equity interest in Bharti Cellular Bharti Tele-Ventures acquired an effective equity interest in Bharti Mobinet (formerly Skycell Communications), the mobile services provider in Chennai. Bharti Tele-Ventures acquired equity interest of Telecom Italia and Bharti Telecom in Bharti Telenet thereby making Bharti Telenet a 100% subsidiary of Bharti Tele-Ventures. SingTel (through its investment company Pastel Limited) acquired STET's equity interest in Bharti Tele-Ventures. Bharti Tele-Ventures acquired an additional effective equity interest in Bharti Mobile resulting in Bharti Tele-Ventures holding an effective 74% equity interest in Bharti Mobile.

**2001**

Bharti Telesonic entered into a joint venture, Bharti Aquanet, with SingTel for establishing a submarine cable landing station at Chennai. Bharti Tele-Ventures acquired NYLIF's equity interest in Bharti Cellular. Bharti Cellular acquired a 100% equity interest in Bharti Mobitel (formerly Spice Cell ), the mobile services provider in Kolkata. Bharti Tele-Ventures acquired equity interest in Bharti Cellular from British Telecom, thereby making Bharti Cellular its 100% subsidiary. Bharti Tele-Ventures acquired an additional equity interest in Bharti Mobinet from Millicom International and BellSouth International. Punjab license restored to Bharti Mobile by the DoT and migration to NTP-1999 accepted. Bharti Cellular entered into license agreements to provide mobile services in eight new circles following the fourth operator mobile license bidding process. Bharti Telenet entered into license agreements to provide fixed-line services in the Haryana, Delhi, Tamil Nadu and Karnataka circles. Bharti Telesonic has entered into a license agreement with DoT to provide National Long Distance Services in India and has been the first service provider to start service in the country. Bharti Aquanet, Bharti Telesonic and Bharti Cellular have entered into license agreements with the DoT to provide ISP services in India

**2002**

Bharti launched mobile services in Gujarat, Haryana, Kerala, Madhya Pradesh circle, Maharashtra, Mumbai, Punjab, Tamil Nadu, Uttar Pradesh (West) circle. Bharti listed on the National stock Exchange, Bombay Stock Exchange and the Delhi Stock Exchange on February 18, 2002. Bharti entered into a license agreement with the DoT to provide international long distance services in India. Bharti launched fixed-line services in the Delhi, Haryana, Karnataka and Tamil Nadu license areas. Bharti became the first private telecommunications services provider to launch international long distance services.

**Company Profile**

Bharti Group has been at the forefront of the fast changing telecommunications skyline in the Indian subcontinent. It has garnered rich experience in all facets of telecommunications technology and services, to emerge as a clear leader in size, range and satisfaction levels.. Bharti Group has many firsts to its credit, ranging from being the first cellular service in Delhi, first private basic telephone service provider in the country, first Indian company to provide comprehensive telecom services outside India (Seychelles), fastest growing VSAT company in India, and first multinational Internet Service Provider.

Group Companies

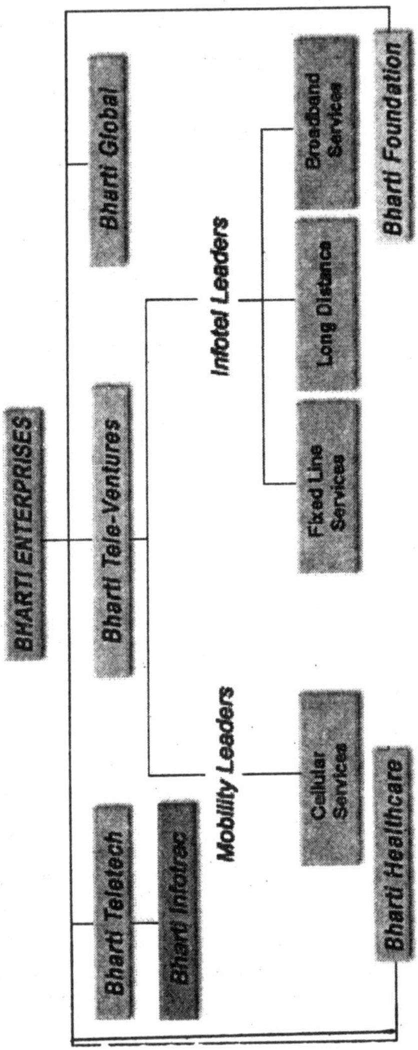

**Bharti Telesoft**

Bharti Telesoft is the software venture of India's leading telecommunication group Bharti Enterprises. It leverages the vast and rich domain expertise of the Bharti Group in telecom and Internet, to develop software products and solutions for the telecom industry. The core business of the company is to provide world-class software solutions in the areas of Telecommunications, Web & Wireless Applications and Customer Care & Billing.

Bharti Telesoft has carefully chosen the direction of its technology initiatives to leverage the expertise built up through experience in telecom and Internet services within the Bharti Enterprises group. The company focuses on software services and solutions, including development of products around current technologies.

The company is organized into two Centres of Competency (CoC), or strategic business units Each has a clear focus on the latest tools, technologies and processes within its domain. These centres are:

- Switching and Network Management
- Customer Care and Billing

The company has international benchmarks in the area of Process improvement and Quality and as a formal statement of its commitment to Quality; Bharti Telesoft has obtained ISO 9001 certification

Instead of being an IT company providing telecom solutions, we pride ourselves in being just the opposite! This translates into a blend of rich telecom knowledge and the best software talent in the country, being made available to customers.

**Bharti Teletech**

Bharti Teletech, the manufacturing arm of Bharti Enterprises, with an installed capacity of 5 million telephone sets per annum, is India's leading manufacturer of high quality telephones.

Today Bharti Teletech is the major PTT supplier in South Asia. It has ISO 9002 accreditation and also an OEM for Sprint Corporation and Siemens. Its range of products marketed under the brand name Beetel constitute a 30% market share in India thereby making it the market leader in the domestic market.

Bharti Teletech has also found a growing market in Russia, Singapore, Sri Lanka, Romania, Bahrain, Qatar, Jordan, Dubai, Yemen, Oman, Uganda, Nigeria, Tanzania, Seychelles, Zimbabwe, South Africa and USA.

**Bharti Healthcare**

The corporate ethos of providing the best to our customers carries extra relevance when it comes to healthcare products. One sector where quality implies the saving of lives and the promotion of healthy living. Offering quality support to the pharmaceutical industry, Bharti Healthcare has been engaged in the manufacture of empty hard Gelatine capsules since 1982.

Bharti's firm commitment to quality and customer satisfaction is duly acknowledgement by the list of prestigious clients including Pfizer, Parke Davis, Wockhardt, Ranbaxy and Glaxo amongst others. Bharti also exports its capsulesto overseas markets like USA, Hong Kong, Malaysia, Thailand, Indonesia, Sri Lanka, Iran, Bangladesh, Syria and Cyprus.

The US FDA has recently assigned Drug Master File (DMF) number to BHCL as an acknowledgement of it's firm commitment to adhere to globally recognized quality standards in the Pharmaceutical industry. BHCL is also an ISO 9002 certified company.

**Bharti Infotrac**

Bharti Infotrac is a fully owned subsidiary of Bharti Teletech which is a group company of Bharti Enterprises, India's premier telecom services company. Our offerings include a range of blended customer care and value added outsourcing services to its clients. Our approach realizes very significant cost savings for our clients, whilst assuring quality and achieving delivery timescales. Bharti Infotrac is capable of taking up large contracts and executing them to excellence using:

- A strong leadership team with significant outsourcing and global experience
- Operational expertise
- Focus on quality and processes
- Best of breed technologies and infrastructure

Bharti Infotrac leverages India's large pool of English-speaking graduates, a world-class delivery facility and the backing of one of India's leading conglomerate to provide exceptional customer interaction services to its customers. As customer care partners, we guarantee the following:

- Excellent quality and consistency
- Reduced turnaround time
- Enhanced service levels while delivering cost savings
- Reduced time to market
- 24X7 customer support services

**Accomplishments**

- The largest private sector integrated telecommunications services group in India in terms of the number of customers.
- Largest Mobile footprint in India, covering 15 of the 22 licensed areas.
- Proven track record of managing growth - both organic as well as by way of acquisitions.
- First and largest private telecommunications services company offering fixed-line services in India.
- Existing foreign shareholders have acquired direct and indirect equity interests in the Company for a total consideration exceeding US$1 billion.
- First private telecommunications company to launch long distance services.

First off the block to launch fixed-line services in all the four circles of Delhi, Haryana, Karnataka and Tamil Nadu.

**Bharti Foundation**

Bharti is one of India's largest private telecom companies. In an environment where information and knowledge-based industries will lead India to a powerful global position, Bharti believes it must continue to make a difference. To this end, Bharti Enterprises has undertaken two major initiatives:

**To promote activities in the social development sector and provide disaster relief.**

Bharti School of Telecommunication Technology & Management: To facilitate advance study and research in telecommunications technology and management.

The Bharti Foundation has been set up with the objective of promoting and supporting activities related to education, health and medical sciences, Indian culture, population control, family welfare, child care, nutrition, environment, etc. Besides establishing educational institutions, it also grants scholarships, stipends and rewards to deserving, meritorious and needy persons. It encourages and supports activities towards advancement of different forms of arts including music, dance, drama, literature, painting, etc., and also provides help to needy and deserving sportspersons. The Foundation also provides support to people affected by calamities such as war, riots, earthquakes, floods, fire, famine, epidemics, etc.

**Bharti School of Telecommunication Technology and Management**

Bharti Enterprises and Indian Institute of Technology (IIT), Delhi - one of Asia's leading institutes for education in engineering and technology - are jointly establishing the Bharti School of Telecommunication Technology & Management for developing young telecom leaders. The School will be a centre of excellence for education and research relating to all facets of telecommunication technology and management. It will host state-of-the-art laboratories and infrastructure and a research environment to attract the best faculty and students. The Institute offers two post-graduate programmes -

- M.Tech in Telecommunications Technology & Management and MBA in Telecommunications Systems Management. It also runs continuing education programmes for personnel of the telecom industry.

**Awards**

Bharti Tele-Ventures, its subsidiaries and management have received several awards and recognitions, including:

- Bharti was recognized as one of the "Leading Lights of Telecom" in Asia in November 2001 in the Asian edition of the "tele.com" magazine with analytical inputs from research consultants Frost & Sullivan.
- The leading telecommunications service provider in India in a survey of Indian companies conducted by Business World in association with Indian Marketing Research Bureau in September 2001;
- The "Techies" award from Information Communications World, an international business magazine, for four consecutive years (1997 to 2000) for brand excellence, network quality, customer service and value added service in our Delhi mobile circle;
- Golden Peacock National Training Award – 1999 to Bharti Cellular for our Delhi mobile operations from the Institute of Directors, a non-profit association in India committed to improving the competitiveness of Indian business by focusing on development of business leaders, for the best human resources and training practices; and
- Ascent – Times of India and Sodexho Pass award in 1999 from the Asia Pacific HRD conclave to Bharti Cellular for corporate excellence in the category of most innovative human resource practices.
- Mr. Sunil Bharti Mittal (Chairman and Group Managing Director) was honoured as " One of the Top Entrepreneurs Worldwide" for the year 2000 and "Stars of Asia" for the year 2001 by international business magazine, Business Week.
- Mr Sunil Bharti Mittal was selected as the "Businessman of the year 2002" by Business India.
- Mr Sunil Bharti Mittal was awarded the "Dataquest IT man of the year 2002".

- Mr Sunil Bharti Mittal was selected the "CEO of the year 2002" by World HRD congress.
- Mr. Akhil Gupta (Joint Managing Director) was adjudged as the Chief Financial Officer for year 2001 for Mergers & Acquisitions activities by EIU.

**Strong Strategic and Financial Partners**

Bharti Tele-Ventures' existing foreign shareholders have acquired direct and indirect equity interests in the Company for a total consideration exceeding US$1 billion.

SingTel is one of Bharti Tele-Ventures' key strategic partners and its position as one of Asia's leading telecommunications service provider gives the Company access to valuable knowledge in implementing tele-communications projects and to its international expertise and managerial resources. Bharti Tele-Ventures' other partners include leading international financial investors such as Warburg Pincus, International Finance Corporation, the Asian Infrastructure Fund Group and New York Life Insurance.

**Joint Ventures/Tie Ups**

Bharti has today many joint ventures with telecom leaders like SingTel, Singapore; E.M. Warburg Pincus, USA; Telia, Sweden; New York Life International, Mauritius; AIF Funds Management Ltd., Mauritius; and IFC

**Technology**

- Alcatel
- Motorola
- Ericsson
- Siemens
- Oracle

- Nortel Networks

**Stakeholders**

Warburg Pincus is a leading global private equity investment firm managing approximately US$11 billion of investment with a further US$5 billion available for investment. Since 1971, Warburg Pincus has raised ten private equity funds and has made over 435 investments across the US, Europe, Asia and Latin America.

Warburg Pincus has substantial focus on India and it has made investments across various economic sectors – telecommunications, financial services, building materials, pharmaceuticals, consumer goods and technology. Warburg Pincus has invested more than US$600 million in India.

SingTel is the leading provider of international and local telephone services, mobile communication services, data communication services and postal services in Singapore. SingTel is also one of the leading integrated communications service providers in the Asia Pacific region. It has 19 offices in 14 countries around the world, extensive networks through out the Asia Pacific region and significant investments outside Singapore, particularly in Belgium, India, Philippines, Taiwan and Thailand. SingTel has a strong track record of adding value to its international investments and supporting their growth

NYLIF is part of New York Life Insurance Company, and is a fortune 100 company and is one of the largest insurance companies in the USA. It offers traditional life insurance, annuities and long term care insurance. NYLIF, through its affiliate New York Life Investment Management, provides institutional asset management and trust services and various securities products and services.

AIF was established in 1994 with participation from Frank Russel, International Finance Corporation, Asian Development Bank and the Quantum group of funds. AIF is a part of AIF Funds Management Limited (AIFML), which manages close to US $1 billion in direct investments across Asia. AIF has made investments in power and transportation sectors in Asia. AIF has made investments in various telecom projects in Asia including wireless, fixed and wholesale carriers.

The International Finance Corporation ("IFC") is an international organization established in 1956 pursuant to Articles of Agreement, which govern its operations. As of January 1, 2001, 174 countries were IFC shareholders.
The principal purpose of IFC is to further economic growth in its developing member countries by promoting private sector development.

In partnership with private investors, IFC assists in financing the establishment, improvement and expansion of private sector enterprises by making investments where sufficient private capital is not otherwise available on reasonable terms. In addition to project finance and resource mobilization, IFC offers financial and technical advisory services to private businesses in developing member countries. It also advises member governments on private sector development matters.

**Snapshots**

**Name of the company**
Bharti Enterprise
**Year of establishment**
1985
**Located at:**
Village Hombran, Ludhiana
**Main products**
telecom terminal, telephone, fax machine, Telecommunications, Web & Wireless Applications, Customer Care & Billing, Healthcare
**Revenue and profit, Annual**
over Rs. 5,000 crore of revenue and
over Rs. 600 crore of net profit .
**Quality certification**
ISO 9002 (BHCL) ,
Bharti Teletech → ISO 9002,
Bharti Telesoft has obtained ISO 9001
**Collaboration**
Alcatel, Motorola, Ericsson, Siemens, Oracle, Nortel, Networks
**Flagship companies**

- Bharti Telesoft
- Bharti Teletech
- Bharti Healthcare
- Bharti Infotrac

**Main domestic market**
Through out India
**Foreign market:** USA, Hong Kong, Malaysia, Thailand, Indonesia, Sri Lanka, Iran, Bangladesh, Syria, Cyprus

# FC Sondhi and Company (Sports Goods)

**Incorporation and Integration**

**Founder Mr. F.C. Sondhi (1906-1983)**

Mr. F.C. Sondhi, a great philanthropist and self made businessman, was born in the year 1906 in Sialkot which is now in Pakistan. Through his own hard work and self education he was able to do well in his academic studies and was called by the then major sports company in United India, M/s Uberoi Limited to work there. He developed a shining reputation for honesty and was put under the personal supervision of Mr. Uberoi himself.

At first he was made the inspector of branches of Uberoi Limited in India to ensure that branch offices were working properly and honestly and then as a reward for his good work he was sent to Rangoon in Burma in 1932 to look after the branch office there. Once again since he was successful in Rangoon, the company sent him to England. Again the branch office in England was quite successful but during the 2nd world war between England and Germany the office was totally destroyed by bombs (it was situated in central London). Mr. Uberoi reluctantly closed down the office and told Mr. F.C Sondhi to return to India. However since no transport was available during the war days, and to go by ship was extremely dangerous, Mr. F.C. Sondhi has to stay in England and tried to make both ends meet by buying and selling various commodities.

Immediately after the war, Mr. F.C. Sondhi started his own small business in the Toy Trade in England in 1944.

Mr. F.C. Sondhi lived in England throughout his life but during the last 20 years of his life he visited India regularly every year and was keenly involved in projects and programmes particularly those for the upliftment of the poor and downtrodden.

**FCS: How it all Started?**

In the year 1944, as already mentioned, Mr. Sondhi started a company in England by the name of F.C. Sondhi & Company Limited. At that time it was dealing only in Toys but after the partition of India in 1947, Mr. F.C. Sondhi left that perhaps he could help the small Sports Goods Industry in Jalandhar by importing some goods from India and selling them in England.

With this idea in mind, in 1950 he visited India and set up a branch of his company in Jalandhar city. The branch was situated at No.1 Basti Nau and he appointed a Manager, Mr. M.R. Khorana to look after the company.

Though the industry was only just beginning to settle down after the upheaval of partition, yet small quantities of hockey sticks, cricket balls, Footballs etc., were purchased from Jalandhar and exported to England.

In 1961 the Indian Government passed a law saying that all the branch offices of foreign companies must be Indianised and the company then was converted to F.C Sondhi & Company (India) Pvt. Ltd., with local shareholders. The company continued to export goods to F.C. Sondhi & Company Limited in England but also to other Sports Goods Importers in England. In fact Mr. F.C. Sondhi established contacts with others in England who started importing from the Indian company. The company continued to be merchant exporter up to the year 1967.

**1967 Onwards: Start of Manufacturing**

In 1967, the present Managing director, Mr. F.C. Sondhi, came to Jalandhar and started the manufacture of cricket batting gloves and cricket leg guards for a well known English company.

The beginning was very modest with just one skilled worker and one hand sewing machine but slowly and gradually over a period of time, manufacturing activities expanded.

Initially work was done in rented premises but slowly and steadily the company started its own factory in Basti Sheikh Road, which is settled in the year 1971.

During the all these years the Mr. F.C. Sondhi came to India regularly to provide guidance and advice to Mr. P.C. Sondhi who was stationed permanently in Jalandhar.

**Profile of the Company**

The FCS family consists of over 300 loyal and dedicated staff and workers.

The entire factory is now housed at Sondhi Nagar on the outskirts of Jalandhar city.

The total area of land there is 20 acres and provides ample room for expansion in years to come.

The factory is beautifully landscaped with flowers and trees and is one of the most environmentally satisfying settings available for a factory in Jalandhar city.

The factory is complete with a cricket ground which is used for instant and confidential testing of the products manufactured.

Presently the products made at Sondhi Nagar include Cricket bats, balls and protective equipment, Hockey sticks and Hockey protective equipment, Footballs and Football Goalkeeper gloves.

**Philosophy and Ideals**

Following are the philosophies and ideals of the company:

- To hold customers in high esteem and to make every effort possible to see that they are satisfied.
- To manufacture and market quality sports goods and to ensure that customers get the best value for money.
- To deal with everyone in a fair, honest and straightforward manner whether he be customer, supplier, staff or worker.
- To give the best possible working conditions, which are healthy and environmentally friendly, to the staff and workers and to afford them whatever facilities possible for their personal growth and development.
- To follow a child labour free policy.
- To remember obligation to the community around the company and in which the company work.
- To manage affairs on modern lines to enable us to deal swiftly and effectively with all who meet us and contact us.
- To continuously follow the pursuit of knowledge through scientific research.
- To achieve cost effectiveness through efficiency.
- To maintain a strong commitment to quality at all times.

**Welfare Schemes**

- FCS believes in mutual respect at all levels and considers the 'dignity of labour' as their need.
- The environment and buildings of the factory are kept clean and tidy; all buildings are well lit and well ventilated. The factory has been designed in such a way that wherever one stands, one can see either trees or green lawns or flowers.

- Free tea and subsidized food given daily.
- Numerous saving schemes are in operation.
- Free medical check up facilities for the employees and their families has been provided from time to time.
- Every winter, subsidized woollen blankets and sweaters are provided to all the employees of the company.
- An annual function is held every year. All employees and their wives and children participate in it. A utility gift if presented to each employee on this occasion.
- A cooperative Consumer store is available on the premises where employees can comfortably do their shopping and the cost of their purchasing is deducted from their next salary.

**Awards, Gifts and Scholarships**

- The company awards a wall clock to everybody who completes 10 years continuous service.
- A small offering is presented to each and every employee on self-marriage or marriage of a child.
- A Best Worker award is given for each skilled category of workers and for the production staff. The award recipient is given a cash prize and a badge to wear so that others are motivated.
- Every winter the company offers subsidized woollens and also a free pair of gloves.
- Every year awards are also presented for attendance.

**Scholarships**

FCS awards 30 scholarships every year. 20 of these are for education of brilliant children of workers and 5 are for education at College/University level. In addition to this there are 5 scholarships for self education for staff and workers.

**F.C. Sondhi Charitable Trust**

The FCS group of companies support and also donate liberally to a CHARITABLE TRUST named after the founder of the company Mr. F.C. Sondhi.

This is a public Charitable Trust which helps those outside the FCS Company.

The trust provides over 300 scholarships and nearly 100 stipends (help to widows and destitute men and women). These figures vary from year to year. (In 1998-99, approximate US$ 12000 was distributed). It also publishes a regular newsletter every month containing spiritual, moral and commercial ideas for those too busy too read such articles in full.

A large number of foreigners also donate liberally to this Charitable Trust and those monies in turn are provided as scholarships and stipends to the poor in and around Jalandhar. No amount is given to anyone without proper verification.

The scholarships and stipends sponsored by well-wishers bare paid entirely to the students and stipend holders. Al other charges, i.e. administration, postage etc., incurred are borne by the Trust itself. The Trust also provides Vocational Training scholarships to enable poor students to get specialized training to earn a better livelihood. It also donates monies to other worthy projects for the poor in Jalandhar, from time to time.

**"Never doubt that a small group of thoughtful, committed citizens can change the world. Indeed, it's the only thing that ever has." Margaret Mead**

**Humble Contribution to Jalandhar City**

Realizing its obligation and with a view to beautifying the city, FCS had adopted one of the roundabouts in the town. It had a statue in the centre illuminated at night by bright multicoloured lights. Its visual beauty was further enhanced by beautiful water fountains.

When the municipal Corporation wanted to speed up traffic in city, they decided that many of the roundabouts needed to be replaced by traffic lights. F.C. Sondhi & co. was the first to volunteer, in the interest of smooth traffic flow, that their adopted roundabout could be demolished.

The statue in the roundabout was of a large hand offering a football. The object was that this should have various interpretations.

- It depicted the hand of God symbolizing the gift of God to Jalandhar since many people in the city have gained employment by making footballs.
- It symbolized the offering of Jalandhar to the visitor i.e., that they can buy footballs here.
- It also symbolized that footballs are made by hand with great care.

As mentioned above, the roundabout has since been removed in 1996. However, due to public requests F.C. Sondhi & Co. have built a small replica of this roundabout on one of the traffic light islands near the original statue.

**Environmental Concerns**

In line with global thinking, FCS has adopted a senior Manager in-charge of environmental concerns. Apart from looking into the reduction in wastage of raw material and disposal of the same, he will be ensuring that consumption of paper is controlled and also that recycling of raw materials and office stationery is done to the maximum extent possible.

In due course of time, it is hoped that company will get ISO 14000 recognition. This will certify that the company are conforming to environmental ideals and contributing to society to provide a healthier & greener environment for generations to come. The company have always had a clean, comfortable and green working environment. Well maintained lawns, flowerbeds and numerous trees can be seen by employees as they work.

**Healthy and Safety Standards**

In addition to environmental concerns or rather as part to it, FCS is busy studying health & safety standards and they are particularly making sure that all their production procedures comply with the necessary global standards. These will include safety measures on machinery, ventilation systems, fire fighting equipment availability and so on and so forth.

**Quality**

**Material Specifications and Testing**

FCS has long believed that if one wants to produce a trouble-free quality product, then one must start at the beginning and test each and every raw material when it comes into factory.

With the help their Research Department and also input from customers, FCS have been able to set up a series of specifications for all major critical raw materials.

These specifications include such as Abrasion Resistance, Breaking Load, Tear Strength, Colour Fastness and Stitch Tear Strength

In some instances materials re not tested in the raw state in which they come into the factory but also after processing e.g. after laminating the PVC for footballs, laminated sheets are again tested to ensure that the strength of the laminate is as A per standards down.

Another example would be the plastic buckle used on a leg guard. FCS has laid down specifications of 85 kgs which could actually hang from this buckle without its breaking. Therefore it is obviously strong enough to withstand any mishap in the field.

The raw material specification is always related to the end use of the product. For instance PVC for the inside of the instep of a cricket legguard which rubs against the cricket shoe must have high abrasion resistance.

This testing done by FCS has given them confidence in their own product as well as giving a lot of confidence to their customers.

**In-Process Quality Control**

The company believe not only in thoroughly testing the quality of the finished product, but also in building quality into the product through in-process quality control.

After the purchase of the raw materials as per the proper specifications, materials are then processed and turned into finished articles. FCS believes that quality can only be achieved by satisfied craftsmen side by side with strict in-process quality controls at every stage of manufacture.

When an order is recovered, the counter sample is checked against the Specification Card of that product to ensure that the correct current counter sample is available. Once this has been determined then the processing of the raw material is started.

For example, when a cricket ball is manufactured, as many as 16 checks are done at various stages to ensure that the quality is up to the proper specifications.

Finally 100% inspection is done of all finished goods.

To educate the production staff, samples and specifications are displayed on the workshop floor.

**"Quality is never an accident; it is always the result of intelligent effort"** John Ruskin

**Field Testing**

FCS believes that a product should never be sold unless it has been tested in the field.

To the extent possible FCS always test its own products, at least under Indian conditions, although simultaneously it is recommended that the customers test the products under the climatic conditions and ground conditions prevalent in their country as well.

On a regular basis one item out of the first lot of each batch of goods is sent through the quality assurance department for field testing. This is given, in majority of cases, to experienced players who are also provided with the test report to fill in and return.

All returned products are studied jointly by the production department and Quality Assurance Department. In this way, any technical, design or material fault which may show up in field-tested product can be immediately located and remedied.

New products are also tested, but normally FCS tries to do this on its own grounds which form part of the Sondhi Nagar Complex.

**Scientific Research**

The commitment of FCS to scientific research originated in 1983 with the development and change in existing products. There was a need and demand for products offering better protection, and for lighter weight products. Simultaneously more competitively priced products, at a lower end of the range, were required which would be affordable to students (or can say instead of students).

Also, the drastic change in playing conditions, particularly in hockey, has necessitated a search for raw materials, new designs and new products.

FCS is totally committed to concept of improvement in all these areas and has its research laboratory along with testing fields where new products can be promptly tried out.

Now design and development centre is functioning independently with two seasoned officers along with a team of highly skilled workers who are, responsible for scientific development of new production. Initial sampling to the customers is done by them keeping confidentiality of the products; design etc. at the same time, this centre is constantly working on new innovative ideas for product development and on new products for diversification.

**Quality Assurance**

In addition to testing of the raw materials when they come into the factory, and the very detailed in-process quality control, goods are not dispatched from the factory without the okay of the Quality Assurance Department.

The Quality Assurance Department is responsible for test checking all goods manufactured in the factory.

This department specially checks each first batch of finished goods coming out of any production department against a new order. The product is first compared with the approved counter sample of the customer. Also, any remarks made by the customer (which are recorded in specification Card of the product) are also seen to ensure that the product is properly compliant. Only after Quality Assurance is satisfied that the product has been made to the customer's specifications and that quality is satisfactory, will they issue a first lot certificate, without which goods cannot leave the factory.

Also, as mentioned elsewhere, continuous field testing is done to ensure that products not only look good but perform well also.

**ISO 9000**

The company plans to get ISO 9000 Certificate to ensure that its management of quality systems is as per the internationally agreed norms. In fact the initial survey done by ISO 9000 consultants show that FCS is already following the majority of the necessary and relevant systems but nevertheless a formal certification is expected.

**Sales and Marketing**

The company follows the following motto:

As Mahatma Gandhi has said, the company believe that:

"A customer is the most important visitor to premises. He is not dependent on us. We are dependent on him. He is not an interruption to work. He is the purpose of it. He is not an outsider to premises. He is a part of it. The company are not doing him a favour by serving him. He is doing us a favour by giving us an opportunity to do so."

**Export Performance**

FCS is basically an export company with over 97% of its production being exported every year.

The major markets to which FCS is exporting are the UK, Australia, New Zealand, South Africa, West Indies & Bangladesh. How ever, in addition to cricket equipment FCS is exporting hockey sticks and football equipment to many other countries and concentrating on those markets is on the increase.

FCS is trying to achieve the same delivery schedules that overseas customers get from the Far East. This is 90 days for ex-factory for an initial and bulk order, and 60 days ex-factory for additional and/or smaller orders.

These days 99% of consignments that are full container loads go through Inland Container Depot which is only 6 kilometers away from the factory. Goods are stuffed there in the containers under own person's supervision. The container is sealed be the customs people then and there, and no further checking is done until the container arrives at the destination.

Containers are sent either by road directly from Jalandhar to Bombay, or from Jalandhar to Ludhiana by road and by train from Ludhiana to Bombay. Since the containers are packed in Jalandhar, the goods arrive at the destination in better condition. The company are getting very good feedback about this from various overseas customers.

**Marketing**

FCS being a Sports Goods manufacturing company, selling seasonal products, always finds that everyone wants their goods at the same time during the year. This is but natural and therefore the effort is always to try and remove the peaks and troughs in the demand for production.

The new marketing policy is very much geared to this end so that maximum utilization of production capacity can be achieved, thereby minimizing the overheads involved. Since customer satisfaction is of prime importance to us, the company try and develop on these lines.

Efficiency and Effectiveness are objectives and the company strive hard towards achievement of the same. Visits of executives to various countries abroad keep us well updated and bring awareness about changing market situations.

Although FCS does not call itself a professionally managed company, yet it does try and adopt a systematic and scientific approach to management, in other words, a professional approach.

**Home Market**

FCS has entered the Home Market very intrepidly.

They are very keen indeed to give world quality equipment with world quality service but at affordable prices.

FCS are trying to keep stock of the main items of constant demand so that can execute orders within 24 hours.

They are also keeping in constant touch with all their customers and keeping them informed regarding dispatch of their consignments.

The response to the Protos brand has in fact been far greater than expectations and the network of dealers is expanding rapidly.

At present FCS are not spending money on advertising and signing up players but prefer to pass the benefit onto their customers so that the customers get more value for his money.

**National Export Award for Outstanding Export Performance**

The Government of India gives numerous awards to various categories of exporters. But perhaps the most prestigious is the National Award for Outstanding Export Performance

This award is open to all exporters throughout India. Multi-million dollar turnover public limited companies, Government owned banks and Government owned trading companies or even the smallest in the scale sector, all are eligible for the award.

Normally there are only 70 recipients each year from all the exporters all over the vast country of India (population 1 billion people).

The President of India personally presents these awards to the recipients.

FCS has had the honour of winning this Award on four different occasions during its history.

**In Tune with the New Millennium**

**Mechanization of Production**

The world is changing at a very fast pace and as one would expect, this is changing business environment around the globe. Gone are the days when the company use to get orders for the full season or the whole year.

The customer is getting more selective and wants the product to match very exact specifications. On top of this, orders are made in small lots and the products need to be delivered in a very short period.

To match the increase in pace and precision requirements of the business, more of the manufacturing process is being mechanized.

The company are mechanizing the various stages of bat manufacture. Band saw and other conventional machines are being phased out and are being replaced by "Special Purpose Machines" (SPMs). The company hope to introduce hi-tech and hi-production machines to make and sand bats and other wooden products. To improve the environment of work place, the company are going to install dust extraction units very shortly. FCS are undergoing an extensive mechanization process with considerable amount of investment. This is being done in all production areas.

The company invite esteemed customers to come and see for themselves.

**Computerization**

The company have installed 21 computers so far in various departments to increase working efficiency.

The company have already computerized accounts (computerized accounts on a local area network of 7 computers), invoicing, Stitching Centre Service Cell, and maintenance of stocks. The company have plans to computerize costing and raw material ordering among other areas.

The company are trying to achieve the goal of a paperless company by installing more computers. The company are also adopting advanced computer technology to make products better and more competitive.

After the company get ISO certification the company will look at an ERP system that will coordinate the activities if the whole organization.

**Email and Internet**

The company are now using email extensively and all communication (with customers who have email) is being done by email including sending Performa invoices etc.

Currently the company have five ports connected to email and in the future the company plan to have inter company email as well.

The company have a state of art digital camera and the company are sending cosmetic designs for approval by email with a digital photograph attachment so that the company save valuable transit and courier costs that were earlier spent in sending actual samples.

Almost all customers now are sending their artwork by email where the artwork is small and can easily fit in mailbox or if it is too big it is sent on CD's. This is saving customers a lot of money as earlier it was sent on films which was very expensive for them.

The company has its own website

http://business.vsnl.com/fcssport

where a copy of the FCS story you are reading has been uploaded!

**Finance and Accounts**

The payment system of a company determines whether the company is able to keep its suppliers happy. The company have adopted a payment system that makes sure there are no delays in payments. The supplier concerned does not need to make continual reminders; instead, the company delivers cheques at the door step of the suppliers. Tardy payments are often a failing of many companies, therefore the company feel proud of reputation as good paymasters.

**Stitching Centre Service Cell**

The company has established Stitching Centre Service Cell in August 1996. This has enabled us to successfully provide Single window Service to 100 odd stitching centres. Among other services, the SCSC is ensuring door to door delivery of goods at the stitching centres in villages and within Jalandhar City.

Taking work to the stitching centres in villages is very environment friendly because it saves those ladies working in those villages coming into town everyday. In other words transport and congestion on the roads is indirectly reduced and at the same time the women in the villages hardly have to walk 5 minutes to come to the stitching centre and can pop up home at lunch time to see that their children care ok (normally looked after by some other member of a joint family).

**Future Plans**

The company has completely shifted to Sondhi Nagar complex and hereby have achieved objective to concentrate efforts at one place, under one roof.

A major renovation process is in progress with old asbestos roof buildings being demolished and modern light airy buildings taking their place.

FCS is working on professional targets such as Just in Time, Computerization, Zero Tolerance on Quality Issues, Stitching Centres, Line Production and Corporate Responsibility.

They hope that by achieving economics to scale, they will be able to offer products to customers at reasonable prices and in shorter lead times.

In addition to the concentration in one place and ion continuous specialization in cricket, hockey and football, the company also plans to spend much more time in scientific research.

As regards computerization, FCS is in the process of planning computerization of the Production departments enabling us to constantly monitor progress of various customers' orders, and linking these to the Sales and Shipping Departments (which are already equipped with computers). Immediately on receipt of orders FCS is able to tell the customers whether or not the order is full container load.

FCS has achieved considerable efficiencies over the last few years and the company feel that by moving to one site in

Sondhi Nagar, this efficiency will grow even more, in the years to come.

**Snapshots**

**Name of the Company**
F.C. Sondhi & Company (India) Pvt. Ltd.
**Year of Establishment**
1971
**Located at:**
Sondhi Nagar, Jalandhar City
**Main products**

- Cricket bats and balls and protective equipment
- Hockey sticks and hockey protective equipment
- Footballs

**Total turnover**
Rs. 22 crore (approximately)
**Domestic**
Rs. 2 crore
**Foreign**
Rs. 20 crore
**Quality certification**
Will be applying for ISO 9000
**Flagship company**
F.C Sondhi & Company (India) Pvt. Ltd.
**Main domestic market**
Through out India
**Foreign market:** UK, Australia, New Zealand, South Africa, West Indies, Bangladesh

# FMI (Measurement Tapes)

**Incorporation and Integration**

FMI Ltd. was started in 1950 with an initial investment of approx Rs. 10,000. This was the money, which Mr. Madan Nayar received in aid from the Indian government after moving from Pakistan to India. For the first time in the country, tape measures were manufactured and it marked the beginning of measuring tools industry in India. The initial unit was started with 30 employees at Iqbal Ganj, Ludhiana. The organization has at present a turnover of Rs.27 Crore.

**History**

FMI Ltd started manufacturing of metal wired tapes in 1950 and in 1965 it pioneered the manufacture of Steel Tape Measures and Tape Rules in the country with American know how. To establish distribution network for serving all European countries, Euro Freemans S.A. was established in 1988 in Barcelona (Spain). Freeman's Measures Limited is amongst the first non–European manufacturer to obtain EEC approval, which itself is a testimony to the fact that its products surpass international quality standards. The company has its own in-house Plastics division, Steel division & four ancillary units, so as to have total control over Quality and Production. Presently FMI Ltd. is serving markets in over 62countries in the world, which include European and American territories. This resulted in an increased market penetration in Europe.

Now FMI Ltd. is the pioneer and largest manufacturers of Tape Measures in Indian Subcontinent and has earned worldwide recognition with its high quality products. Since 1950 we have been making measuring tapes. What has changed is the range of products we have introduced over time to serve every need in the engineering industry. What hasn't changed however is our commitment to precision. Because we know that in this business every micron counts. Precision, quality and a firm belief in perfection has resulted in constant up gradation of technology and expansion of the existing production facilities to meet your changing and exacting demands which means having the best of men and machines

**Profile of the Company**

**Product**

The product categories are bifurcated into various kinds mentioned below:

- Pocket tapes
- Long tapes
- Micro tape
- Torpedo level

The main products of the company are Measuring Tapes of all types- Metal Wired, Glass Fiber, Steel Tapes, Rules, Scales, Cutters and Spirit Levels. FMI Ltd. is also engaged in manufacturing and export of a variety of hand tools, which include Pliers, Hammers, Spanners, and Pipe Wrenches etc.

**Mission**

**Commitment to Perfection through Quality and Customer Satisfaction**

FMI Ltd. strives to meet customer's aspirations, satisfaction and confidence in quality, reliability, aesthetics and economy through high innovation, creativity, Zero Defect approach by constant up gradation of quality and human excellence to stay in global mainstream. FMI Ltd. designs its products in such a way that they have above average quality. When FMI Ltd. announces "New and Improved Products" it means it.

**Certifications**

FMI Ltd. has quality certification ISO 9002. Company year after year from 1997 to 2001 has bagged Export Excellence Award from Engineering Export Promotion Council (EEPC). It is the first non-European manufacturer to obtain EEC approval, which itself is a testimony to the fact that its products surpass international quality standards.

**Distribution Network**

We are the pioneers, largest manufacturers of Tape Measures in Indian Sub continent. Precision and quality have earned our company worldwide renown, with well-established market in over 62 countries including U.S.A., U.K., Germany and most competitive countries like Taiwan. We meet over 70% of the Indian market demand.

**Management's Perspective**

The management of FMI Ltd. touches upon various aspects of the present day challenges of globalization and competitiveness of Indian firms, which needs to be analyzed. In India the various factors of production are considered to be costlier.

Thus the efficiency and effectiveness is quiet reflected in the productivity level. Even taxes are being imposed heavily and not doing favour to the Indian business. Despite labour reforms, the position on labour front is very gloomy. The management also thrown some light on the Chinese labour whose wages are same but considered to be far more productive.

For tackling the global channels companies will have to go for cost reduction even if scarcity of options are there. The management argues that role of government in supporting business and said that although protective policies like soft rate of interest for credit, relaxation and exemption from labour loss, subsidized raw material and technological support provided by the government have helped a lot but threats and pressure from the global environment has created more hurdles by shielding Indian Business In order to improve efficiency incentives schemes to be given. The management said that information technology benefits are real for traditional business as information flow speeds up and economies are also realized. The organization is benefiting from new techniques like Re-engineering and Enterprise Resource Planning, which are making systems more effective. In today's competitive era human resources is an intellectual capital, which acts as a competitive edge for an organization.

The success of an organization depends on capability of its work force. Human Resources are a source of a balance, motivation and good discipline. Regarding educational institutes the views are that the B-schools like IIM's provides very rich and practically oriented education. And thus emphasis should be on practical exposure in various regional institutes in our country so as to come up with the industry requirements.

It is only through the real- time education that the students can mould their skills according to the requirements of the industry. The ability to adapt to the changing business environment must be present to face the challenges of real business. The managers and technical graduates of today should be honest and should have integrity.

The calibre and analytical bent of mind is the need of today, which is quite uncommon in our country. The management also encouraged worker's participation in management is at times an eye-opener to the management. He added that after getting ISO 9002 certification the management started encouraging the departmental heads to contribute to the organizational meetings. The results obtained were more than expected. Even the grass root workers started bring innovative ideas and suggestions. When asked about the future of Ludhiana Industry in the light of emergence of low-cost competition from countries like China, there statement related to the survival of the fittest. Only big companies with large resources and ability to control cost can face the threat from China. Large companies can achieve the economies of scale and hire consultancies to improve upon their skills. Small companies with scarce resources are not in a position to take on low cost competition. Further, the government has to take drastic steps to simplify the procedures. The board also emphasized on the importance of specialization for penetration into local or international markets. Talking about the future operational plans, it was disclosed that FMI Ltd. is planning to diversify in measurement related products only because other fields are too crowded.

| **Snapshots** |
|---|
| **Year of Start**<br>1950<br>**Located at:**<br>Ferozepur Road, Ludhiana<br>**Main Products/ Operations**<br>Measuring Tapes of all types – Metal Wired, Glass Fibre, Steel Tapes, Rules, Scales, Cutters and Level Vials.<br>**Total Turnover**<br>Rs. 2700 Lakh<br>**Domestic Turnover**<br>Rs. 1600 Lakh<br>**Foreign Turnover**<br>Rs. 1100 Lakh<br>**Certification**<br>ISO 9002, EEC approval<br>**Main Markets being Served Domestic and Foreign**<br>Domestic 60%<br>Export 40% including Europe, USA (in all 62 countries all over the world) |

## Incorporation and Integration

The story of Sonalika International started 33 years back when due to vagaries of weather, crops got perished because the same could not be processed in the absence of proper farm implements. Although there was visible increase in crop yield but traditional ways of threshing took many days to process the crops. More so, weather conditions were not always helpful, resulting into enormous loss/sufferings not only to the producers but also to the consumers. There was Nation's need to have modern farm machinery to help the farming community. Mittal group of Companies rose to the occasion and pooled all resources and efforts towards farm mechanisation to improve the plight of the farmers. The result was production of high quality multi crop threshers and other agriculture implements. Due to trouble free and excellent performance, the threshers became the household name among the ruralites. This encouraged the company to produce more quality implements which were very well received and soon captured the Indian market. Today, the farm products of Sonalika have major share in the Indian market and only meagre share goes to other brands. It is manufacturing more than 75,000 agriculture machines which is a record in itself.

## Company Profile

Spread over an area of 50 acres located at Hoshiarpur Jalandhar road, the plant has been given a complete face-lift and has been made ultra modern. There are spacious halls to house different sections for specific jobs. The plant is mechanized and has been fully computerized. The different departments are being manned by the cream of the industry assisted by skilled and dedicated workers. Each tractor, which rolls out of the factory, is subjected to strict quality controls. The company has achieved prestigious ISO 9001 certification in view of its world class R&D, quality controls & systems. Sonalika under the stewardship to Shri L.D. Mittal, Chairman, International Tractors Ltd., has made rapid strides within a short span of 6 years. It has not only made its presence felt in the Tractor Industry but has made in-roads into the market share of popular brands. Its valued and satisfied customers are multiplying and have crossed 63,000 mark.

**Journey...**

Sonalika International after making a mark in the farm implements for over 33 years diversified its activities and started its tractor's wing in 1995. They developed the first tractor DI - 740 and soon this product caught the fancy of farming community and it has gained such a popularity as has not been achieved by any brand so far that too during short span of a few years. The company is manufacturing tractors conforming to the actual needs of the farming community and not just to produce Tractors and force their sales on the ruralites. The Sonalika International has moved forward with confidence and has not looked back. Success continues to embrace the company and encourage it to develop more models from time to time suitable to the pockets of the farmers and catering to their actual needs. Accordingly 12 models have since been developed and marketed ranging from 25HP to 60 HP. These tractors have created a stir in the tractor market due to their outstanding performance.

**The story so far....**

ITL has developed a tractor engine in 50 HP range which conforms to Euro II norms and which incidentally is the first engine in India, that has been developed by Hoshiarpur Plant of Sonalika International. It is really a golden feather in the cap of the company. Its engineers and workers by dint of their hard work and technological advancements have been able to show this splendid achievement within a few years and this break - through has not been achieved by any other tractor company so far.

An Agreement has been signed with world automobile Giant Renault Agriculture of France in July 2000. There has been exchange of technical know - how and Renault technology has been introduced in the Tractors being manufactured in ITL factory at Hoshiarpur. This will help in providing Tractors to the Indian farmers with latest world-class technology at the lowest rates and this will also increase the efficiency of tractors and income of the farmers.

**Family Tree**

Sh. L.D. Mittal
(Chairman)

Sh. Deepak Mittal
(Jt. Managing Director)

Sh. A.S. Mittal
(Managing Director)

**Group companies**

- International Tractors LTD
- Sonalika Agriculture Industries
- Sonalika Capital Ltd.
- Punjab Agriculture Industries
- Casting Corporation of India

## Philosophy and Goal

The credit for the distinctive position earned by the company goes to the great visionary and soft-spoken Chairman Shri L.D.MITTAL assisted by Managing Director Shri. A.S. MITTAL and Shri Deepak Mittal Joint Managing Director. The Company in the years to come is destined to scale still greater heights. The dedicated team of workers and engineers are lending their full help to make Sonalika International the No.1 in the entire country, which is its ultimate goal. According to Shri Mittal, this phenomenal growth is the result of hard work coupled with dedication at all levels. On the top of it, company has never compromised on quality. This is precisely the *secret of success* of the company. Shri Mittal further states "We have been after a class technology so that Indian farmers get the best value for their hard earned money."

## Quality and IT

The Hoshiarpur plant of the company has been given a complete face- lift with all in house facilities backed by computerized and automatic machines and some of them are prized possession. The world-class systems, standards, R& D and quality controls are an asset to International Tractors Ltd., which has been awarded

## Markets Reach

After having done exceedingly well in the domestic market the tractors are finding their way to global markets also. Consignments to Sri Lanka, France, Bangladesh, Nepal and African Countries are being despatched regularly. Shipment to United States and Australian markets are at the final stage.

**Distribution Setup**

The company believes in selling and excelling true to its business principles and providing service after sales to create further confidence in the customers. The company has more than 600 dealers having servicing facilities and beautiful showrooms.

**After sale service...Building up of relation**

Our Engineers/Marketing's top officials are regularly contacting the Sonalika Tractor users by visiting their villages. As per feed back available the sonalika Tractor owners were surprised to see a Tractor representative visiting their place. This proves amply that visits of Sonalika officials have created a confidence in the farmers and they in turn have wished the company a great success which in fact is helping the farming community to increase their field-yields through farm implements and a complete and perfect Tractor. These are only a few of the 100 of stories, which are pouring in offices of the Sonalika Dealers. Similar exercises to visit the clients at their home place and to enquire about the health of the tractors and exchange pleasantries have been held in other parts of the country. This process is on to build a complete rapport with the farmers.

Apart from this, the company has opened its own servicing centres to augment process of giving efficient service to the customers at the nearest points. The mechanics of the dealers are being given training at their work place and at Hoshiarpur plant in a phased manner so that they familiarize with the new tractors and repairing and servicing is done more efficiently and scientifically. There is a quick response to the servicing complaints. The review of the servicing complaints / suggestions is daily done at company's Hoshiarpur Plant between 4 to 5 PM under the Chairmanship of Joint M.D. The servicing complaints if any are taken up and remedial action is taken wherever necessary.

**Product Profile**

Sonalika has already created a dent in the tractor industry by capturing the hearts of the farmers all over-India by producing and marketing quality tractor for the use of small and big farmers. The number of models has reached *12 ranging* from *25 HP to 60.HP*. Sonalika has already been certified as *ISO 9001 & ISO 14001* company. Sonalika Tractors with excellent pulling power, superb design and low consumption of fuel have proved their superiority over others.

**Performance**
**Growth in Tractor Sales (Nos.)**

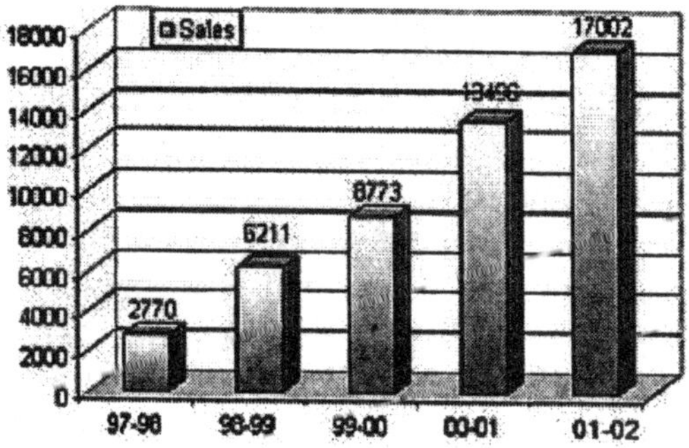

**Group Turnover**

**Group Turnover as on 2002 are as under:**

| | 1996-97 | 1997-98 | 1998-99 | 1999-00 | 2000-01 | 2001-02 |
|---|---|---|---|---|---|---|
| Tractors (Nos.) | 396 | 2770 | 6211 | 8773 | 13496 | 17002 |
| Agriculture Machinery (Nos.) | 5000 | 7500 | 12000 | 18000 | 24000 | 32000 |

**Achievements and Awards**

- Joint Venture with Renault Agriculture of France
- Sonalika awarded ISO 9001 and ISO 14001 in recognition of quality and standards. International Tractors Ltd. is the 2nd such company in India, which has received this certification. The scope of registration covers design, development, production and installation. The registration is a quality mark. Sonalika has also been certified as ISO 14001 which is another golden feather in Company's Cap and another stamp of quality.
- First Indian Tractor Engine (750 III) Conforming to Euro II Norms In recognition of Services rendered In Tractor Industry
- Pride of Country awarded to Sh. L.D. Mittal, Chairman
- Gold Medal for excellent quality in production of tractors was given to Sh A.S. Mittal Managing Director Sonalika International
- Udyog Bhushan Awarded to Sh. Deepak Mittal JMD
- International Tractors Limited, the rapidly growing Tractor Company, has been awarded the ITID Quality Excellence Award. This award has been instituted by the institute Of Trade and Industrial Development.

- CMERI Govt. of India Transfers Design and Technology to Sonalika

**Moment of Pride**

- Prime Minster Refers to Sonalika Tractor in Diamond Jubilee Celebrations of CSIR, Govt. of India
- Sonalika Tractors Lauded by European Farmers in SIMA Fair-France
- Ultra Modern Plant Inaugurated by Chief Minister of Punjab The Chief Minister of Punjab inaugurated the Ultra Modern Plant of the company at Hoshiarpur. Some of the machinery fitted in the plant is the prized possession of the International Tractors Ltd, which other tractor companies do not have.
- International Tractors Ltd. with Sonalika International Brand name shot into limelight once again when it signed MOU with Renault Agriculture France in an impressive ceremony on 30th April 1999.
- Sonalika joins hands with world renowned Renault Agriculture of France. Sonalika International has collaborated with world-renowned automobile giants Renault Agriculture France (with annual turn over of US $ 34 billions). The joint venture is three pronged, financial, technical and lastly joint marketing. A global marketing company has come into existence with head - quarters at Mauritius, which will be responsible for global marketing of Sonalika Tractors. This joint venture will usher in an era of technological advancements into Sonalika Tractors when world class technology will be transferred into Tractors being manufactured in our plant by Renault Agriculture, France. This collaboration will also help in earning much needed foreign exchange for India. The senior engineers of Renault Agriculture,

France, are working round the clock in Hoshiarpur Plant of the company and giving effective and efficient supervision to improve quality and technological innovations of our Products.

| **Snap Shots** |
|---|
| **Name of the company**<br>International Tractors Ltd. Hoshiarpur<br>**Year of establishment**<br>1995 (tractor wing)<br>**Located at:**<br>Jalandhar Road, Hoshiarpur<br>**Main products**<br>Tractor<br>**Total turnover**<br>Tractors (Nos)17002<br>Agriculture machinery (Nos) 32000<br>**Quality certification**<br>• ISO 9001<br>• ISO 14001<br>• First Indian Tractor Engine (750 III) Conforming to Euro II Norms<br>**Flagship company**<br>International Tractors Ltd. Hoshiarpur<br>**Main domestic market**<br>Whole of-market<br>**Foreign market:** Sri Lanka, France, Bangladesh, Nepal, African Countries |

## Leader Valves (Machinery Parts)

**Incorporation and Integration**

Leader Valves Limited is a leading manufacturer of Valves & Boiler Mountings in India producing more than 8,00,000 valves per annum. The company was setup about five decades ago when India was on the threshold of industrial revolution and there was no good valve manufacturer in the country. It has over the years built up an excellent track record of following the policy of customer satisfaction. It has also obtained ISO- 9001: 94 certifications from Lloyds Register of Quality Assurance and the company is on the approved list of main valve Consumers & Consultants of the country. The company has API Spec. Q1 and API 6D monogram for Oil and Petro Pipelines.

**Profile of company**

**Year of Establishment**

1950

**Management**

The company is managed by an efficient Board of Directors & Well-Qualified professionals.

**Aim**

The company aim is to give long term commitment to customers, working in close co-operation, ensuring Total Quality & reliability through continuous product Development / Improvement Programmes.

**Nature of Company**: Limited Co.

**Area of the Factory**

Total Area: - 53576 Sq. Mt.

Covered Area: - 20290 Sq. Mt.
**Electricity Load Sanctioned**: - 3425 KW
**Employee Strength:** 1200 dedicated & motivated people are working round the clock to produce best Quality Valves for the Industry. The details of the employees are as under:
Engineering Staff = 85
Departmental break up as follows:

- Marketing & Sales
- Design & Development
- Production Planning & Execution
- Calibration
- Materials Management
- Quality Assurance
- Ferrous Foundry
- Non Ferrous Foundry
- Servicing
- Special process including Heat Treatment & Welding
- Electrical & Mechanical Maintenance.

Administrative Staff = 103
Department break-up as follows: -

- Finance
- EDP
- HRD
- Shipping
- Environment & Safety
- Security
- Stores
- Library

**Work Force**
Total Strength = 1012
Skilled = 700
Semi-skilled = 156

Unskilled = 156

**Annual Turnover**

At present the plant is working at 60 % of its installed capacity due to sluggish market conditions.

Turnover for the year 2002-03: 430 millions

**Casting Capacity**

The castings are produced in The company own foundries, which are equipped with latest technology and modern laboratories. The company Non-ferrous foundry is having two Induction furnaces of 1000 Kg. & 750 kg. capacity respectively & The company can melt around 500 Tons copper alloy castings per month per shift basis. The nonferrous castings are produced by shell moulding process. The company ferrous foundry is equipped with one Ton Induction furnace with two Crucibles and ARPA 1300 moulding machine along with Mechanized Sand Plant. With the ongoing modernization program, the output of the Ferrous foundry will increase to 3000 tons per annum of Radiographic Quality Steel and alloy steel castings.

**Forge Shop**

The company forge shop is equipped with "Rovetta Isgec" 350 ton capacity forging press for making brass forgings & 300 ton extrusion press besides other small capacity hammers & induction heaters/ furnaces. There is also available a 1000 kg. Friction Drop Forging hammers for producing forgings for value up to 50 NB.

**Workshops**

Work shops have more than 400 machines including SPM's and CNC Machines capable of carrying out all types of Precise machining operations. The company have installed state of art CNC machines such as Juaristi CNC horizontal machining centre for machining gate, Globe & Check Valves up to 36inch, Praga Mitsibushi CNC Horizontal Centre Model MPA – H50A for machining valves up to 14inch, and CNC SPM to machine Butterfly valves. Recently The company had installed two CNC-1) Hessap Make Vertical Turning Machine & two Maxmuller Make Horizontal Turning Machine.

**Quality Assurance**

The company maintain strict control on quality in all stages of production right from raw material to shipment. The company have in-house Quality control Lab. Which is equipped with UTM, SPECTRO analyzer, Impact testing machine, Hardness testing machine. The company have in house facility of all NDT equipments such as Radiography, UT, MPI & DP. Added to this Qualified level II professional who carry out NDT operations. The company have facility for Radiography of castings, Die penetration and magnetic particle inspection of material. In house Spectrometer for physical analysis & specialized tests are furnished on demand. The company 10 Q.A. Personnel's are trained and qualified in accordance to SNT-TC-IA for carrying out non destructive examination of jobs. Company have its own Standard Room for calibration of measuring Instruments, Gauges & temperature Recorders etc.

**Continual Improvement Programme through R&D and HRD**

Leader being an ISO 9001 company, all its designs/products are validated for specified service by using In-house testing facilities or by using facilities at recognized test houses. The product development/Improvement is done under the supervision of highly experienced & qualified engineers.

LEADER is committed to its Employee Development program by imparting technical training on a regular basis to ensure that The company staff is capable of rendering best possible support to The company Customers at any time. The company 6 officials have successfully completed the course of Lead Auditors of Quality Management System to ISO 9000. The company has successfully tested its products for Pull test as per API 591.

**Product Range**

The company are able to offer complete range of valves as well as being able to develop special valves for critical applications. The company Product range includes:-

- Ferrous/Non-Ferrous, Gate/Sluice/ Globe/Check /Reflux Valves/Butterfly Valves/Ball Valves/Plug Valves & Expansion joints etc; from 6mm to 900mm in pressure Rating Class-125 to 2500. The company also manufacture "FIRE-SAFE" Gate, Globe, Check & Ball Valves.
- Boiler Mountings i.e. Pilot Operated Pressure Reducing Valves, Safety Valves Single/Double Post Safety Valves/Steam Stop Valves, Injectors, Steam Traps, Relief Valves, Parallel Slide Valves, Non-return Valves etc. in Ferrous/Non-ferrous materials from 15 mm to 200 mm.
- The company specialize in Actuated Gate, Globe, Butterfly & Ball valves.
- Marine Valves
- Special purpose Valves to meet specific requirements of the Customers.

**Special Testing Facilities**

- Vaccum Testing Facility
- Helium Testing Facility
- Cryogenic Test Rig & Testing Facility
- Fire Safe Test Rig & Testing Facility
- Endurance Test
- Pull Test as per API 591

**Sales Strategy**

A well defined distribution and sales network through agents and regular personnel contacts by The company qualified, experienced professional's directly with custommers. The company have very wide network of sales not only with all the major centres in country, but with smaller towns as well. The company are spread allover India through the network of the company about 270 dealers. The company have branch offices at Mumbai, Delhi, Bhubaneshwar, Cochin, Coimbtore & Chennai. Baroda office is in the offing.

**They are proud of their Patronage**

**National**

- Engineers India Ltd. (EIL)
- Asea Brown Boeri
- Indian Oil Corporation Ltd. (IOCL)
- National Mineral Development Corp. Ltd.
- Indian Petrochemicals Ltd.
- Gas Authority of India Ltd.
- Bongaigaon Refinery & Petrochemicals Ltd.
- Oil & Natural Gas Corporation Ltd.
- National Thermal Power Corporation Ltd.
- I A.E.C. Boilers

- Bharat Heavy Electrical Ltd.
- J.N Marshall Ltd.
- Garden Reach Shipbuilders & Engrs. Ltd.
- Ranbaxy laboratories Ltd.
- Mazagon Dock Ltd.
- Batala CO-OP. Sugar Mills Ltd.
- Fert. Corp. of India Ltd.
- TATA Iron & Steel Company Ltd.
- National Fertilizer Ltd.
- Larsen & Tubro Ltd.
- Rashtriya Chem. & Fert. Ltd.
- MECON, Ranchi
- Hindustan Petroleum Corp. Ltd.
- Techno Electric & Engg.
- Reliance Petroleum Ltd – Jamnagar
- Spic-Je! Chennai
- Technical Development Committee
- Tata Projects Ltd.
- LLOYD'S Redister Industrial Services (I) Ltd.
- TATA Consulting Engineers
- DGS & D
- Bureau Veritas Industrial Services (I) Ltd.
- Engineering Projects India Ltd.
- Nuclear Power Corp. of India Ltd.
- Project & Development India Ltd.
- Indian Register of Shipping
- MN. Dastur & Company Ltd
- BAX Counsel Inspection Bureau & Many Others
- Bharat Heavy Plate & Vessel Ltd.
- State Electricity Boards & Many Others.
- UHDE India ltd.

- Directorate of Q.A. (Warship projects)
- FEDO
- Mumbai Municipal Corporation.

**International**

- Malbranque, France
- Colonial Hardware, Colombo, Sri Lanka
- Mikon Int. USA
- Khulna News Print, Bangladesh
- Al-Bassam, UAE
- Supply Solution, Germany
- Kuwait National petroleum Co.
- Bechtel International
- Saudi Transformers, Damman
- Daelim, Korea
- T & I Singapore
- Secit s.p.a. - Italy
- G.E. International U.K.
- Trade Promotion Centre, Cairo, Egypt
- Saudi Transformers Co. Ltd., Saudi Arabia
- Hyundai, Korea
- Ansaldo Energia s.p.a, Italy
- Technip s.p.a. - Italy
- Yamato Special Steel Co. Ltd, Japan
- Elitebliss Ltd. – Keigley, U.K.
- Valsteam Engineering SA, Portugal
- Scana Godtkaer, Denmark
- Inter Power Ltd. Malta
- International Agency, Malta

| Snapshots |
|---|
| **Name of the Company**<br>Leader Valves Limited<br>**Year of Establishment**<br>1950<br>**Located at:**<br>Jalandhar City<br>**Main products:**<br>Ferrous/Non-Ferrous<br>Gate/Sluice/Globe/Check/Reflux<br>Valves/Butterfly<br>Valves/Ball<br>Valves/Plug<br>Valves & Expansion joints<br>"FIRE-SAFE"<br>Check & Ball<br>Boiler Mountings<br>Actuated Gate<br>Butterfly & Ball valves<br>Marine Valves<br>**Total turnover**<br>Rs. 43 crore<br>**Quality certification**<br>ISO- 9001: 94 certifications from Lloyds Register of Quality Assurance<br>The company has API Spec. Q1 and API 6D monogram for Oil and Petro Pipelines.<br>**Flagship company**<br>Leader Valves Limited<br>**Main domestic market**<br>Through out India<br>**Foreign market:** France, Sri Lanka, USA, Bangladesh, UAE, Germany, Kuwait, Korea, Singapore, Italy, U.K, Egypt, Saudi Arabia, Japan, Portugal, Denmark, Malta |

## Ranbaxy Laboratories (Pharmaceuticals)

**Incorporation and Integration**

Ranbaxy Laboratories Limited, India's largest pharmaceutical Company, manufactures and markets generics, branded generic pharmaceuticals and active pharmaceutical ingredients. It stands amongst the top ten generic companies worldwide.

The Company's products are sold in over 100 countries with manufacturing operations in 7 countries and a ground presence in 34 countries. It has employed diverse strategies, including exports, alliances, partnerships and acquisitions to gain the flexibility needed for viable and profitable business operations worldwide. The Company was incorporated in 1961 and went public in 1973. For the twelve months ended December 31, 2003, Global Sales at USD 969 Mn (Rs. 45,165 Mn) registered a robust growth of 22%. Overseas markets accounted for 76% of the global sales. USA and Europe contributed over 50% to Global Sales with a combined turnover of USD 500 Mn. With the recent acquisition of RPG (Aventis) SA, Ranbaxy has become the 5th largest generic Company in France and has expanded considerably, its overall presence in Europe.

**Key Persons**

**Mr. Tejendra Khanna**

Mr. Tejendra Khanna was elected Chairman at a meeting of the Board of Directors of Ranbaxy Laboratories Limited held at New Delhi, on July 5, 1999. Mr. Khanna, former Commerce Secretary to the Government of India, and a former Lieutenant Governor of Delhi is widely regarded as an expert in International Trade and Public Administration.

**Portfolio-Current:** Chairman, Ranbaxy Laboratories Ltd.

**Portfolio-Previous**

04-01-1997 to 20-04-1998: Lt Governor and Administrator of the Union Territory of Delhi, the National Capital.

16-07-1993 to 31-12-1996: Commerce Secretary of Govt. of India and Principal Civil Service Coordinator of India's bilateral, regional and multilateral trade relations.

25-05-1992 to 16-07-1993: Food Secretary, Govt. of India, concerned with the development and administration of India's food – security policies.

14-01-1991 to 20-04-1992: Chief Secretary to the Govt. of Punjab. Head of the Civil Services and chief Coordinator of all Government programmes.

17-02-1989 to 14-01-1991: Chief Controller of Imports & Exports, Govt. of India in the Ministry of Commerce:

05-08-1986 to 10-02-1989: Financial Commissioner, Revenue, Govt. of Punjab

07-10-1983 to 05-08-1986: Secretary to Govt. of Punjab, Irrigation, Power & Public Works

07-06-1980 to 01-02-1982: Principal Secretary to Chief Minister, Punjab; Secretary, Science, Technology & Environment; Food Supplies, Labour Employment Secretary. Punjab Govt. Commercial Counsellor, Indian High Commission, Deputy Secretary, Ministry of Commerce, Govt. of India, M.D, Punjab, State Industrial Development Corporation.

01-06-1961: Joined the Indian Administrative Service Life Member of the Indian Institute of Public Administration and the Bharatiya Vidya Bhawan – an organization devoted to the dissemination of Indian cultural and philosophical values.

**Mr D.S. Brar**

He was instrumental in developing the Pharmaceutical exports business of the company in early 80's which later became synonymous with major growth and expansion of company's portfolio. In addition to the International business, he looked after the Animal Healthcare & OTC businesses of the company. In 1986, he took over the Pharma business in India along with Chemical Manufacturing Operations. In early 90's he led the company's expansion into overseas markets creating joint ventures, affiliates and subsidiaries in major countries like China, Russia, U.K., South Africa and the USA. In 1996, he took over as the President of the company and was appointed CEO & Managing Director in1999.

**Portfolio- Current:** CEO and Managing Director, Ranbaxy Laboratories Ltd.

**Other Current Positions**

- Director of the Central Board of Reserve Bank of India (RBI), which is the Central bank of India
- Director on the board of Barista Coffee Company Limited
- Director on the Board of India Trade Promotion Organisation (ITPO)
- Board Member of National Institute of Pharmaceutical Education and Research (NIPER)
- Chairman of Confederation of Indian Industry (CII) National Committee on Drugs and Pharmaceuticals
- Chairman of Federation of Indian Chambers of Commerce and Industry (FICCI) forum on Foreign Direct Investment (FDI)
- Member of Prime Minister's task force on Pharmaceuticals and Knowledge Based Industries
- Member of multi-disciplinary group for creation of knowledge parks in India (set up by the Ministry of Chemicals & Fertilizers

**Company Profile**

**Journey ....**

2003

- Ranbaxy receives The Economic Times Award for Corporate Excellence for 'The Company of the Year,

2002-2003

- Ranbaxy and Glaxo SmithKline Plc (GSK) accelerate their discovery programmes through a global alliance for drug discovery and development. While Ranbaxy will leverage its early product development strengths, Glaxo would use its expertise at late development stage to complete the development process.
- RBx 7796, Ranbaxy's first NCE in the respiratory segment successfully completes Phase I clinical trials and steps into Phase II.
- Ranbaxy files an IND application for RBx 9001, its second NCE for the treatment of Benign Prostatic Hyperplasia (BPH)
- Cipro XR 500mg and 1g, based on the technology developed by Ranbaxy, were launched in USA by Bayer AG.
- Ranbaxy launched the first branded product Sotret (Isotretinoin) for 10mg, 20mg and 40mg capsules in USA.

2002

- Ranbaxy files IND for an Anti-bacterial Oxazolidinone - RBx 7644
- Ranbaxy launched Cefuroxime Axetil post approval from USFDA for 125mg, 250mg, 500mg Tablets, first approval granted to any generic company for this product
- Ranbaxy receives permission from DCGI to conduct Phase-I clinical trials for RBx 7796 (Anti-asthma)

2001

- Ranbaxy took a significant step forward in Vietnam by initiating the setting up of a new manufacturing facility with an investment of US $ 10 million.
- Ranbaxy achieved a turnover of US $ 600 million for the year 2001 and moved closer to achieving the target of 1 billion dollar by 2004.
- Ranbaxy USA crosses sales of US $ 100 million, fastest growing company in the US.

2000

- Ranbaxy files IND Application for Asthma Molecule RBx-7796 after successful completion of pre-clinical studies.
- Ranbaxy acquires Bayer's Generics business (trading under the name of Basics) in Germany.
- Ranbaxy forays into Brazil, the largest pharmaceutical market in South America and achieves global sales of US $ 2.5 million in this market.

1999

- DCGI grants approval to conduct Phase I Clinical Trials for RBx2258, and the trials commence from June 10, 1999.
- Bayer AG, Germany and Ranbaxy sign an agreement where Bayer obtains exclusive development and worldwide marketing rights to an oral once daily formulation of Ciprofloxacin, originally developed by Ranbaxy.

1998

- Ranbaxy enters USA, world's largest pharmaceuticals market, with products under its own name.
- Ranbaxy filed its first Investigational New Drug (IND) application with the Drugs Controller General of India (DCGI) for approvals to conduct Phase I Clinical Trials.

1997

- Ranbaxy Laboratories Limited crosses a sales turnover of Rs. 10,000 million, with its exports reaching an all time high of Rs. 5,000 million.

1995

- Acquisition of Ohm Laboratories, a manufacturing facility in the US. Inauguration of FDA approved, state-of the art new manufacturing wing, at Ranbaxy's US subsidiary Ohm Laboratories Inc.

1994

- The new Research Centre at Gurgaon, (near Delhi), becomes fully operational.
- Established Regional Headquarters in London (UK) and Raleigh (USA).
- The Fermentation pilot plant at Paonta Sahib is commissioned.
- Ranbaxy's GDR listed in Luxembourgh Stock Exchange.

1993

- Company enters into an agreement to setup a Joint Venture in China Ranbaxy (Guangzhou China) Limited.
- Ranbaxy enunciates it's corporate mission 'to become a Research based International Pharmaceutical Company.

1992

- Company enters into an agreement with Eli Lilly & Co of USA for setting up a Joint Venture in India to market select Lilly products.

1991

- New state-of-the-art facility for Cephalosporins set up at Mohali
- US patent granted for Cephalosporins.

1990

- Ranbaxy is granted US patent for Doxycyline

1988

- Ranbaxy's Toansa plant gets US FDA approval.

1987

- Production start-up at the modern APIs plant at Toansa (Punjab), makes Ranbaxy the country's largest manufacturer of antibiotics/ antibacterials.

1985

- Ranbaxy Research Foundation is established.
- Stancare, Ranbaxy's second pharmaceutical marketing division, starts functioning.

1983

- A modern dosage forms facility at Dewas (MP) in India goes on stream.

1977

- Ranbaxy's first joint venture in Lagos (Nigeria) is setup.

1973

- Ranbaxy goes Public.
- A multipurpose chemical plant is setup for the manufacture of APIs at Mohali in India.

1961

- Company Incorporated

**Vision Garuda**

At Ranbaxy, ONE is not merely a word, but a sacrosanct work philosophy. On one hand, it denotes individualism and on the other, it represents oneness, teamwork, unity... with respect for each individual. And the mission to become a Research-based International Pharmaceutical Company is driven by a strong emphasis on employee empowerment at every level. Encouraging entrepreneurship, practising delegation, rewarding commitment and creating opportunities for every single team member... a family of over 8000 individuals with a collective passion for exploring new frontiers of knowledge and success.

This highly empowered ONE team is set out to traverse the most challenging path towards realising the Vision for 2012 – Vision GARUDA... the aspiration to achieve significant business in proprietary products by 2012, with a strong presence in advanced markets. This team stands committed to Galvanise Aspirations for Ranbaxy's Unceasing Growth in the Decade Ahead by Harnessing the power of ONE

**Vision as per Mr. D.S. Brar**

"There is a renewed sense of excitement and pride across Ranbaxy, as we reflect upon the year gone by. We are within striking distance of the Billion-dollar Vision we had set for ourselves for 2004. The business events of each passing year, and the last was no exception, seem to amplify our chances of realising our vision. As we move sure-footed, towards becoming a Research-based International Pharmaceutical Company, we smell the compelling call of success.

A decade ago we dared to dream of a Ranbaxy that would become a Research-based Pharmaceutical Company. Emboldened by success and seasoned by our journey from the developing markets to an international milieu, we are setting the score for our next symphony. We believe that in the coming decade, we will be a speciality pharmaceutical company that will see a stronger presence in the advanced markets. Proprietary products will give impetus to future growth, while generics would keep the rhythm. Even as we savour the performance of another successful year, excitement and anticipation punctuate our preparation for the future - identifying new competencies we need to build, and gaps we need to bridge, to ensure another winning score."

**Board of Directors**

At the helm of the entire operations is the experience and able direction of the people who make it all happen. Ranbaxy acknowledges their inspiring stewardship and indefatigable work.

Mr. Tejendra Khanna
Mr. D.S. Brar
Mr. V.K. Kaul
Dr. Brian Tempest
Mr. Malvinder Mohan Singh
Dr. P. S. Joshi
Mr. Surendera Daulet Singh
Mr. Harpal Singh
Mr. J. W. Balani
Mr. N. Kampani
Mr. V. Bharat Ram
Mr.Vivek Mehra
Mr Gurucharan Das

**Allied Business**

- Animal Health
- Ranbaxy Fine Chemical Limited
- Ranbaxy Diagnostics

**Ranbaxy Fine Chemical Ltd**

With a **mission** "To become an efficient and reliable supply partner of high purity fine chemicals for Manufacturing Processes, Quality Assurance and Research & Development" and an ISO-9002 Certification, Ranbaxy Fine Chemicals has been doing pioneering work in its field.

**Committed to Customers**

"Committed to Customers" has become a familiar phrase with us. It is not only supplying products which meet customers' specifications but also high standard of production, delivery and customer service. Our endeavour at Ranbaxy Fine Chemicals Limited is to critically monitor total cycle time from an order entry to on-site delivery for ensuring lasting partnership with our customers. We at Ranbaxy Fine Chemicals Limited take pride in living up to this challenge. In order to meet your diverse needs we offer chemicals in various grades of quality to suite the respective fields of application.

**Quality Assurance**

Quality assurance have long been a tradition with Ranbaxy. Quality is priority in all activities carried out in our company. With the feedback given to our field staff who are in constant touch with you, you have helped us in achieving increased production volumes with continuous decline in Quality Complaints. Our Quality Manual is our most important document.

**Laboratory Chemical Data System**

Analytical data is on-line available on electronic media enabling an uninterrupted, re-traceability of Product History. Batch specific analytical data is available with our Marketing offices in the form of Certificate of Analysis (COA). Standard Test Procedures are shared with Customers on request.

**Analytical Capabilities:** We constantly upgrade our Analytical capabilities, by enhancing the skills of our chemists through training and adding sophisticated world class instruments to ensure the reproducibility of our results.

We have Atomic Absorption Spectrophotometer with graphite furnace and VGA for ppb level analysis of metallic impurities. FTIR for identification of our new range of Products, Double beam UV-visible Spectrophotometer for HPLC grade solvents are some of our sophisticated instruments. Our GC analysis is done on capillary columns for superior resolution.

**Statistical Quality Control:** Annual Analytical Trends help us in continuously upgrading our Specifications. On request we supply statistical trends for past supplies for specific product.

**Technical Services Group:** All our product development and manufacturing services are supported by a Technical Services Group comprising of Scientists, Engineers and Analytical Chemists. The team works in close coordination with customers to ensure availability of any kind of information related to product application, specification and safety. Customized manufacturing and product enhancement, according to the need and requirement of the customers being their other areas of contribution.

**Safety: Prime Concern:** Chemicals should be handled by Qualified individuals familiar with their potential hazards. Safety Data Sheets are available for all products in our range MSDS data bank is just a call away.

**Ranbaxy's Animal Health division**

Strives to improve the productivity of poultry and livestock farmers and the joy pets bring to their owners, by offering them world-class products to maintain their animals in a state of excellent health! It serves veterinarians in India, who are guardians of animal health....

Ranbaxy Animal Health markets a comprehensive **product line** for Poultry, Livestock and Companion Animals, including:

- Pharmaceuticals for anti-infective and other therapy.
- Feed additives for animal feed.
- Poultry Vaccines for disease prevention.
- Parasiticides for pets and livestock.

Ranbaxy Animal Health is a **portfolio** of more than 100 poultry, livestock and companion-animal products directly to veterinarians poultry and livestock farmers and distributors. Many of these are innovative products lead them to pet categories.

**Quality Control**

Its products are manufactured under strict quality control procedures in Good Manufacturing Practices certified production facilities, using modern scientific tools and techniques.

**All India Reach**

The Animal Health division has 20 Primary Distribution locations over 400 stockists, 2000 retailers, and over 170 technically qualified and highly trained marketing and sales personnel. Our team is in touch with over 200 direct accounts, including large feed mills, dairy co-operatives and poultry breeding farms; the Ranbaxy field force covers 15000 prescribers and consultants every months.

**Organization**

The Division has three Business Units

- Poultry
- Livestock
- Pets

**Market Success**

The Animal Health Divisions on the fast track. Growing at double the industry rate. The Division has in the last five years leap-frogged from 20th to the 4th position in sales revenue. With the No. 1 slot in Poultry Health products.

**Commitment towards Total Animal Healthcare**

Ranbaxy is committed to total animal healthcare. That's why the Division is broadening its product portfolio by sourcing and manufacturing, diagnostics, biological and additives plus. It is exploring traditional systems of medicines like plant-based drugs for the growth and productivity booster segments.

What's more Ranbaxy is researching new generation and Biotechnology based products; and specializing in sunrise areas like petcare, aqua that will further consolidate its leadership position in the future.

**Ranbaxy Diagnostics**

Ranbaxy Diagnostics is part of Allied Business operations of the company. The division initiated its operations in 1987 and is a major player in the diagnostics market with a market share of 7 percent plus. The sales showed a growth of 14 percent in year 2001 against the market growth of 10 percent . The division is amongst the top 5 companies in the diagnostics industry in India.

**Mission**

To provide complete customer satisfaction through products offering

- Accuracy
- Quality
- Reliability backed by efficient service

The division offers a wide range of products, which coupled with high technical skills of marketing team and an efficient distribution chain have given it a competitive advantage in the market. Keeping in focus the importance of service, the division continuously strives to meet the customer needs and requirements. The well qualified and trained marketing team of about 90 persons ensure that customer queries are addressed in the shortest possible time. Ranbaxy diagnostics provides complete solution to the needs of clinical laboratories and blood banks is fast emerging as a one stop destination.

**Customer**

The diagnostics business caters to about 4500 customers all over the country. The customer base which includes certain leading hospitals, laboratories and blood banks throughout the country.

**List of Customers includes:**

- Bombay Hospital, Mumbai
- Apollo Hospitals, Chennai and Hyderabad
- All India Institute of Medical Sciences, N. Delhi
- St. John's Hospital, Bangalore
- SRL Ranbaxy, Mumbai
- Dr. Lal's Laboratory, N. Delhi
- Christian Medical College, Ludhiana
- AMRI Apollo, Kolkata
- Sri Chitra Trinamool, Trivandrum

**Distribution**

With a strong focus on prompt customer service, the division distributes its products either directly or through 150 stockists located in various regions throughout the country.

One of the major highlights of the system is that the product are distributed under an efficient cold chain. The cold chain is available both at branch level (15 locations) and at stockists' premises where walk-in freezers are available assuring that the products are maintained at the desired temperature.

**Quality Assurance**

The division is committed to marketing products that conform to strict quality specifications. In its fully equipped quality assurance laboratory, the products are subject to stringent quality control. To ensure performance of products at customer place, every single batch of products is subject to accelerated stability studies prior to release for sale. This is done to ensure the stability and performance of reagents under extremes of temperature and humidity. Our manufacturing facilities are approved by Drugs Controller General of India, Ministry of Health and State Drugs Control Authority, New Delhi.

**Portfolio of affiliates/JVs of Ranbaxy**

The Company has an expanding international portfolio of affiliates, joint ventures and representative offices across the globe with JV's/ subsidiaries in USA, UK, Germany, France, Spain, Ireland, Netherlands, India, China, Brazil, South Africa, Japan etc.

Ranbaxy operates in India through its marketing arms such as:

- Pharma
- Stancare
- Croslands
- Rexcel
- Solus

- Rextar
- Blue R
- Ranbaxy CV
- Super Speciality

**Achievements and Rewards**

While Ranbaxy aggressively pursues the internationalisation of its business, the growth strategy equally focuses on enhancing market share in India. The Company has a strong Brand marketing team and distribution network in India. It is ranked at No.6 in BT* 500 and was conferred with The Economic Times Corporate Excellence Award for 'The Company of the Year' 2002-03. Four of its brands rank among the top 25 products marketed in India.

Ranbaxy is ranked No 7 by Far Eastern Economic Review, in it annual review of leading companies of Asia.

**Research and Development**

The Company has established state-of-the-art multi-disciplinary R&D facilities at Gurgaon (near New Delhi), India. Emphasis on NCEs (New Chemical Entities) for long term value building and on NDDS (Novel Drug Delivery Systems) in the medium term are the key anchors of future growth.

Ranbaxy is accelerating its initiatives in NDDR (New Drug Discovery Research) and NDDS (Novel Drug Delivery Systems). It is one of the largest investor on R&D in the Indian pharmaceutical industry with an R&D spend of approx. 6% of its sales in 2003. Ranbaxy's continued focus on R&D has resulted in several approvals in developed markets and significant progress in NDDR. The Company's major research focus is in the areas of, Urology, Anti-infectives, Respiratory, Anti-inflammatory and Metabolic disorders segments. Its first NCE, RBx 2258, for Benign Prostrate Hyperplasia (BPH), has been licensed to Schwarz Pharma AG of Germany to develop, market and distribute the product in USA, Japan and Europe, while the Company has retained the rights for all other markets. RBx 2258 is presently in Phase II clinical trials in India. Ranbaxy's Anti-asthma molecule, RBx 7796, is also undergoing Phase II clinical trials. Besides these, the Company has other molecules in its NCE pipeline, which are at different stages of drug discovery and development.

To accelerate its research programme, Ranbaxy has joined hands with GlaxoSmithKline Plc for a global alliance in the area of drug discovery and development. Ranbaxy's collaborative research initiative with Medicines for Malaria Venture, Geneva, to develop a new drug for Malaria, reflects its commitment to eradicate such diseases from the world. The Company has also partnered with Clinton Foundation HIV/ AIDS Initiative, to provide HIV/ AIDS drugs at an affordable price to patients in Africa & Caribbean region.

Ranbaxy's foray into NDDS has led to several proprietary know-how "platform technologies" resulting in many products under developmental/commercial stages. Its first NDDS innovation once -a -day Ciprofloxacin has been licensed to Bayer AG, the originator for select markets. Ranbaxy's NDDS focus will be in developing prescription products and value added dosage forms and expand its platform technologies

**R & D – Achievements**

Ranbaxy R&D team of talented research scientists is continuously striving to upgrade its capabilities and realise the company's mission of becoming "Research based international pharmaceutical company.

**Products Launched**

| No. | Product | Molecule | Countries |
|---|---|---|---|
| 1 | Keflor MR | Cefaclor | India, SA, Poland, Hungary, Singapore, Malaysia(Total 18 countries) |
| 2 | Sporidex AF | Cephalexin | India, USA, SA |
| 3 | Coriem XL | Diltiazem Hcl | India, Malaysia, Myanmar |
| 4 | Difnal DR | Diclofenac Sod. | Malaysia, Singapore |
| 5 | Difnal OD | Diclofenac Sod. | Malaysia, Singapore |
| 6 | Roletra D | Loratadine Pseudoephedrine | India |
| 7 | Altiva D | Fexofenadine Pseudoephedrine | India |
| 8 | Romesec DR | Omeprazole | Malaysia, Singapore |
| 9 | Cifran OD | Ciprofloxacin | India; Licensed to Bayer AG for further development |
| 10 | Zanocin OD | Ofloxacin | India |
| 11 | Riomet OD | Metformin | India |

**Pharma Research:** Over 40 products launched in India in 2002.

**Chemical Research:** Development activity undertaken for synthesis of 24 APIs in 2002,process know-how developed & commercialised for 12 APIs .

**IDRA:** IDRA achieved filing of 980 new registrations across 102 countries in 2002. Ranbaxy also received regulatory approvals for 455 products across 74 countries.

**Manufacturing Facilities**

An organisation's capabilities and intent are strongly reflected in the product it manufactures. In other words, the manufacturing competencies and facilities echo truly, the R&D extent and the ability to implement it for the best of the market it targets.

Ranbaxy's manufacturing strengths have established it as a producer of world-class generics, branded generics and a major supplier of its range of Active Pharmaceutical Ingredients.

Ranbaxy has world-class manufacturing facilities in seven countries namely China, Ireland, India, Malaysia, Nigeria, USA and Vietnam. Its overseas facilities are designed to cater to the requirements of the local regulatory bodies of that country while the Indian facilities meet the requirements of all International Regulatory Agencies. Some of the agencies such as MCA-UK, MCC-South Africa, FDA-USA and TGA-Australia, have audited and approved Ranbaxy's manufacturing facilities for the compliance with international Good Manufacturing Practices and have registered its products for safety, quality and efficacy.

**Products**

Using the finest R&D and Manufacturing facilities, Ranbaxy Laboratories Limited manufacture and markets generic pharmaceuticals, value added generic pharmaceuticals, branded generics, active Pharmaceuticals (API) and intermediates.

The Company remain focused on ascending the value chain in the marketing of pharmaceutical substances and is determined to bring in increased revenues from dosage forms sales.

Ranbaxy's drive for internationalisation is guided by a well planned brand strategy. The Company having in its basket over 25 global brands which will strengthen Company's position in international arena.

**Active Pharmaceutical Ingredients (API) Facilities**

Ranbaxy's API business over the years has grown consistently. In a macro environment of extra ordinary competition and challenges, the API division has moved from strength to strength. It supplies "World Class API's" to leading generic companies in more than 50 countries, which give the API business a truly global complexion. The business today contributes 12% of the Global Sales of the Company. The focus being on the regulated markets with Europe and USA being the mainstay of this business. Supplementing the sales achieved in these territories is the excellent performance in China, selected markets of Asia, Far East and Latin America.

The API division has in its portfolio over 50 products covering a wide therapeutic range such as Cardio-vasculars, Anti-infectives, Anti-ulcerants, Anti-diabetics, Anti-depressants, Anti-virals and others.

The objective of this business is to provide total solutions to the customer with regard to the API starting from samples and trial quantities, right up to regulatory assistance required for registration and regulatory compliance.

**Ranbaxy's API division is an ideal partner for APIs due to its**

- GMP Culture
- FDA/MCA approved plants
- Good quality

· Regulatory and R&D support
· Robust Pipeline
· Good Therapeutic width
· Differentiated products providing early market entries
· IP related strengths- Well Grounded Patent Opinion
· Pre-emptive Capacity Planning
· Commitment through Long term Contracts
· Speed to Market
· Customer Orientation

**Dosage Forms Facility**

Ranbaxy produces and markets high quality generics, valued-added generics and branded generics across the globe.

These are available at:
Dewas, India
Paonta Sahib, India
New Delhi, India
Jejuri, India
Goa, India
Lagos, Nigeria
Malaysia
NJ, USA
Guangzhou, China
Ireland

**Market in India**

In India, Ranbaxy is the largest pharmaceutical Company by sales with a domestic market share of 4.83%(July 2003 MAT) and is ranked third on the retail market. It prides itself for a strong Brand marketing team with 3 brands amongst Top 25 today while Cifran & Sporidex features among Top 10 brands of the industry.

During the year 2002, the Company registered a sales growth of 8.2%. The Company re-organised its marketing and sales teams to reflect better alignment of products/ field deployment with the threpeautic area concept to bring synergies in marketing effort . The contribution to the Company's sales from the chronic segment was 33% and from the anti-infectives category was 41%. During the year Ranbaxy launched 29 new products/line extensions of which 20 comprised the chronic segment including 3 Anti-HIV products. Ranbaxy outperformed the market in the areas of Anti-infectives, Gastrointestinal and Dermatological segments (Source : ORG MAT June 03).

The region is represented in India by its marketing arms-Pharma, Stancare, Croslands, Solus, Rexcel, Rextar, Blue R, Ranbaxy CV and Super Speciality.

**Foreign Markets**

**Middle East, Sri Lanka**

Ranbaxy is the only Indian Company to have made significant forays into the Middle East region over the years. It has full-fledged marketing operations in UAE, Bahrain and Oman.

The year 2002 saw the region achieve a robust growth of 44% over the previous year. The secondary sales in the retail segment recorded a growth of 31%, outperforming the market (10.6%).

UAE, the single largest market in the Middle East, grew by 61% over the previous year. Two new products, Cifran and Enhancin Suspension, launched in November 2002, were favourably accepted.

In Oman, Ranbaxy continued to maintain its leadership position in the private market for the third successive year. Despite a declining market, secondary sales grew by 24%.

Ranbaxy was the first Indian Company to be registered in Saudi Arabia. Ranbaxy also became the first Indian company to be registered in Kuwait with the first shipment being dispatched in November 2002.

Ranbaxy attained the status of being the first Indian pharmaceutical company to be recognised by the Ministry of Health, Lebanon.

With the business objective of 'Achieving Sustainable Profitable Growth', many new initiatives were taken - the sales force was further strengthened to expedite entry into new markets and support the overall service distribution network.

In Sri Lanka, Ranbaxy ranked amongst the top 5 companies in the region, with a sales growth of 40%. Sporidex ranked No.1 in the Antibiotic segment (MS Q4 2002, MAT). The Company entered 3 new segments, Pain Management, Anti-histamines and Anti-diabetes, with the launch of 7 new brands - Cepodem, Altiva, Colcibra, Rofibax, Caverta, Covance and Pioglar.

Ranbaxy believes in multi-agent concept where the company is open to having more than one agent in a particular country to look into different lines of business. As a result Ranbaxy is also looking out for agents in countries where it is already present for exploring new opportunities of business.

Ranbaxy is presently exploring opportunities for inorganic growth through acquisitions and co-marketing alliances in the region. One of our strengths is to foster mutually beneficial relations with the right people to gain the critical 'local' advantage in International markets.

**Other Foreign Markets**

- Europe

- United Kingdom
- Germany
- Poland
- Russia
- France
- CIS
- Lithuania
- Ukraine
- Africa
- South Africa
- Nigeria
- Egypt
- Ivory Coast
- Zimbabwe
- Zambia
- Mauritius

**Beyond Product**

Ranbaxy has been making constant efforts to provide the best in products and services. The realisation of its responsibilities as a pharmaceutical company goes beyond providing the products it manufactures. It endeavours to provide the right opportunities to those who could make contributions in the field keeping issues like **Environment, Safety and Community Healthcare** at the core.

**Environment, Health and Safety**

Behind every business are the essential values and ideologies on which the core edifice of the business grows. At Ranbaxy, these values are intricately woven in the fabric of its work ethics. It does not come as a surprise then that the enthusiasm to provide the best pharmaceutical products and new discovery drugs is finely balanced with the responsibilities towards its immediate physical environment.

At Ranbaxy, regulatory consents, compliance with consent conditions, adequate resources, environment-impact assessment and environment management systems form the five absolutes for achieving corporate objectives defined by the EH&S policy. Environment Impact Assessment Studies are carried out periodically to assess the effect on local environmental conditions effected by the various plants.

In an endeavour to ensure maximum safety, Ranbaxy encourages employee participation in activities organized on various occasions like National Safety Week, etc. To identify potential hazards, all new production processes undergo a thorough scrutiny, before the manufacturing process begins. To conduct in-house hazard studies, the Company has trained a large pool of managerial employees. All manufacturing and R&D locations were subjected to a detailed safety audit and risk assessment exercise, carried out by Tata Risk Management Services Limited during the period 1996-98, and the recommendations made in the audit report have since been implemented.

Ranbaxy takes great pride in its EH&S policies. After all Good Health and Safe Unpolluted Environment are legacies that it would like to hand down to the future generation.

**National Safety Awards for the Year 2001 and 2002**

**Ranbaxy Science Foundation**

Ranbaxy Laboratories Limited incorporated Ranbaxy Research Foundation in 1985 with an implicit mission of giving impetus to research activity and help in reviving India's great scientific tradition. The Foundation instituted Ranbaxy Research Awards to recognize original outstanding contributions in the fields of Medical and Pharmaceutical Sciences. Every year the Foundation invites nominations for 4 awards – 3 Awards for Rs. 1,00,000/- each in the fields of Medical Sciences in Basic. Applied and Clinical Research and 1 Awards of Rs. 1,00,000/- each in the fields of Medical Sciences in Basic. Applied and Clinical Research and 1 Awards of Rs. 1,00,000/- in the field of Pharmaceutical Sciences. So far 62 scientists have been honoured by the Foundation. Ranbaxy Research Foundation was later reconstituted as a separate society as Ranbaxy Science Foundation and registered under the Societies Act in May 1994.

Late Prof. V. Ramalingaswami, was the founder Chairman of the Ranbaxy Science Foundation a non-profit organization. Now RSF is chaired by renowned scientist Dr. Nityanand

**Social Responsibility**

Ranbaxy has a strong element of Corporate Social Responsibility inscribed in its values and its concern for the society extends well beyond its business motives. The company does not view success and achievements in terms of commercial gains only but firmly believes that corporate social responsibility is the key for providing a deep symbiotic relationship that exists between the company and the environment it functions. Over two decades ago, in 1979, in the wake of grim health scenario of India, Ranbaxy realised the urgency to reach out to those who had little or no access even to basic health care and instituted 'Ranbaxy Rural Development Trust'.

The main objective of the programme was to deliver primary health care to the underserved and underprivileged section of the society to achieve positive health for them and thus to contribute to the national objective 'Health For All'. As the scope of the programme and company's commitment grew, in 1994, a professionally managed, non-profit, independent body '*Ranbaxy Community Health Care Society' (RCHS)* was established against the backdrop of full moral and financial support of the company.

**Mission**

To be a premier community based organization in primary health care to achieve positive 'Health for All' in our service areas.

**Values**

- Service to community is fundamental to our work.
- Provide quality services.
- Treat all without discrimination.
- Promote active community participation to achieve our goals.
- Monitor achievements and continually improve.

**Community Participation**

It was recognized that over 70 percent of the deliveries in RCHS service areas were conducted at home by either untrained or improperly trained 'dais'. On one hand, lack of skills was causing many neo-natal deaths while on the other these 'dais' acted as counsellors to pregnant women and enjoyed easy accessibility and acceptability. Thus, as a strategy, two-phase intervention was planned where the RCHS Medical officers were trained to train the 'dais' in the first phase and training of 'dais' from the community was done in the second phase.

RCHS has established community based local groups like health committees, women groups and other interactive groups like "dais", "anganwari" workers, volunteers, adolescents and breast-feeding support group to promote community involvement and self-sustainability.

**Scientific Approach**

RCHS firmly believes in a focused and integrated approach to the basic issues of health care that are elementary and directly responsible for the state of community health in RCHS service areas. With a view to plan future strategies for need based interventions, RCHS regularly monitors and records all vital events such as live births, infant deaths, maternal deaths and abortions etc. For example, the main causes of infant and maternal mortality as identified in RCHS areas are Low Birth Weight, Diarrhoea, Pneumonia, Birth Asphyxia, Hypothermia, Anaemia in pregnancy including obstetrical causes like Sepsis or Haemorrhage. Special attention is given to promote ORS in Diarrhoea and early diagnosis and appropriate treatment of Pneumonia. Focussed work with precise risk groups like pregnant women, lactating mothers, newly married eligible couples and adolescent girls to prevent low birth weight and anaemia in pregnancy, including referral services for dealing with obstetrical emergencies are some of the steps taken in order to bring down the infant and maternal mortality rates in RCHS area. It was further derived that out of all RCHS service areas, the urban slums of Dewas in Madhya Pradesh faced the highest infant and maternal mortality rates. Hence, in addition to the above measures, appointment of 1 Social Worker and 1 ANM was done to address the multi-faceted problems pertaining to the area.

**HR at Ranbaxy**

Our future will be made by the steps taken by our People today. In recognition of this partnership, Ranbaxy is committed to providing each member of the Ranbaxy Family:

- a vibrant & exciting work environment
- significant rewards
- an opportunity to realize their potential

As a rapidly growing organization we look forward to partnering with dedicated professionals who believe in our mission, share our values and respect our dreams. Do explore the opportunities Ranbaxy can provide.

**Future Plans of Ranbaxy**

With a target of achieving US $ 1 Bn sales in 2004, the Company is now aspiring to achieve US $ 5 Bn sales by 2012 and be amongst the top five generic players. To translate these objectives and to optimise value creation, the Company has adopted a multi-pronged strategy. Acquisition of generic brands overseas, strong emphasis on brand marketing in the US and Europe, entering high potential new markets with value added product offerings, will be the major thrust areas in the coming years. Ranbaxy's global consumer healthcare business in India recently launched three herbal brands under New Age Herbals range, further strengthening its OTC range of products.

The Company is making a transition from a generic Company to a specialty pharmaceutical Company and aims at achieving significant business in proprietary prescription products by 2012 with a strong presence in developed markets. Together with the strong commitment of it's around 9000 multicultural workforce, Ranbaxy continues to aggressively pursue its strategies to become a Research-based International Pharmaceutical Company

**Ranbaxy Pharmaceuticals Inc. (RPI), USA**

Ranbaxy Pharmaceuticals Inc. (RPI), USA, was created to achieve the vision and mission of Ranbaxy Laboratories Limited, its parent company, to become a research based international pharmaceutical company.

RPI, a wholly owned subsidiary of Ranbaxy Laboratories Limited, established operations in the USA in 1994, and began marketing products in 1998 after receiving FDA approval for Cefaclor, a broad spectrum anti-infective agent. After 10 years of operations, RPI has achieved significant milestones by achieving sales of $413 m in 2003 - a growth of 39% over the previous year.

Ranbaxy Laboratories Limited is positioned today as the tenth largest* generic pharmaceutical company in the world. RPI has built on RLL's 43 years of pharmaceutical experience and expertise. Combine that with RPI's commitment to develop new and innovative products, our rapidly expanding generics, brands, and OTC product lines, and the advanced manufacturing capabilities of OHM Laboratories; and RPI has positioned itself as a robust and capable player in the US market.

| Snapshots |
|---|
| **Name of the Company**<br>Ranbaxy Laboratories Limited, India<br>**Year of Establishment**<br>1961<br>**Located at:**<br>Mohali<br>**Main Product**<br>Pharma<br>•Stancare<br>•Croslands<br>•Rexcel<br>•Solus<br>•Rextar<br>•BlueR<br>•RanbaxyCV<br>•Super Speciality<br>**Total turnover**<br>Rs. 3,222 crore ( 2002 yr),<br>For $3^{RD}$ Qtr of 2003-04, Rs. 885 Cr.<br>**Stock exchange listing**<br>BSE and NSE<br>**Flagship company**<br>Ranbaxy Laboratories Limited, India<br>**Main domestic market**<br>Through out India<br>**Foreign Presence**<br>Manufacturing operations in 7 countries, ground presence in 34 countries. |

# Shreyans (Paper and Textiles)

**Incorporation and Integration**

Shreyans group came into existence in the year 1987. Mr. D.K. Oswal took over the change of the Shreyans Paper Mills Ltd. and Adinath Textiles. The initial investment made was Rs. 6,00,00,000. The group initially focused on Paper and Textiles and had a turnover of Rs. 2,70,00,000. It started off with 400 employees. In 1990, the Co. set up another spinning unit of cotton yarn Shreyans Spinning Mills. The name of Shreyans paper Mills Ltd. was changes to Shreyans Industries Ltd. on Oct.20, 1992 and then onwards the Shreyans Industries Ltd. has two units namely Shreyans Paper Mills and Shree Rishab Paper.

Since then group is marching consistently on the path of growth. The group has interests in textiles, paper and finance. Dynamic and moderate Mr. D.K. Oswal, a doyen in the cotton spinning industry chairs the group. Mr. D.K. Oswal has more than 30 years of experience in the textiles industry. He was previously MD of Vardhman Spinning for 22 years. Mr. Rajneesh Oswal, the eldest son of Mr. DK Oswal has 7 years of techno-commercial experience and at present holds the position of Vice Chairman of the Shreyans group. The promoters of the group belong to the well – known Oswal family of Ludhiana, which is well known in their business, intellectual all over the world and very high presence in the industrial arena of India.

The group has high presence and good potential in the papers and textiles industry with well-set manufacturing facilities. The group has in its fold three manufacturing set ups viz:

**Adinath Textiles Limited**

Shreyans Papers

Shree Rishab Papers

**Profile of the Company**

The Shreyans group is one of the leading industrial groups of Punjab. The major operating companies in the group are as enlisted below:

| Company | Year of Commencing Commercial Operation | Activity | Present Capacity |
|---|---|---|---|
| Shreyans Industries Ltd. (Shreyans Paper) | 1979 | Cream Wove<br>Coloured Paper<br>Duplicating Paper<br>Maplitho Paper<br>Offset Paper<br>Super Printing Paper | 30000 Tons Per Annum |
| Shreyans Rishabh Paper | 1994 | Cream Wove<br>Surface Sized<br>Printing Paper<br>Maplitho Paper<br>Offset Paper<br>Rail Ticket Paper | 25000 Tons Per Annum |
| Adinath Textiles Ltd. | 1987 | Hand Knitting Yarn<br>Fancy Yarn<br>Machine Knitting Yarn<br>Carpet Yarn in Acrylic | 34000 Metric Tons Per Annum |

**Shreyans Paper Mills Limited**

Shreyans Paper Mills limited was established in the year 1979 with Mr D. K. Oswal as the Chairman. The initial investment made in the unit was Rs. 6,00,00,000 with 40% of equity, 55% borrowing, and 25% subsidy. It was the first of two paper units in the folds of Shreyans group now. It has the production capacity of 75 tons per day. The turnover (including domestic & exports) of this unit is Rs.150 crore. Writing and Printing paper is manufactured here. It utilizes residue like straw, wheat straw and sugarcane residue there by converting waste into wealth. Its product i.e. Paper is being sold all over India through Dealer Network.

The unit has received several productivity and quality awards over the last 10 years. It has received prestigious National Productivity Council Award for three consecutive years in 1988,1989 and 1990. It has received the best consumer service award in 1987. This award being contributing silently to the conservation of our precious forests reserves. The group is totally domestic with no foreign collaboration.

The R &D section is equipped with ultra modern equipments to ensure quality products to its valuable customs. R&D lab equipped with lad Digester, Lab valley Beater Brightness, opacity and gloss testing Machine, Burst strength tester, Double Folding Endurance Tester, Gurley, Porosity, smoothness tester and Cobb Tester. State of art automation system Valmet Qxd 9000 installed from Valmet (Canada) to keep Strict Control on ash contents. Grammage variation and moisture to percentage to produce quality papers.

The unit also has a rare distinction of being in only unit, which has installed under US ATD test program. Due to the success of this technology at Shreyans papers and a commitment to clean environment the same plant was installed at Shree Rishab Papers, which is running successfully. The main competitors of this unit include Varinder Agromills Ludhiana and ABC Paper Mills Hoshiarpur. The unit is listed on all major stock exchanges of India. Its stock is listed on Ludhiana, Mumbai, Kolkata, Madras, Ahemdabad and Delhi Stock Exchange.

**Product Profile**

| | |
|---|---|
| Cream Wove | Inland Letter Paper |
| Coloured Paper | Postal Envelope Paper |
| Duplicating Paper | Offset Paper |
| Surface Sized Printing Paper | Cover Paper |
| Azure Laid Paper | Super Calendered Paper |
| Maplitho Paper | Rail Ticket Paper |
| Stamp Paper | Super Printing Paper |

**Shree Rishab Papers Limited**

It is an agro-based unit of Shreyans Group located in village Babah Distt. Nawansehar. Shreyans group has taken this unit from Birla Zenith Papers mills a unit of Zenith Ltd. in the year 1994, which is presently known as Shree Rishab Papers. It has product profile similar to that of Shreyans Paper Mills Ltd. It is similar unit having annual capacity of 25000 M.T. Unit is supplying its products to Indian Railways, Postal department, Universities and educational boards through out India. Unit has excellent technology inputs and parameters in the industry. Unit also has state of art automation system measures 2002 EL (ABB) installed from ABB to have strict control over ash contents, grammage variation and moisture % contents to produce quality papers. The main competitors of India are Varinder Agromills Ludhiana and ABC Paper Mills Hoshiarpur. Its products marketed all over India through a network of Dealers. Its product enjoys a substantial market share. The Company is listed on all major exchanges of India i.e. Ludhiana, Mumbai, Kolkata, Madras, Ahemdabad and Delhi.

**Adinath Textiles Limited**

Adinaths textiles limited company, based at Ludhiana is the largest worsted-spinning unit in the Indian subcontinent with installed capacity of 12000 spindles manufactures the hand knitting yarn, fancy yarn, machine knitting Yarns and carpet yarn in Acrylic with vast variety to meet ever sort of count combination demand of its prospective customers, Equipped with the latest technology imported from Italy, France and Belgium the group products exemplify unwavering commitment to total quality. The raw material used in the company is both imported and indigenous fibers. The unit is catering to domestic market in the hosiery sector and hand-knitting sector. Although its product finds customer all over world but it is specifically marketed in Northern India consisting of Punjab, Himachal Pradesh, Chandigarh, Delhi and in the International market it finds customer in Bangladesh, SARAC Countries, Hong Kong etc.

Adinath is also catering to the export market and presently exporting mainly to Bangladesh, Hong Kong and Middle East markets. Unit has latest R&D equipment to keep strict quality control at various levels of production annual capacity of the plant is 34000 M.T. The lists of competitors include Vardhman Spinning & General Mills, Malwa Cotton & Spinning Mills, Punjab Worsted Mills, Anshupati Mills and other Ludhiana Based Mills. The total turnover from the unit is Rs. 29.94 crore. It is listed on Ludhiana, Mumbai, Delhi, Calcutta, Madras and Ahmedabad stock exchanges.

**Import Profile**

| | | |
|---|---|---|
| Acrylic Fiber | 3 Denier | Bright, Vcl, Raw White, Tow, Fiber |
| Acrylic Fiber | 3 Denier | Bright, Dyed Tow |
| Polyester Fiber | 3 Denier | Bright, Vcl, Raw White& Dyed |

| Polyester Fiber | 10&20 Denier | Trilobal, Vcl, Raw white |
|---|---|---|
| Nylon Fiber | 6,7,10,30, Denier | Super Bright, Vcl, Raw White |
| Cationic Dyes | 100%strength or more | Looking for competitive suppliers from China and other countries |
| Dispersed Dyes | 100%strength or more | Looking for competitive suppliers from China and other countries |

**Mission**

Shreyans aims to be an utmost class paper and textiles organization producing diverse range of products for the global paper and textiles market. Shreyans seek to achieve customer delight through excellence in quality and customer service. Shreyans is committed to be a responsible corporate citizen.

**Group Philosophy for Growth**

The shreyans group has always striven to be in step with the changing times. It believes in a process of continuous transformation to face the emerging challenges of market led domestic economy and global economic integration the group has been on a steady growth path and is building competitive strength in products, processes, markets and people for sustainable growth in the coming in the coming years.

**Expansion and Diversification**

Shreyans group has plans in the near future for capacity enhancement at both its paper plants. Horizontal expansion by setting up facility for office stationery manufacturing. Converting plant for maplitho & copier paper to diversify into information sector by going into call centres, medical transcriptions software exports etc.

**Technology Sharing**

Shreyans group is looking for technology up gradation and technology sharing in the following areas on global basis.

Improvement in quality of pulp (Agrò based)

Improvement in quality of paper (Agro based)

Water Management system (In agro based Paper units)

**Group's Perspective**

The group attributes success of the business to dedicated efforts, hard work and team spirit. According to the group, human resources should be given prominent significance over and above the other resources. They believe that it is only this resource, which makes use of other resources, and thus this resource has always been given pivot importance in the group policy frame.

The group believes that Ludhiana Industry is mature enough and has the capability to meet any challenge. In the past also, after USSR division it was able to look after other European and USA market and today too it has developed a very good reputation in new markets. But what matters the most is that the Ludhiana industry looks at State Government for having better opportunity and environment free from Babu Raj. Mr. Oswal is confident that Ludhiana Industry has a bright future and already it has got a very good name in world's cycle industry and garment industry.

The group is of the opinion that Indian firms have the gut power not only to face the global competitiveness but also has the capability to excel it and make its presence felt. This fact is well established by India when Indian IT industry becomes a world's most after sough industry and today all country is looking on India for well-trained manpower. In engineering industry also India has made its presence well accepted in the world industry. The group feels that time is not far away when India will be super power in the world.

Since the group has successful working in the Paper Industry, it is looking for future ventures in this area for both forward and backward integration of the present production facilities. The group is also thinking of venturing into technology transfer on turnkey basis in area of continuous raw material feeding and chemical recovery fields were they have the experienced manpower to handle such projects.

In the present scenario since IT has made the global business possible on a very high scale and distance and location boundaries has almost banished. In order to benefit from this sector, group is also looking for suitable ERP software to be implemented.

Shreyan a responsible corporate, wishes to play a very positive role social commitment and to develop on a continuous basis various social welfare scheme for the community. They have set the chemical recovery plant and plan to do much more for the community.

Shreyan are the pioneer in few fields such as it is a first company which had recovery plant installed in the Paper Mill. Further it enjoys good image in the industry as quality wise it is leading in the market with 70 % of supply of its product to the government department. The group visualizes itself to be India's No.1 Paper conglomerate in the coming future. Further it believes that it has edge in the field of technology transfer. Regarding management education provided by educational institutes the group believes that with the opening up of economy and global competition, the management education has gained importance & the professional institutes should enforce practical orientation to the various theoretical concepts of the courses.